Praise for Stammering Against Truth

Truth teller, Wen Gibson, manages to engage with the issues of severe, ongoing abuse and the psychology of parental abusers, as well as how incestuous fathers not infrequently interact with other sadistic abusers. To survive, a child dissociates, compartmentalising childhood traumas that, in response to a range of triggers, nevertheless continue to emerge, impacting the full range of functioning.

Wen is very likable, fully authentic, and a talented writer. Her book is the careful synthesis of a life-long quest to understand and process what happened to her and how it impacted on feelings of shame and confidence and on relationships. Many brave individuals subjected as children to incest and related traumas will readily find in this account deep parallels, while those without such histories will find an enhanced understanding of how such victims are so often silenced.

Dr Warwick Middleton, fellow of the Royal Australian and New Zealand College of Psychiatrists, professor, School of Medicine, University of Queensland.

*

It is a long, long time since I read a book that I couldn't put down. Amidst the horror and shocking abuse, Wen still found room for beauty and joy. Her journey of self-discovery unfolds beautifully. It is told with dignity and resilience. I honestly cannot fathom how she survived to be the loving person she is.

Susie Roberts, artist, musician and retired career counsellor.

Wen needs to tell her story. Writing this book has been part of her healing process. If others reading this have had similar experiences and are struggling, Wen's words will encourage them to keep going, so that they too can find their true self. *Stammering Against Truth* gives hope and the knowledge that they too can come out of this successfully.

Janelle Kenna, Australian volleyball representative player, educator and children's author of Caterpillar Capers.

STAMMERING

Your mother hates you

AGAINST

Your father uses you to save himself

TRUTH

The true story of surviving the unspeakable

Wen Gibson

First published by Busybird Publishing 2024

Copyright © 2024 Wen Gibson

ISBN:
Paperback: 978-1-923216-49-5
Ebook: 978-1-923216-50-1
Audiobook: 978-1-923216-51-8

This work is copyright. Apart from any use permitted under the *Copyright Act 1968*, no part of this publication may be reproduced, stored in a retrieval system or transmitted in any form or by any means, electronic, mechanical, photocopying, recording or otherwise, without the prior written permission of Wen Gibson.

The information in this book is based on the author's experiences and opinions. The author and publisher disclaim responsibility for any adverse consequences, which may result from use of the information contained herein. Permission to use any external content has been sought by the author. Any breaches will be rectified in further editions of the book.

Cover Image: Our little gang. Trevor, Wen and Graeme at the rock pools in Broome, WA, 1966.

Cover design: Busybird Publishing

Layout and typesetting: Busybird Publishing

Busybird Publishing
2/118 Para Road
Montmorency, Victoria
Australia 3094
www.busybird.com.au

For Graeme

Some of the names of the people in the following story have been changed to protect their identities. This is my story – how I remember it. Any errors are my own and unintentional.

Warning

This book includes scenes of emotional, physical and sexual distress and violence. Please take care of yourself as you read it, especially chapters 19 and 20.

Contents

Praise for Stammering Against Truth — i

Foreword - By Associate Professor Anthony Korner — 1
Preface – The ground — 11
Introduction – On speaking up — 15

Part I
Struggling

Chapter 1 - A centre for a family gone wrong — 19
Chapter 2 - Playing truant from my voice — 30
Chapter 3 - The start of belonging — 38
Chapter 4 - My mother — 49
Chapter 5 - A never-ending sea of pain — 59
Chapter 6 - Conflicting loyalties — 66
Chapter 7 - Dreaming — 75
Chapter 8 - Escaping — 83
Chapter 9 - Rape and love and being on the ceiling — 91
Chapter 10 - A life without Graeme — 97
Chapter 11 - A perfect finish — 108

Part II
Searching

Chapter 12 - Another beginning — 123
Chapter 13 - Jannette — 136
Chapter 14 - Navigating love and connection — 153
Chapter 15 - Do I matter? — 172
Chapter 16 - Starting again — 185
Chapter 17 - Living, not dying — 195
Chapter 18 - Being a bonny lass — 205

Part III
Finding

Chapter 19 - Remembering ... 219
Chapter 20 - A child murder ... 233
Chapter 21 - Bullies ... 245
Chapter 22 - Saying no ... 258
Chapter 23 - Trusting my knowing place ... 265
Chapter 24 - My words are round perfect stones ... 277
Chapter 25 - No longer hidden ... 292

Epilogue ... 304
Gender as cure ... 304
My Wish for You ... 308
Acknowledgements ... 309

Foreword

By Associate Professor Anthony Korner

Many people in our community believe people never change. This memoir challenges such beliefs by demonstrating just how profoundly people can and do change.

Wen Gibson writes from the heart. She also writes with great skill. There is a real sense of care in the way she tells her unfolding story. It is a narrative of amazing resilience, through what could be described as a 'long dark night of the soul'. In this case, the long night extends over decades, although with sufficient glimpses of new dawns to show how Wen found a way through, where many may have succumbed. She never lost sight of the child's journey, from the vulnerability and dependence that characterise the beginning of all human lives. For Wen, this beginning was further complicated by severe trauma, neglect and abuse. Ultimately, this is a story of healing and recovery.

We experience with Wen how perceived powerlessness (human vulnerability) is also the essence of who we are, necessary to the full realisation of our humanity. Her narrative unfolds in an existential drama taking the reader to places of horror, but also to moments of great beauty and transformation. In reading it, my idea of what it means to be human was altered. I expect I won't be the only one.

It turns out that words are essential to the process of healing and integration, much as this is sometimes questioned. People might ask what difference talking makes. In this foreword, I'll take a look not only at words but also at images, the feeling body, and the ways we hold ourselves together in the face of overwhelming threat and trauma. I will examine the internal conversations people have with themselves, and how the power of words impacts people's self-image. The role of relationships will also come into focus – in particular, the special bond felt between twins. There are things revealed by Wen about the twin experience that will be new to many.

In the introduction, we hear about Wen's lifelong struggle with a stammer – a hereditary condition that subjected her to bullying and made it an eternal battle to get words out in speech. For reasons that later become evident, it often felt safer for her to stay silent. On the other hand, we read that the written word is 'magic' in her life. Her writing takes on coherence, initially in the keeping of a diary, later in writing poetry and writing in therapy, and finally in writing her 'words' in this book.

A couple of words or phrases stand out. I will always remember Wen as the little girl who put her heart in a clock. As the reader gains access to this moment, there is another word that resonates: 'waiting'. This isn't waiting as an adult understands it. It is a situation where a small child is *in extremis* – in a situation over which she has no control. Time becomes endless; waiting, an experience of terror where things repeat and no other reality exists. Either the child is *in extremis* in the hands of abusers, or in a fog where there is an inevitability about what will come again. What does one do with one's heart in such a place? The answer, for Wen, is in the phrase above. At the same time as her heart was displaced, there was, paradoxically, a sense of words being locked in her heart. Or hidden in a brown paper-wrapped parcel. They remained there, anonymous, hidden and unavailable for a long, long time.

It is only much later that another word, 'stone', comes into play through Wen's phrase 'round perfect stones'. I was puzzled by this initially, but as I read on it became clearer. Stones have a solidity that feels like being anchored, providing a sense of continuity and substance rather than an existence chopped up and insubstantial, founded in pretending to be what others want as a means of survival. Wen discovers cornerstones and stones that settle in the heart until they finally become accessible and available for release into the world. We don't always associate language with solidity, but this seems to be the case here.

So far, I've focused on words that have come from Wen herself. There were words in her life that came from others but were directed at her – words like 'bad' and 'stupid' and phrases like 'it's all your fault'. The constant repetition of such barbs takes a toll. They become internalised as a traumatic script – for many years the only way Wen could see herself. No matter what she achieved, this remained as a heart of darkness from which there seemed little prospect of escape. It's only after a long journey that she gained sufficient perspective to see the real origin of these detonating verbal attacks.

Let's move on to images – images have great power. They have a history in the mind that precedes the acquisition of the mother tongue and the capacity for verbal expression. In many traumatic situations, for many people, certain images become engraved in the mind, sometimes dominating one's consciousness. In this book, there are many images, some beautiful or peaceful, even transcendent, while others are shocking, violent and likely to disturb the reader (note the trigger warning after the title page).

Importantly, Wen begins in the preface by drawing our attention to an image of love: 'If I dared to peer within, I saw, shining up through the vibrant reds of the bleeding cut lines of myself, a pair of pure blue eyes.

They were the eyes of my younger self staring up at me – the eyes of my little-girl self.' This capacity to see her child self was only possible after decades of feeling lost. It reminds me of words familiar from the popular song 'Amazing Grace': 'I was lost and now am found.' The phrase 'cut lines' suggests a certain kind of brokenness, acknowledged by Wen even as her healing gains momentum. Through the cuts, the vibrancy of the child spirit is sensed within.

At one stage, it might be said that Wen turns images into words by keeping a diary. This practice becomes an important tool in her eventual recovery. We come to know various scenes of trauma over the course of the book. Chapter 1 takes us to the time when Wen's childhood achieved some (relative) measure of stability – the period when she moved in with her grandparents. From there, we are taken on an odyssey. If the Homeric Odyssey (and its equivalents in other cultures) is considered the archetypal human journey, Wen's Odyssey can be considered a modern exemplar, as she takes us on a personal journey of experience.

We move forwards and backwards in time. In external reality (the objective view), time only appears to move in one direction, whereas from the mind's perspective ('psychic reality'), we can become time-travellers. Wen's trauma was largely hidden from others and from herself, breaking into her eight-year-old life as nightmares. While able, in the main, to keep up appearances, she senses something hidden and chaotic sequestered within.

In the adult world, we learn not to be superstitious – to be sceptical about the existence of ghosts, goblins, vampires and such monsters. For many children, monsters are real. In a loving family, a 'monster' may only be experienced fleetingly, perhaps in a moment of parental anger that is soon resolved, sometimes with an apology to the child. In other families, however, the situation is far more difficult, with no prospect of escape from the monsters. It is not the monsters of fairy tales that are of concern: children enjoy reading fairy tales about all sorts of dangerous mythical creatures. Rather, it is the actual people in the child's sphere, those who have no regard for the child's humanity and treat the child as an object, who are most terror-inducing. These creatures in human form lack a sense of humanity towards others; it is they who make the blood run cold.

One such person is Wen's father, a man who is not, in her very earliest memory, sensed as a threat but who becomes increasingly dangerous and threatening when Wen is still a preschool child. The trajectory for him is a downward spiral – a descent into the perpetration of abuse, the inability or unwillingness to protect Wen from others and complicity in a corrupt gang, leading to Wen's entrapment. As is commonly the case, there is no acknowledgment of wrongdoing. Simply a response of blaming the victim. As far as can be seen, the father ends up an unhappy and embittered man. There is no redemption story for him.

Wen's father undergoes a malignant personality transformation. There are other characters in the book who have gone even further down a moral descent into organised criminality. We are introduced to this situation well into Wen's adult life, even though she is speaking of events that happened in early childhood. At a certain point, in a therapeutic setting, she is triggered into an experience of violent and shocking images, involving great detail and explicit sexual abuse. These are the basis for the trigger warning at the beginning of the book. For Wen, there followed a long period of months, possibly years, of drawing images and writing about them, in keeping with her earlier adoption of writing as a preferred form of expression.

In this book, she is finally able to speak the truth for her child self. Wen informs us of the efforts that have already been made to bring these perpetrators to justice. Evidence is provided to support the story she recalled. One of the hopes in publishing *Stammering Against Truth* is that there may be others who recognise the images and the people in them. Maybe some measure of justice could still be served.

In the world of mythology, looking directly at a monster is a dangerous thing to do. Yet this is exactly what happens in the scenes that relate to the paedophile gang. Somehow, almost-three-year-old Wen finds the courage to fix her gaze on a man holding a knife and threatening to cut or kill her. In such a precarious circumstance, her capacity to look the man straight in the eye felt like the thread by which her life hung. It was an extraordinary act of bravery.

Most of Wen's childhood is characterised by the need to be on guard against the dangers around her, particularly those posed by parents and some other adults. This is associated with a narrowing of consciousness and constraints on what can be felt. Feeling is the level of experience that provides a bridge between our physicality and our mental lives. There is an element of feeling always present in consciousness.

One of the ways things begin to change for Wen, long before she has any sense of understanding of what she is going through, is the discovery, in play with her brothers, of the sense of aliveness that comes from being in 'flight' – whether riding bikes fast, on horseback, in sports (especially volleyball) or simply exploring the world in which she finds herself. In such moments, she experiences exhilaration that is lacking in other contexts, particularly when in contact with her parents. Later, as a young adult, Wen speaks of feeling most alive when on a 'knife's edge', at a time when she is literally teetering on a precipice. As she explores foreign climes and alternative systems of healing and spirituality, there emerges an experience, at the level of feeling, foreshadowing her later capacity to put experiences together into a coherent narrative. This is of great importance, providing hope that had been in scarce supply.

At times during her stay in India, Wen's body is on the verge of failing her as she becomes gravely ill. Barely clinging to life, she sees the possibility of a way forward. She begins to believe that, even in her despair, she might navigate a way towards health and understanding who she really is. It is as if a map is beginning to form. By the time of writing the book, we see further developments in feeling and relatedness, with an eventual sense of transcendence in relation to the trauma that had for so long defined her.

It would take too long to discuss all the relationships that we encounter in Wen's story. Many characters provide her with hope: teachers, friends, (maternal) grandparents, coaches and strangers met on the road. As a rule, these are people who have a kind gaze and gentle manner. Some get close to Wen, although for a long time she struggles with intimacy, particularly in relation to sexuality. Of course, there are other characters in whom Wen only finds a recurrence of trauma: those who are cruel, who use force or coercion, against which Wen finds it impossible for many years to respond with the 'fight' that she sees other people display. This is a source of shame and confusion.

The relationship I want to focus on here is the relationship with her twin brother, Graeme. This twinship involves an extraordinarily close bond, with the sense of lives having been shared from the time together in the womb. Together with her older brother (Trevor), and Graeme, there is a 'gang of three' who support each other, escaping the toxicity of the home environment and providing some measure of human connection at a time when it is most needed. The sense of connection with Graeme is concrete, intimately tied up with Wen's sense of self; she only feels alive and intact when with her twin. In early adult life, fate intervenes and the bond is broken. For Wen, it feels as if her life is over. She attempts suicide and strives against despair. While others struggle to understand the depth of pain she experiences at this loss, she eventually discovers she isn't alone and that other twins have experienced such searing pain at the death of their twin. The twin bond, for Wen, is beyond words – something that is never renounced and always treasured.

At various points in the narrative, the author uses terms that come from the world of psychopathology. In the preface, we are introduced to 'dissociative amnesia'. Later, there are references to psychosis and postnatal depression. Significantly, Wen negotiates these pathological states and phenomena outside mainstream psychiatric care. While she has two important therapy experiences in Scotland, these avenues of help are not part of the National Health Service or publicly funded psychotherapy. One is important in unlocking the flood of images referred to above, with a second therapy characterised by gentleness and compassion, and seen to be more nurturing.

While dissociative amnesia is referred to specifically, other forms of dissociation can also be seen in the text, including: 'shutdown' responses, where Wen becomes less present to her environment; 'out-of-body' experiences under extreme stress; and periods of numbness and loss of the sense of ordinary reality both in herself and the environment. There is also the experience of fragmentation, or disintegration – a form of dissociation that is overwhelming and acutely distressing, sometimes referred to as primary dissociation. These kinds of responses are an obstacle to self-awareness and realisation. In the literature on dissociation, there is widespread recognition of it being a response to trauma, as evidenced in Wen's life. There is debate as to whether it should also be seen as a capacity. In Wen's case, it prevented her from experiencing a level of pain that may well have overwhelmed her capacity to cope. By keeping experience dissociated (i.e. sequestered within networks not available to consciousness), lives become limited in some ways although at least some forms of adaptation and maturation still occur. Perhaps we can see that dissociation may have had a role in keeping Wen alive.

When lives are broken up by dissociative experience, the person often has a sense of frustration – of a life lived through guessing what others expect them to do, rather than being able to discern one's own desires and possibilities. Wen is frequently frustrated and perplexed at what is happening to her. At one point, the confusion culminates in a degree of fragmentation and disorganisation that leads to out-of-character chaotic behaviour, where she pushes those closest to her away to the point that they leave her isolated in India. Later, she refers to this episode as most likely involving psychosis. Fortunately, the friends who were driven away later make active attempts to reconcile with Wen. This kind of effort at relationship repair is new to her.

References to postnatal depression come later, at a point when Wen has gone a long way towards creating a life for herself. She finds that her own childhood did not provide her with any sort of healthy model for parenting and she needs to find her own path rather than repeat the patterns that had become ingrained through experiences with her mother. The required change takes time to accomplish, although things eventually get a little easier.

Another aspect of Wen's resilience and self-discovery involves her experience of gender and sexuality. Seeing herself as outside the mainstream in many respects, protesting against government policies and finding solidarity with other women trying to challenge patriarchal domination, Wen develops experiences of intimacy and sexual relationships with both men and women. Whilst being confounded by a world that wants to see people in binary terms in relation to gender, it becomes important for Wen to find ways of being within herself and with others that go beyond stereotypical definition. This is crucial to becoming herself and coming to terms with her traumatic past.

Gradually she learns to 'fight' for herself, where for years she had defeated herself by shutting down and becoming 'powerless' at moments of interpersonal challenge. This shift from 'feign' to 'fight' meant developing a capacity to sustain herself, with the emergence of a sense of personal freedom.

We read how Wen faced repeated abuse at the hands of her father and the men to whom she was exposed. Survival in these circumstances borders on the miraculous. Tellingly, this isn't seen by Wen as the 'original wound'. Rather, it is in the relationship with her mother that Wen sees the ultimate source of her trauma – a mother who was relentlessly critical and cruel, who was incapable of seeing Wen as an infant or child who had any value at all in her own right. A mother who could not, it seems, return her baby's gaze. Wen never felt seen by her mother.

What does a child do when her mother, her primary source of support, hates her (or him) for no reason? When the mother denies her own failings and blames her daughter for all misfortunes. Such questions are important in a world where the most vulnerable humans – children – quite frequently become objects of hate. Part of the answer lies in the human capacity to *seek* – to find what one needs in the environment, though such seeking may take us to strange and unexpected places.

This book outlines one person's journey in the face of such a predicament. For the child, it is necessary to do what they can to preserve a relationship in order to survive. For those who want to know more, I suggest you read on.

Associate Professor Anthony Korner, PhD, FRANZCP, MMed (Psychotherapy), MBBS (Hons)Director, Master of Medicine and Science in Medicine (Trauma-Informed Psychotherapy), The University of SydneyFaculty of Medicine and Health, Western Clinical School, Westmead

Preface – The ground

I want to tell you straight up that I am a survivor of neglect and abuse: physical, emotional and sexual. For a long time, being alive was only about surviving and the debilitating self-hatred that went hand in hand with it, clawing at my insides. I believed something was wrong with me and it was my fault. If I could fix myself and find another version, I would be OK.

I spent years attempting to escape from myself by crossing countries and continents. I know now that running and looking outside was not the answer. That journey repeated the message already forced on me: that I wasn't good enough, that I wasn't worthy.

The answer lies in diving inside, making sense of this struggle, and rebuilding myself from the ground up. I needed to learn how to be friends with the core of me and to discover my voice, which was silenced.

It starts and ends with me: my struggle, my searching, my finding. We're going to do that diving. I warn you, it's unjust and downright ugly at times.

The first draft of this story was the start – a seeping pile of blood and intestines spilled out on bare pages. A mass of words. Here, we're going to pare it back to its bones. Hopefully, you'll continue with me.

Together, we'll learn that when the beginning of life is full of suffering, there is a way through. There is a method to healing – of cradling life in both hands and claiming it as our own.

At eight years old, I neatly packaged and then forgot the content of the early trauma – a process called 'dissociative amnesia'. In a half-hour drive from one house to another, when my grandfather helped move us from my father's house to his own, I forgot what my father did. I forgot my mother's primitive hatred acted out on me, although she came with us and her hate continued.

Dissociative amnesia, the rarest of dissociative disorders, is linked to intolerable distress. My even rarer version was known as 'localised dissociative amnesia': memory loss of specific periods of life and particular events. Most episodes of this are short, lasting days or weeks, but it took me until my mid-twenties to remember the forgotten period.

When I moved to my grandparents' house, I crossed a line in space and time that allowed me to bury the memories in my unconscious. I wrapped them in brown paper to pretend the parcel wasn't important, but inside, it was a different story. Inside, it was beautiful in its mix of colours.

If I dared to peer within, I saw, shining up through the vibrant reds of the bleeding cut lines of myself, a pair of pure blue eyes. They were the eyes of my younger self staring up at me – the eyes of my little-girl self. She carried the trauma for me. I'd put her inside the package, along with the terror and pain. I'd abandoned her so I could escape the memories she held. This is how my older self moved on. She'd split from my younger self and the memories.

*

I am a fraternal twin with a boy, Graeme. Ours is a bond formed in utero – a melting sense of no boundaries with another, of utter knowing. We spoke without speaking before we knew there were words. He was with me from the beginning of my life and I carry a sense of being one of two – a half of a single whole. This knowing sustained me when I was alone.

*

This story is about surviving … but it's also much more.

It's about how I learned to live, fully and joyously to the edges of my skin – the skin that is mine now, when many others have owned it. I claim my flesh and underlying muscles, exhilarating in their strength and movement. My heart beats steady and reassuring in my chest, stuffed full of the love I have for the people in my life, personally and professionally. I have gone on to work in the field of healing, as a psychotherapist and counsellor.

'Why?' is an often-asked question at the beginning of therapy, as people share their life stories, trying to make sense of what happened. We may never find the why of another person's actions, but we can piece it together from scattered clues. Here, I do that for myself, finding how two parents treated their children in an abusive and neglectful way. And how I managed to survive.

There's a statement many survivors hate to hear: that there are hidden strengths to be found within the trauma and in making sense of the mess inside. I wanted to deny it when it was first said to me, but now I know it's true.

Those of us who have survived horrors are especially sensitive to emotion and the currents in a room. We are usually hypervigilant and on edge, and hold, for others, an awareness of the impacts of pain, until they can hold it for themselves. The abusive adults are often defending against seeing and taking responsibility for what they are doing. The emotions have to go somewhere so the abused children often carry the disowned emotions of the adult abusers, such as guilt and shame. That's part of the mess and what needs to be sorted and worked through, then given back to those responsible.

I continually use this skill of emotional awareness in my work and private life.

The greatest gift is in making friends with my powerlessness. I was a victim. Being a victim defined my character. It wrapped my personality to its chosen means of survival: dissociation. I lived it out repeatedly. But now I see it for what it is. The sense of being powerless is at the core of each person, because we have all been babies and children and dependent on caregivers. Some better, some worse. Some good enough, some not.

I've uncovered, in the depths of powerlessness, a supple, tender strength that bends and moves and doesn't break.

If we deny this place because of the overwhelming pain that it also holds and attempt to live above it, as I did for many years, we live in a pseudo-strength. That place is brittle, liable to shatter when the stresses battering it become too great. That kind of strength doesn't know how to sway. Instead, it braces before any hurts. Held stiffly, it risks cracking apart, which is what I did, again and again.

If we can learn how to drop into the pain, we can find a subtle, quiet presence where we can allow it all.

Allow.

Not forgive or condone or agree or rage against. Simply allow.

It's a still, bottomless pool of knowing and soft, caring love – first to ourselves and then rippling out.

That is how we change the world, one tiny ripple of breath at a time.

Introduction – On speaking up

For a lifelong stammerer like me, writing is magic.

Stammering is a genetic abnormality linked to subtle differences in how the brain develops and processes speech. It's usually more predominant in males, although it passed through the female line in my case.

Force never works with my stammer. Shame follows. It swamps me. There is nowhere to hide. I see my mother's face laughing into mine and hear her words taunting me. That's when I want to run. I'm falling into my dangerous place: a pit without hope. I'm stupid because I can't talk properly. The old stories and messages flood me.

Compare the struggle of speaking to typing words.

My written words flow effortlessly, limited only by imagination and my fingers running to catch up to my thoughts. I can risk the syllable that sits most appropriately next to its neighbour, not worrying if it has too many parts to manage in a single breath.

I'm articulate on a page and free to name what I want, the boss of silent language, skipping and lunging across the page. Those magical 'f' words, fluency and flow, elbow out any hesitancy.

If only you knew how the inside of me differs from the outside. Hundreds of phrases and sentences sit in queues, buzzing and fighting to escape. Instead, they have to wait for me to find a way to say the dreaded sounds out loud.

Now I have, silently, on these pages. Can you hear them as well?

Part I

Struggling

Chapter 1

A centre for a family gone wrong

Friday 13 February 1970 was a perfect day. It was the day I wrapped up my memories and buried them inside, turning my face to stare at the horizon my grandfather was driving us towards. I was eight years old.

My grandfather was taking us to live with him and my grandmother at their Rowland Street home, having given way to his daughter's demand that he save her from her marriage. My mother, Joan, didn't have a separate income or savings and women's refuges were yet to be established. It was inevitable that Grandad had to be the one to rescue us.

I remember staring at the back of his head from the rear seat of the Holden. My grandfather had short back and sides and a stiff, upright posture. The fine, greying hair on top of his head flopped slightly to one side, suggesting a softness. But I didn't know this man. I wondered what he was thinking as he drove without speaking. His silence allowed my mother to keep up a running commentary as we crossed Townsville from Currajong to North Ward – about six kilometres.

I hated saying the word Townsville. I always stammered on it. I wondered why it was called 'town' and 'ville' together. Didn't the words mean the same thing? But I found out that when Europeans first settled in the area in 1864, the name Townsville was to honour Robert Towns. He helped finance the building of the port near the mouth of Ross Creek. A port was needed in the north of Queensland, as the area was being opened up for cattle grazing and growing sugarcane. Then gold was found in Charters Towers in 1871, about 110 kilometres further inland. It became the largest goldfield in Australia.

Naming words of any kind were tough for me to say. My name was the worst word of all. I could never say it in one go. After getting stuck, I was usually too embarrassed to attempt anything more.

When we'd first arrived in Townsville from Broome two years earlier, we'd stayed with our grandparents for a few weeks. That time had been fraught with arguments between my grandfather and father. I'd kept out of their way. Then, when we moved to Currajong, my father policed their visits to us. Now, I was already tuning into my grandfather's moods.

I did it instinctively. I needed to suss out the adults around me. My feelings were often a jumble. I put them on hold and turned my attention to the outside – to the other person. It was safer that way.

My mother sat in the front of the car, holding my month-old baby brother in her arms. My younger sister snuggled next to her. There were no child restraints or seatbelts in 1970. The bench seats allowed us to squash together. We three older children shoved against one another in the back. We knew to keep our voices to a whisper.

My mother kept turning around and glaring at us if we forgot. She had a round, puffy face, pale blue eyes that seemed to turn a deeper blue when she was angry, and short, nondescript hair. She hadn't put on her red lipstick or special going-out clothes. In the rush to get us ready for the move, she was wearing a worn house dress that hung from her large frame.

Earlier that morning, as soon as my father left the house for work, she announced, 'You're not going to school. You're all staying home today. We're going. We're leaving your father. I've had enough of his damn moods and having more bloody kids.' She paused, staring at each of us in turn, almost like she was daring us to contradict her.

'Five of you damn kids is enough for any mother. I'm not doing it again, do you hear? I'm getting out while I still can – before he damn well destroys me.' And just like that, my world changed.

I stood, dressed in my school uniform, looking at her. Then the removal van arrived, followed by my grandfather.

In the weeks leading up to that day, Joan had secretly collected our belongings into cardboard boxes that Grandad had ferried to his home. I'd come home from school to find clothes missing. She hadn't said anything to any of us kids about what she was planning.

One time, I'd caught her emptying my wardrobe. She'd hissed at me, 'Don't you dare say a word to your father!' As if I would. I still hadn't understood she was preparing to leave him.

North Ward, one of the oldest and most popular suburbs in Townsville, sat on the north side of the city. It overlooked the main beach, called The Strand. The suburb sloped gently up from the Coral Sea to the foot of Castle Hill. The Hill's bare rock-face stared over the houses towards Magnetic Island and the largest port in Northern Australia. The skyline was broken by the half-dozen cranes needed to move the containers on and off the large cargo ships lined up at the wharves. Townsville was the main exporter of zinc, copper, lead, fertiliser, sugar and molasses.

North Ward had kept many of its original houses. The early settlers had realised they needed to shield their homes from the fierce tropical sun during the dry season and then deal with the torrential rain that occurred in the wet months. They had built verandas for shade and raised the houses on timber stumps to prevent flooding and improve ventilation. This also helped deter snakes and goannas from entering the homes.

The wealthier person wrapped their entire house with a wide veranda framed by intricate wrought-iron or wooden latticework. Those less well-off lived on narrow blocks and built plain homes with shallow verandas shading the front and rear of the house. These early homes were now surrounded by buildings using the wonder product of the 1950s: fibrous cement sheets, simply known as 'fibro'. Homes built with fibro walls topped by a corrugated iron roof met the need for cheap, affordable housing following World War Two.

This was the style of the house my grandfather pulled up in front of – a simple rectangular home raised about two meters above the ground on concrete stilts. Front steps led up to what used to be a small veranda. The house looked up to the commanding presence of Castle Hill.

A wire-mesh fence, edged by a flower bed, marked the front of the triangular block. The front yard was a neat, green carpet – a sharp contrast to the next-door neighbour's ten-metre-high row of mango trees standing in a yard full of deep leaf litter.

I walked up the steps and stared at the room that opened in front of me. My grandfather had converted the veranda into a bedroom. He said it was mine. But then I realised the new front door opened straight into my bedroom. Clear sliding glass doors separated my bedroom from the lounge room, leaving an open gap at one end that was previously the walk-through. The glass doors hadn't been made into a solid wall and the walk-through didn't have a door.

Yellow floral curtains hung in bunches along the length of the glass wall but there was no way my grandmother was ever going to allow me to pull them closed. I knew I couldn't ask her. I shrunk inside myself and became a mirror of that room: perfectly tidy on the outside, with all my confusing thoughts hidden from view.

The message was clear. Nothing was allowed to spill out and mess up that room. I looked at the bed with its wrinkle-free chenille bedspread and how it sat at right angles to the wall beneath the window. It faced the wide expanse of the hill. I stood still, trying to take it in.

I no longer lived with my father in the scary house in Currajong. I shivered. It was too soon to believe it might be true.

That first night, I changed into my summer pyjamas in the bathroom after waiting my turn. The television was on in the lounge room. The three adults were not yet ready to retire. They each sat in their single armchair and faced the screen. The row of fluorescent lights above the glass wall shone into my room. It was awash with light and noise as I attempted to sleep.

*

My grandfather gave up his dream of retiring from the water department of the local council. He continued working as a labourer with Charlie, the plumber, to support us, as he was the only earner. His home had been built for four but now held eight. My twin Graeme and older brother Trevor had moved into the third bedroom. Joan, along with Sarah, my younger sister by four years, and the baby James had been squashed into the second bedroom.

First thing on a weekday morning, and at odd hours through the night and weekend, I would hear the plumber's truck start. The sound carried easily from Charlie's house, which was further up the slope of Castle Hill. It worked in place of a telephone, which my grandparents didn't have. My grandfather would spring into action and then wait at the edge of the footpath for Charlie to collect him. He would return hours later, often mud-splattered and weary. He'd kick off his boots and stomp around the kitchen, telling us of burst water mains or laying concrete pipes. He often swore about the waste of water. Townsville was in the middle of a drought.

*

Grandad usually rose at 5 am, leaving Grandma to sleep. First, he would go into the kitchen to boil the electric jug, then he would come to my room. Each morning he would reach under the mosquito net, pull the sheet off my feet and tug my toes to wake me up. I would trail him to the kitchen and help him make the tea. Then I would sprinkle sugar over margarine spread on white bread, which we would take out to the back landing. It was small, about a meter square, with painted timber flooring and a metal railing. Wooden steps led down to the backyard.

I would sit next to Grandad on the top step. It was the perfect viewing platform to watch the sky lighten as we ate our sugared bread and drank our tea. We often didn't speak, but it was a comfortable silence. I had fitted myself into his life by becoming his sidekick and did what he wanted, without speaking or complaining. He seemed to welcome me.

I would imagine the day was holding its breath with us, helping to draw out our still, quiet moments. Then it would rush to gather us up for the jobs waiting ahead. This was signalled by the sun starting to peek through the mango trees and the chickens' increasingly loud clamour to be fed. Grandad would stand up, grab the mash he'd already soaked and take it down for the chooks.

My grandfather usually wore khaki six days a week. On Sunday, he would wear navy trousers, a starched white shirt and an old-fashioned, narrow tie. It was often too hot for a coat as he stood at the gate of the rugby league ground. The gate was diagonally across the road from our house. Here, as he took the entry tickets, he would smile a greeting at the queuing line of mostly wide-tied, beer-bellied blokes who came to watch the games. He would repeat the weekly joke to a select few and earn a raucous laugh in return.

During the week after school, I would meet Grandad under the palm trees lining the walkway to the entrance of the clubhouse. He would tell me what jobs needed doing, such as trimming the hedges, and I would tell him what I thought, like that the lawn needed mowing.

Perched on the upturned bin, I often snuck glances at his whipcord figure. He pushed the mower as if his life depended on the neatly cut buffalo grass. We were an often-seen team around the clubhouse, keeping the grounds well groomed – each blade of grass not daring to lean out of place.

*

My grandmother, Annie, turned sixty not long after we arrived. She was short, about five feet tall, and round in the middle, with sun-damaged skin from living in the tropics. She spoke quietly and didn't draw attention to herself. Annie's hair was her pride – a luscious, rich black. It was cut short like all the women's hair in my family, but it shined in the sunlight when she scrunched it into waves after washing it.

Grandma ran the house to a strict routine. Everything had its place and each job was done on time. It was like clockwork and I loved it. It allowed me to know exactly what was going to happen each day. After the chaos of living at Currajong, the new routine helped soothe my hyper-alert system.

Affection wasn't expressed openly between my grandparents, but their understated presence was enough to settle me, except when my mother was in the room. With Joan, I was constantly on edge.

I would sit on the carpet at my grandmother's feet in the evenings and watch her crochet. She would listen as I stammered through any softly attempted words. She wouldn't stop me or try to say the word or pick on me or say I was stupid. I gave up on Joan being my mother and turned instead to my gentle grandmother.

I'd stammered for as long as I could remember. When I had to speak, I would scan ahead to consider any possible words that I might have to use, in case there was a word waiting to trip me up. Half my mind was always checking sounds and the physicality of speaking.

I would twist sentences into strange shapes to avoid sounds I knew I would get stuck on. The other person would often look at me confused – I had lost the meaning of what I wanted to say. I often gave up. I couldn't speak like the people around me.

It didn't matter how hard I tried, I always came out hesitant. My stammer shrouded so many of my words. Then, a block would appear out of nowhere and stop me flat. My throat would push against the stuck sound if I continued to try to force the word out – I couldn't. That word was never going to come out, no matter how much my mind wanted it to.

My mother outgrew her stammer but mine persisted. She taunted me. She'd got rid of her stammer when she was a kid. That made her better than me. I was useless, she said. I was pathetic to be so stuck. Joan often used this as her revenge. She hated the easy friendship that was developing between me and my grandmother and would criticise me for no reason. My mere presence would set her off.

Joan would stand over me, having cornered me against a wall. Her muscled arms were always ready to grab me if I dared turn away from her onslaught of words. I'd have to stand there and take it.

I felt lost in the face of her torment, but I couldn't let her see that. It would give her more ammunition to use against me. I pretended not to care by keeping a bland, almost mocking face. I walked this fine line of defiance, implying that she couldn't hurt me, but inside I felt defeated. I never knew how to get it right or what she wanted from me. I couldn't understand why she hated me so much, yet loved Graeme.

I imagined that when my mother first viewed us, her twins, she saw the perfect split of sexes laid out in front of her in little cloth-wrapped forms. A girl child side by side with a boy. It was the ideal setup to play out the message that seemed to have been passed down through the women in my family: that boys are to be valued and loved, and girls are to be used and abused.

We had become our mother's focus for her unresolved self-loathing. She had made Graeme good and me bad. My stammer was the proof she needed. I would save my words for Grandma and shut up the moment my mother walked into the room. It enraged Joan further.

I longed for each evening and the time when I was allowed to escape to my bed. I would pull the mosquito net down around me. The white gauze gave me a sense of containment, like pretend walls that would keep me safe.

*

Of a night, my grandmother would sit well back in her tan vinyl armchair. Her hands were usually busy hooking and twisting some number 80 thread. I would watch the double crochet spiral onto a circle of chain stitch and imagine that this was the centre for our family gone wrong. I often wondered about the pattern of my grandmother's life before we arrived.

Had it always been washing on Monday, Wednesday and Friday, with the big sheet and towel wash on Saturday, and Thursday the shopping day? On Wednesday nights, my grandmother would circle the specials advertised in the newspaper and write out the shopping list. In the afternoon she often made a quick dash around the corner to the local store, Aherns, to fill the gap for that night's meal.

Friday was usually spent cleaning the house. It started with a dust, then a wet wash and dry, followed by a polish. The bath was washed out last of all. Saturday was baking day. She cooked the weekly cakes, four-egg sponges, chocolate crunch and foam biscuits needed to get us through the week. At night after dinner, on the days allowed because of the drought, Grandma watered the lawn and the pot plants that sat in neat lines at the front of the house. She saved the row of smiling gerberas, standing proud and tall in the flowerbed that edged the front fence, for last. She weeded the lawn before breakfast, after picking up the leaves fallen from next door's mango trees that overhung the yard.

Money was always tight but sugar was a staple. It was spooned into our tea, on our cereal and sprinkled on bread first thing in the morning. When David Jones advertised a special on sugar, we were all driven into the store to line up. We'd purchase four bags of sugar each, the amount allowed, and come home with twenty-four two-pound bags.

Cheese, a dreamt-of luxury, was only allowed on Saturday morning, and then only two thin slices each. I would carefully arrange the yellow rectangles on top of thick-cut slices of toast and savour each bite.

After a breakfast of scrambled eggs and preparing the roast lunch, my grandmother would spend Sunday listening to six records chosen with offhand care. These were placed in the record player, silent in the loungeroom Monday to Saturday and opened only on Sunday – to hear the singer Slim Dusty's songs: 'Where the Dog Sits on the Tucker Box', 'A Pub with No Beer', or 'Tie me Kangaroo Down'. Scottish marching bands and Harry Secombe might follow.

My grandmother taught me to place the heavy crystal vase of plastic roses in the middle of the polished dining room table to mark the completion of a meal. The vase sat on one of her crocheted doilies. Only then would she find some peace, to hook and twist the fine cottons.

Chapter 2

Playing truant from my voice

The trauma I carried in my body needed to go somewhere. It couldn't just disappear. It came out in the same nightmare for months and then consistently over the years. My father had terrified me with stories of World War Two and the blitz in London – how the street where he'd grown up, in Islington, had been reduced to rubble – and how lucky we were compared to him as a child.

This had somehow transformed into the scene of my regular nightmares. Most nights, a string of spitfires flew towards me, their guns blazing a double stream of bullets into my brain. My face and my flesh were destroyed. I was left, burned and bloodied in the street. I awoke, trembling and terrified in the dark.

I searched for a sliver of light slanting in from the street outside, to check to see if my skin was bleeding. Disorientated, I couldn't believe I wasn't hurt. I was still caught in the nightmare. I often wanted to get up and walk around to break its hold, but I couldn't. I refused to pull up the mosquito net and put my foot over the side of the bed and onto the floor. I was terrified of the monster that lived under my bed. It would grab my ankle and pull me under.

These terrors played out in nightmares and continued to live inside, in the split-off part of me. I lived above the split. I knew to stay away from that line, but in staying away, I made that buried part bad and hated myself for having it. There was something wrong with me that made me different from other people, yet I pretended to myself and the world that I was all right. It cost me. It was exhausting to keep it shut down. It turned me into a cardboard cut-out of a person.

All my attention became focused on trying to live up to my grandparent's expectations. I made my bed every morning and then never sat on it. My room was kept immaculate in case visitors came calling. Grandma gave me a white dressing table with a large mirror and a little padded stool. She added a crystal duchess set that sat on pale-pink doilies. The finely curved vases held delicate bunches of crimson plastic flowers. I often sat on the stool, where I settled into the feminine elegance, entranced by its beauty.

The crystal pieces became my friends as I imagined them alive. They spoke to me, saying, 'Hey, we see you.'

The solid arms of the dressing table held me when I ran from the wrongness inside me. They told me I was a girl. It was the first positive confirmation of my natal sex. It helped me stand up to my mother's continual shaming of my girl form. I was still on edge but began to relax, even though my bedroom was only for sleeping, never for mess.

*

The household was overwhelmed by the needs of my baby brother, James. My grandparents' demand for order was stretched to its limits, but slowly, they too were won over by having this chance to love again. James became the centre of the three adults' attention. The baby released a longing in my grandmother. She adored him. He was the child she could now indulge when her children had been brought up under struggle and hardship.

I heard the stories of her life during the blackouts that occurred at least once a week. Various workers' unions were often out on strike. Many were fighting for workers' rights and the ability to strike in itself – the federal government was attempting to impose anti-strike laws. This had led to widespread defiance by the unions.

In the flickering candlelight, I imagined the scenes of my grandmother's life as she spoke. During the Depression, my grandfather worked to repair and upgrade the railway line between Townsville and Mount Isa – over 1,000 kilometres in distance through the arid Queensland outback. My grandparents, with their two young children, lived in a tent at the edge of the tracks, progressing along its length as the work was completed. My mother remembered being a little girl playing in the dirt between the spinifex, surrounded by sun-bronzed, mostly single young men. One gave her a doll – her first. She carried it everywhere, refusing to let it go.

Grandad was refused enlistment in the Australian Army during World War Two due to his poor eyesight – a blow to his male ego as all his brothers fought. This slight seemed to stay with him. He always seemed to be trying to live up to his idea of a real man but somehow failing.

He then worked at a string of jobs: in a fish and chip shop in Brisbane, as a butcher in Townsville, running a boarding house for men one street back from The Strand, and then taking over the canteen at the local sports reserve of a weekend while working for the council during the week.

Joan was taken out of school at twelve years old to provide an extra pair of hands in the boarding house. She was again surrounded by single men. She told how she had to starch and iron the men's cricket clothes – their 'whites'. The trousers were starched so stiffly they could stand up on their own. If they didn't, several of the men would throw them back in her face.

*

James adored Grandma and called her Mama in his child's voice. Joan demanded the title she didn't work for. It was a constant power struggle between the two of them over who was his real mother. Grandma did most of the mothering as Joan was incapable of putting herself to one side and attending to her son. The situation somehow always became about what Joan needed and she made sure we heard about it.

Joan often fought with her mother, but Grandma would turn away and leave Joan to it, having learned that was the best way of dealing with her daughter. Grandad couldn't cope with the tension in the house. He blamed the women for spoiling the child, then gave James some of his lemonade or squares of chocolate – part of his private stash kept in a corner of the fridge.

We older kids looked on as Grandma made James special chicken dinners – a treat in a land of cheap cuts of beef. I forced myself to swallow the still-red corned beef boiled in salted water and then baked egg custard, which threatened to come back up, while James was served ice cream for dessert.

We enrolled at Central State School, the oldest school in Townsville, built in 1869. The school was moved to its present location, the site of the original gaol, in 1879. The school's two-story administration block was the former residence of the police inspector. It's an elegant stone building with French doors and arched openings. The blocks of classrooms were built on the site of the former cell blocks for male inmates and swept around what remains of the stone prison wall, now all painted a brilliant white. The concrete slab of the female cell block marked the lines of the court for playing handball.

Later, some of us dared each other to sneak into the old psychiatric ward. It sat, locked up, adjacent to the school but easily entered by determined students. It was terrifying to peek through the eye hole in the door and then stand in a padded cell. The heavy material lining the floors and walls was discoloured a dirty grey. I imagined being locked in – trapped and surrounded by the cloying, sweat-soaked muskiness that still lingered. It added to my nightmares.

Graeme and I first started at the school in Grade 4 with Trevor in Grade 5. To get to school we walked past the sports reserve and through Queens Park. Local Indigenous children loved to surprise any new kids. They jumped out from the tangle of vines of the massive fig trees lining the park, scaring us.

The Bindal and Wulgurukaba People are the first people of the Townsville region. Their important symbols are the shooting star and carpet snake. But little of their culture was known to me or spoken about when I lived there as a child.

That first day, they made a show of threatening us with fists and teasing us with swear words, but in our little gang of three, we held our own. It set the pattern for our walks to school. Later, when Trevor went to high school, there were only two of us. Graeme wasn't a fighter, but I would stand in front of him, staring the other kids out. Once they knew I was serious, they would leave us alone.

On our first day at school, I said goodbye to my brothers, who were both in different classes, and found my classroom. I stood inside the door to let the other students push past. My teacher spotted me.

'Good morning. My name is Mrs McVane. Your place is over here.'

Mrs McVane led me to my seat and waited while I settled. She crouched down until she was level with me, holding on to my desk to keep her balance. She welcomed me with a smile that lit up her eyes.

'What's your name?'

I looked down and tried to say my name. 'WWW-Wen-Wen-Wen-dy.' I got it out.

Mrs McVane stayed silent. She was waiting for me to look up. When I did, she gave me a little nod of recognition. She knew what it cost me to speak.

Mrs McVane's ginger hair was tied back in a ponytail that bobbed when she walked. She flitted like a butterfly from desk to desk, pausing in front of a student and then giving them all her attention. She laughed a lot and showed me how to learn when it had been an unfathomable maze. From that first meeting, she didn't force me to speak in front of the class. She let me show her the answers I'd written in my book.

I looked into her sea-green eyes and risked a grin. I spent hours after school perfecting my assignments, drawing and printing out the words in spaced-out lines. I developed a sense of pride in my work. Between her and my grandparents, I was developing a strong work ethic, as I embraced this new concept of order and hard work. Life wasn't about fun – it was about having everything perfectly in place and doing my best.

*

Christmas arrived – my first without my father. The adults were busy preparing as extended family were coming. Strangers soon filled the rooms. They all talked at once as they sat on a mismatch of chairs. The food they'd brought to share was spread out before me in unfamiliar shapes, colours and smells. It sat waiting, inviting me in, on a long table covered with a starched, ironed, white linen cloth. A small plastic Christmas tree stood in one corner. I couldn't remember having one before. There were a few presents under the tree.

Aunty Estelle introduced herself and handed me a small parcel wrapped in silver Christmas paper. A little smile danced on her lips. She prodded my hands, *go on*, when I hesitated. I pulled apart the sticky tape to discover the picture of a rearing jet-black horse, neck arched and nostrils flaring. It stared up at me from the cover of a book – *Black Beauty*. It was my first ever book.

I slipped outside to the back of the house to be alone. I found chapter one. The words lost their shapes as I became Black Beauty, pulled apart when he was whipped, then put together when a kind owner was found. I lived his broken knees and his work as a carriage horse, and stumbled with him when he was forced to gallop over sharp stones.

Except for a few fairy tales Joan read to my brothers at bedtime in Broome, neither of my parents read. Joan proudly stated that she'd never read a book in her life. My grandmother would read the advertised food specials as my grandfather grabbed the rest of the newspaper, but one of his favourite sayings was that only bludgers sat around reading books. I'd have to read in secret or pretend it was for homework.

When I returned to school in the new year, I discovered the library. In the breaks, I escaped to its aisles where I was transported to endless places. I became the characters in the books. I was Jade, the girl dressed as a boy and going to sea as a pirate. Maybe I could do that too and my mother might leave me alone. I found Elyne Mitchell's *Silver Brumby* series and roamed the Australian high country, racing through the mountains with the palomino stallion, Thowra. I lived in the Wild West and the author JT Edson became another favourite. I devoured the library, working my way through the shelves.

I broke free of my stilted body and played truant from my struggling voice. I found an untamed abandon in these imagined other lives, but I had to keep my emotions hidden at home because Joan would use them against me. I was often jarred back into reality by a critical comment from her – like a knife thrust into my belly.

If I couldn't say a particular word and was forced to answer, I made up an easier set of words. A yellow dress became green because I could say green. Or I stopped mid-sentence, going silent, any further words deserting me. When I was tired it was often too hard to produce even a single sound.

When I went to bed, I hid under the mosquito net. I blocked out the light glaring in and the noise from the television, and imagined I was a spy – the first female James Bond. I wanted to be in MI6 when I grew up.

I couldn't wait to escape to my bed and re-enter my make-believe world of espionage and spies. I kept one story going for weeks, picking it up each night. I tried to stop myself from going to sleep because then I'd wake to my nightmare or another day, and the torment of speaking. There was always some adult demanding I try.

Chapter 3

The start of belonging

I wanted to be a boy yet I hated being mistaken for one. This frequently happened because of my hair. I didn't look like a girl. I longed for the life of my brothers – of not having to help with the laundry or wash and dry up for hours. But being a boy was a dream. The next best thing was to join them in their room, but I was told it was out of bounds for girls.

My mother called me a tomboy and laughed in an unkind way. My body was somehow lacking. I ached to be like the other girls at school, but I didn't know how. Maybe if I looked more like them … I decided to ask my mother for permission.

'Um um, I was www-won-wondering … can I gr-grow my hair l-long? All the g-g-girls have l-long hair.'

I stood in front of my mother, sweating after the effort of forcing the words out. I'd watched her until I thought she was in a better mood. I'd practised saying the words, but still, I'd stammered. I was determined to at least hold my ground. That was something I could do silently.

My mother stopped what she was doing but didn't answer me immediately. She stared straight through me for some time, thinking.

'Get in the car.'

'WW-What? Now? But www-what about home-ww-work?'

'Get in the car, I said. Can't you do anything I tell you?'

I sat in the front seat next to her and she drove towards the local shops. I didn't know what she was up to until she parked in front of the hairdressers. I refused to move from my seat but she shoved me towards the door.

'Get out. You're getting your hair cut and that's it!' She got out of the car and walked around to my side. She yanked me half out. I gave up and got out, following her into the hairdressers – not making eye contact with anyone.

'Can you cut her hair now?' my mother asked the hairdresser.

'Yes, sure. I have a space, but her hair doesn't look like it needs a trim …'

'I want you to cut it all off.'

The woman looked at me, then carefully said, 'Maybe you could think about …'

'I said I want you to cut all her hair off. Are you going to do it? Or do I need to go somewhere else?'

'Mm … OK …'

She started cutting my hair, not saying another word. She stopped and glanced at my mother, only for my mother to tell her to keep going. When it was almost a crewcut my mother said she could stop.

The next morning, I didn't want to get out of bed.

'I think I-I-I'm sssick …'

'You're going to school and that's my final word.'

I dragged myself to class, my school hat pulled low over my eyes. I sat still as the room bustled into life. I couldn't look at Mrs McVane when she said good morning to the class and stopped in front of my desk.

'What's wrong?' She stooped down low, trying to meet my eyes.

I shook my head. I couldn't speak.

'Can you tell me …?' She tried again but I started crying.

After a pause, she turned to the rest of the class and told them to leave me alone.

*

I retreated into a bleak place, barely functioning. On another school day, I needed to go to the toilet but I was frozen on my chair. I couldn't speak in front of the other students or put my hand up. I sat there not moving until I peed on my seat. The seeping puddle was hot against my skin.

The bell went and the children started to leave. Their chairs scraped the wooden floor as their excited chatter surged around me. I sat in the warm puddle with my head bowed. Mrs McVane quickly realised the problem.

She called a girl over. 'Emma, could you please wait with Wendy while I go get a towel?'

'Yes, sure.' Emma perched on my desk, swinging her legs. Mrs McVane returned with a towel and a clean set of clothes from the school's second-hand clothes store. She cleaned me up and helped me slip into some dry shorts.

'It's normal you know. Kids are always having accidents. That's why we keep spare clothes.' She smiled at me and kept talking. When I chanced a quick peek, Mrs McVane stopped and waited for me to look again. Quiet now, she held my gaze, her eyebrows raised, until I gave a little answering nod to her unspoken question.

'Now you can go home,' she said to me. She turned to Emma. 'Emma, can you please walk Wendy home? She lives near you. Would that be OK?' Emma nodded her agreement and went to grab her school bag.

'I'll see you both tomorrow in class. And Wendy, you'll be OK. Do you believe me?' She sounded so certain. I nodded.

We walked together in silence at first, and then Emma started talking and asking questions. I gave short replies. She didn't laugh at me. I discovered Emma was kind and funny. She became my first girlfriend; I'd only hung around my brothers before. I visited Emma after school. She lived up near the plumber, Charlie.

I couldn't believe how Emma could babble on – an almost continuous string of words, something I'd never done. If I attempted to say something and got stuck, she filled in the silence with a burst of words.

It was easier to go to her place. I cautiously sat on Emma's bed – something I didn't dare do at home – and marvelled at the mess in her room. Her mother welcomed me when she came in with a plate of biscuits for us to share.

In making friends with Emma, I stepped out of my narrow, tightly held existence and into an unknown world. It suggested that maybe I could do this: make friends, fit in and even join a conversation. It was the start of belonging.

I discovered sport, joining the school's vigoro team. Vigoro was popular in North Queensland. It was the girls' version of cricket but played with a teardrop-shaped bat and two balls: red and white. It's much faster than cricket as it doesn't have overs and is always bowled from the same end. I joined a local club, Castles, and played competitive club games on the weekend.

My grandparents, having been avid tennis players when younger, enrolled us at the local Lawn Tennis Association and we played on Saturday mornings. I was good at it and won my age competition. My grandparents were proud when they saw my photo in the local newspaper. Our vigoro team won the season too, and I received a handful of awards. Another picture in the paper. I made a new friend, Jennie, and we played in the school teams together.

Life outside of home was now full of laughter and excitement, of having girlfriends who welcomed me into their homes. It didn't matter that I got stuck on words.

*

I was 10 when I met my Uncle Eric for the first time. He was my mother's brother and Aunty Estelle's husband. He'd just returned to Townsville after several years of fighting in Vietnam with the Australian Army. He visited us one afternoon after we'd returned from school and stayed for dinner. I was surprised at how big he was – not fat, but burly. He towered over me but was careful with his size. He gently took my hand when he first said hello at the front door.

His hand was rough with thick callouses. Grooves outlined his deeply tanned cheeks and crisscrossed his forehead. He had dark, puffy patches under his eyes and shadows that seemed to shiver behind them. He spoke in a low, scratchy voice and came with the smell of cigarette smoke. Neither of my grandparents smoked – they were both dead against it.

I watched Eric from the corner of my eye as we ate the special roast dinner in his honour. My grandmother continually jumped up to wait on him as my mother plied him with information that he wasn't interested in. I helped clean up and then followed him out onto the back landing. He dwarfed the space.

Eric leaned on the top of the metal railing as he lit a cigarette. He glanced at me and said, 'You know, your grandad hasn't changed in all the years I've been away.' He laughed, shaking his head, and lifted one foot to perch on the bottom railing.

'He's just the same, the stubborn old coot. He couldn't even give me my own bottle of beer. What does he think I've been doing all these years? I'm a grown man, for God's sake … I very nearly didn't come back. Do you know that?' He glanced at me then looked away.

'So many didn't. What a celebration! Of what? One bottle of beer between the nine of us.'

He didn't expect an answer but I nodded at his words, hoping he could see me. I wanted him to know that I was listening. I remembered my taste of beer: a single swallow from my tall glass. It was sour and smelled strange. I didn't like it, but I was glad to be included. Even James was given a taste. He'd pulled a funny face and nearly spat it out but quickly caught himself. I'd laughed.

'Dad and his set-in-stone ways.' Eric shook his head, then knocked the cigarette ash into the black china-cat ashtray that he was holding in his other hand. The ashtray was usually tucked away in the sideboard.

'I've never been allowed to smoke in this house, yet they keep this ashtray for me and bring it out each time.'

It was dark now. He looked up at the millions of stars clustered in a vast sweep across the night sky. He turned to me and asked, 'Do you know what the blanket of stars is called?'

I shook my head, still not daring to say a word.

'It's the Milky Way.' Eric pointed to a cluster of stars. 'That one there is the Southern Cross. You find it by its two brighter guiding stars. Can you see them?' He turned to check, so I nodded again. He continued smoking. Then, still staring out over the chook yard and banana trees, he quietly stated, 'You wouldn't want to know what the war was like.'

His eyes hinted at images still caught in their gaze that didn't belong to Rowland Street. And then he talked, in a faraway voice, gruff with unshed tears.

'The Viet Cong cut lengths of bamboo from the jungle. Then they sharpened the ends. They pushed one end into the soil, hiding the poles in the vegetation that lined the paths we had to walk along. The paths were very narrow.' Eric shook his head again.

'It was all we could manage to do – to machete a thin path from that crazy jungle. It was so dense. So we couldn't see the poles. We didn't even guess they'd done it. We'd only just cut the bloody path, for God's sake. They were so silent and fast at doing it. The bamboo poles slanted inward at 45 degrees. But then the Viet Cong would open fire. We were ambushed, so we jumped into the jungle … but my mates were speared on the poles.' Eric shook his head, almost as if he couldn't believe his own words.

'I lost so many mates. We could never find the buggers but I could feel their eyes, constantly watching us, like a physical weight. Do you know I was a mine sweeper?'

'No,' I whispered – my first word to Eric.

'It was my job to walk at the front of the men and sweep for mines.'

I stood still, not wanting to break the flow of his words but they had ground into silence.

His pain woke an answering rawness in me. I knew I had a similar place: of confusion and chaos and hurt. It was almost as if I could glimpse the door – as if from the end of a long corridor. This man had inadvertently awakened my knowing, but this intimate sharing was one-sided – only Eric's secrets and what kept him awake at night. There were no words for mine, so I shut it down and turned away from myself.

Eric turned to me and asked, 'Do you know how to wish upon the stars?'

'No,' I said, louder this time.

He then taught me the words, 'Star light, star bright, I wish I may, I wish I might have the wish I wish tonight.'

The outside me looked up to the starlight and longed to believe that it was possible, while the inside me sat waiting, abandoned and alone in the dark.

I was eleven on 11 January 1973 when the governor-general formally declared an end to Australia's involvement in the Vietnam War.

*

When I grew towards my early teens, I hated that my room was the converted veranda without real walls and a door I could shut, yet I loved that I could sleep in it alone. The rest of my family slept in bedrooms at the other end of the house. James now shared with Graeme and Trevor, making a boy-only space, leaving Joan with Sarah. Those two behaved like girlfriends together.

I looked on, unable to make a noise or mess in my fishbowl of a room. The boys kept closing their door, shutting me out. I heard their music through the wall; the band, Paper Lace, playing 'Billie don't be a hero' and 'The night Chicago died' – Trevor's favourites. Graeme loved any songs by John Denver, especially 'Leaving on a jet plane'. I sat on the front steps and silently mouth the words along with the songs.

My room allowed me space to roam at night. I wasn't scared of the monster under my bed anymore, although I still checked. Most nights, I crept to the fridge. Then, careful of the light of the opened door, I ate a few squares from Grandad's private hoard of chocolate. I didn't eat too much. I found out later that all of us were stealing his chocolate – four children sneaking into the kitchen whenever Grandma was in the garden. I made a few hurried escapes from the fridge when I heard my grandmother's hard heels clunking up the back steps. Grandad never let on.

*

One afternoon, in that difficult time before dinner, Grandad was pacing up and down the hall between his bedroom and the kitchen. His head was down and his hands were clenched into fists. He'd get to one end, then promptly turn around as if he couldn't make up his mind.

My grandmother banged the pot she'd washed onto the draining board. I jumped, the dishcloth in my hand. I'd been waiting for her to hand it to me. She turned sharply towards her husband. Her face was strained; her lips, tight. She stepped around me and followed him down the hall.

Her frustration spilled out in angry words.

'It's all your fault. Call yourself a man. What a laugh. You're never bloody here, you bloody bastard. You leave me to do everything!' She continued shouting as Grandad faced her. 'It's you! It's always you that makes it worse. If you could only help, but you leave me every time. You walk out and go to that bloody club. You make it worse, don't you see? It's you!'

He stayed silent but my grandmother wasn't finished. The dam had burst and she wasn't stopping. 'I hate you. I wish I'd never married you … and now this! All these bloody kids to look after. All the washing, all the bloody mess all the time. Do you ever help pick up? No. You just leave and go mow the bloody lawn.'

That was the final slight. It pushed my grandfather over the edge. He shoved her, attempting to get past, but she fell backwards onto the floor, banging her head. This was his chance. I saw it cross his eyes. He straddled her with his legs and grabbed her around her neck. I stood frozen as I watched his hands tighten around her throat. Her face changed colour. She stopped struggling. He kept going. He didn't stop.

I couldn't move or breathe or help.

I couldn't work out if it was seconds or hours.

His face slackened as he slowly loosened his hold. His eyes registered what his hands had been doing. He looked at them, almost as if they'd done it alone. His face was pale as he collapsed back against the wall. My grandmother gasped a sudden ragged breath.

For long, mute minutes, he leaned there, his chest heaving, staring at his wife as she continued struggling for breath. She lay there, not daring to move. The wall held him. Then he pushed himself up and stumbled away. I heard him go down the back stairs.

My grandmother continued gasping, freer now that he was gone – a broken, too-real doll. I'd never seen her lie on the floor before. Her dress was above her knees, exposing her legs turned out at odd angles. I could see the soft white flesh of her thighs above the tan line. She was always tidy and contained. I couldn't understand how my grandmother was lying in the hall. From being pale, her face had flooded with colour. She cradled her throat with her hands.

Something cracked in my chest as I watched silent tears slip down the side of her face. I stepped towards her, kneeled and put my smaller hands lightly against her gnarled and sun-damaged ones. Her skin felt scaly. Warm. She turned towards me and I helped her up into my arms, where she sobbed. After Grandma calmed down a little, we sat together at the table. I made us both a cup of tea. We sat quietly, not saying much, comforted by each other's presence.

A while later, my mother crashed into our silence. She was oblivious to what was going on. In her overloud voice, she demanded to know why dinner wasn't ready. Why weren't the plates on the table? My grandmother ignored her. I stood up, found the plates and arranged them.

Life went on, but my grandmother increased her visits to her sisters and my grandfather worked extra shifts with the council. I walked tentatively around them as if I were in a dream of shadows and couldn't find my way. The world had lost its sparkle.

Chapter 4

My mother

I call my mother by her name: Joan.

I first refused to call her Mum in the early 1970s when I realised she hated it. I'd found a way to hurt her. It was a sliver of revenge when I didn't know how else to stand up to her overwhelming presence. We'd been waging a war against each other. It was a loud, dramatic, raging one for her and a silent, bewildered one for me. I was desperately trying to hang on to myself in the face of her inherent right to tell me how wrong I always was.

Joan, like her brother Eric, was taller than the average person. She was big-boned and fleshy, with breasts that swung beneath her thin cotton shifts because she didn't like wearing a bra, only a thin camisole. It did nothing to stop her nipples from pushing into me when she demanded I hug her. She wore her dresses too short, and it made me uncomfortable; in fact, everything about her made me squirm.

When I called her Joan, I watched for the anger sweeping her face. By the time I was eleven, we were too even in size for her to grab and fling away. With vague memories of her doing this, her hands too tight under my arms, but not the details, I knew I couldn't trust my mother. I compared myself to my friends and how they interacted with their mothers. I couldn't comprehend their varying degrees of closeness.

Both my grandparents were one of fourteen children and grew up in outback Queensland: Grandma in Prairie and Grandad in Richmond. When their siblings visited us, Joan held court, as over time she too relaxed. She had grown more insistent, as she didn't have a husband who shut her up. She wasn't scared of her parents.

One Sunday morning, after I turned twelve, two of my grandmother's sisters came for morning tea. I set the table with care, proud to be trusted with handling my grandmother's best china. I spaced the cups and saucers neatly around the table and waited for the water to boil to fill the big silver teapot. It was my job to make the tea. My mother found her place and looked around the semi-circle of people.

'Come on Mum, we're all waiting,' Joan called to her mother. Grandma was the last to sit down as she brought the sponge cake and tray of biscuits. She handed the cake knife to my mother, knowing Joan would want the attention. My mother portioned out pieces of the vanilla sponge and then took her own. After a few bites, she looked directly at me but spoke to her aunts.

'She's stupid, you know. Do you know what she did when she was a little girl?' Joan turned to look at them.

'She ate half the lino on the kitchen floor. It was when we lived in Brisbane, on View Street. Aunty May used to come and visit and couldn't believe it either that a child would eat the mucky lino on the floor. It was disgusting.' She laughed. 'It was so eaten away we had to replace it before we moved. Norm was furious. He hated spending money, the bloody miser, but it was a rented house and we needed our bond back.'

I couldn't look up. I knew they were all staring at me. I was a dirty, shameful creature.

'Ex-excc-cuse m-me,' I said and fled to the adjacent kitchen.

I tidied up and boiled the jug for more tea. I was often the butt of Joan's jokes, but I struggled to understand this new information. Her usual putdown was calling me the bull in the china shop, but this was different. I listened, safe on the other side of the kitchen counter, my face hidden behind the overhead cupboards.

Joan continued, telling more snippets of when her children were young. No one else spoke. Her words washed through me and opened a door into my past. I remembered eating the kitchen lino in the house at Chermside in Brisbane. As I remembered, I became that child. I was young, maybe two years old.

I knew that the boys were good but because I was bad, I was separated and put in the kitchen. I lay on the hard lino on the floor and listened to my brothers in the lounge room with our mother. I pressed my face hard against the gap under the closed door, and with my eyes shut, I imagined I too was playing. It helped if there was a draft to cool my face and carry their voices, but in the steamy humidity, it was too hot for a breeze.

My stomach hurt, folding in on itself, demanding food, while the shadows crawled across the walls. I faded into a restless sleep, waking hungry, then wet. Cramps gnawed at my stomach.

After a time, I discovered the lino that covered the floor. I lifted a corner, started nibbling then chewing on the rubbery substance. The swallowing hushed my growling belly and gave me something to do.

The gritty underside and jarring crunch of little stones caught in the back of the lino sent shivers through me, but I liked the smooth top. I spied a cockroach and grabbed it, stuffing it in my mouth. From then on, I looked for more of them. The spikey bits on their legs scratched my gums but they were more filling than the lino. I made a game of who was faster.

Ten years after this happened, I stood in my grandmother's kitchen in Rowland Street and remembered feeling their little legs and the bitter taste of cockroach wings in my mouth. How could she laugh? Her story helped explain why I always wanted more food. I never felt full, but can a two-year-old child give up? Because inside me there was an empty pit of despairing nothingness.

I felt flattened by the memories until I remembered how my father would come into the kitchen. He would come when the shadows smudged the far side of the room and sweep me up into his arms. I was his girl.

My father was the same height and build as my mother – a matching pair, both solid and thickened around the waist. When she reddened from too much sun, he turned a deep olive-brown. His even, white teeth shone from within his tan when he grinned. They complimented the sheen of his slicked-back hair, which was held in place with Brylcreem – the popular men's hair product. That, along with his accent and charming smiles, marked him as different: they shouted 'Englishman'.

Daddy would pour that charm on me when he swung me around and took me through to the lounge room. Joan would glare from behind his back. Sometimes he wasn't happy when he came home from work and didn't come into the kitchen. On those occasions, I heard him storming around the house like a rampaging thundercloud. But mostly he found me and we would play happy families until the fighting and shouting erupted.

Later, when my father wasn't watching, Joan would grab me under my arms and carry me to my room. Once there, she would throw me through the air. I remember flying backwards until my head whacked the wooden bars of the cot.

At the morning tea, Joan puffed out her chest and announced that she purposefully kept Graeme and me apart. She told the aunts it was because I always bit Graeme when we were together. She claimed I was a destructive child and she needed to protect him from me.

Her words confirmed my feelings of always being separate. But then I pictured the photographs of us as toddlers and how she presented us to the outside world. She showed us off, her twins, dressed alike in boy/girl versions of the same clothes in our double stroller. My favourite picture was of Graeme and me in a matching tartan set, complete with caps.

On the occasions when I was with my twin, I would ache to feel him close, a skin-and-flesh need I couldn't satisfy. It was a visceral longing for our preborn state of total enmeshment.

*

As I grew into a teenager, I pieced together parts of our earlier life from Joan's stories. Her words continued to prompt thoughts of different scenes, but they never broached that well-wrapped parcel of cut-off memories.

*

Another story Joan told to hold centre stage was about Trevor in Brisbane. Trevor was seventeen months older than Graeme and me. He was born in London after my father, Norm, went home to England with Joan. Norm wanted to show off his new bride to his parents. Then, when Trevor was nine months old, they returned to Townsville by cruise liner – the main transport in those days. The trip took six weeks and we were born six and a half months later.

Joan laughingly told the story of how Trevor packed a little case with all his precious possessions and left the house in View Street one afternoon. He must have crossed several busy roads because he was found miles away and several hours later. A woman spotted him wandering in the night and took him to a police station. When questioned, Trevor said in his little boy's words that he was looking for a new mummy and daddy. He'd wanted a new home.

Trevor had been four.

*

At another gathering, Joan went further back in time. She said I was born as the lunch bell rang at the Mater Hospital in Townsville. She was proud she could produce a child at noon, with Graeme born 15 minutes later. We were separated into different humidicrib incubators for several months, having been born severely underweight and six weeks premature.

Her words woke distinct sensations – this time of the nasogastric tube down my left nostril and glaring overhead white lights. Joan said the nurses struggled to find a milk formula that we could tolerate. I knew my brother was somewhere in the room but I couldn't reach him.

This telling made sense of the sharp sensation of loss I felt when I thought of my twin brother. It reinforced my knowledge of being with him in the womb. I remembered feeling him wrapped against me, as a presence and a consciousness. We had talked silently. It was me who had wanted to get out of the space we were in. It had been getting too squashed as we were shoved against each other. Graeme had been content staying put. This had set the pattern of our future relationship: me always pushing and Graeme happy to potter along. Or better still, sitting in a shady spot where he could daydream.

Joan said that when our father arrived at the maternity ward, he took one look at our tiny forms through the nursery window and told her, 'It would be better if they died.'

Joan finished the story by saying, 'He walked out, not visiting again, the bastard. I was the only mother without a bunch of flowers by her bed.'

*

Stories of Broome became my favourites. We had flown as a family from Brisbane to Darwin where we lived for a year, before settling in the Western Australian town in 1966. I avoided thinking about Darwin, as it left my stomach in knots, whereas memories of Broome pulled me in with its welcoming colours and wide-open land.

Broome at that time was a remote town of First Nations locals who moved freely through it, with Chinese, Japanese and Indonesian immigrants, who made up the bulk of the workforce. There was a smattering of white-skinned folk like us.

I remembered the red dirt that coated my skin a different colour, the sharp cliffs and crazy rock formations and the distant sound of the surf that I could hear in the quiet of the night. I pictured the long wooden wharf that jutted out into the endless blue, with the pearl trawlers tied up at its sides, and how the skies would turn to dirty white and surging grey when the storms roared in from over the ocean.

Norm was second in charge of the Overseas Telecommunications Commission station, and we lived in an OTC house. Norm was still nervous, but in Broome, he seemed to relax a little. He started smiling and would take us to the now-popular tourist attraction Cable Beach to play in the sand. The sand gave way to stone shelves at one end of the beach. Here, the retreating tide would expose rock pools full of plush, red sea anemones and scuttling crabs.

Back then, Broome was rough and ramshackle, poised between the bustling boom of the natural mother-of-pearl trade and the development of the cultured pearl industry that later helped turn the town into a thriving resort destination. The Asian immigrants had come to dive and harvest the mother-of-pearl, as well as collect the occasional natural pearl. Mother-of-pearl had been used for buttons, buckles, cutlery handles and as inlay in furniture, but the development of plastic was taking over many of those items and the mother-of-pearl trade was in decline.

Norm would oscillate between smiles and fierce moods that flared up and kept raging for days. We learned to keep out of his way. His favourite form of punishment was grabbing any two of us and smacking our heads against each other, which he had started doing in Brisbane. I was often left dazed, my ears ringing. It worked a treat.

If I wasn't fast enough to hide us both, Norm lashed out at Graeme whenever he was within range. Graeme forgot to watch out for our father. Norm demanded quiet when he came home from work or after the night shift when he had to sleep during the day. We learned to duck into any child-sized space to escape him. It was easier in Broome, as the house was on two-foot-high stilts. We dashed under the house.

Once there, Trevor, Graeme and I cuddled together in the dirt, sometimes for hours. We hid behind one of the square concrete stilts until it was time for bed, or hunger drove us out. We made up games, pretending the tin squares on top of the stilts that stopped the ants from entering the house were hats for soldiers, and fight mock battles, sticks as our guns. We made friends with a carpet snake that had also found refuge under the house. We snuck out to eat the tart yet sweet rosellas from the bushes lining the side of the yard.

Graeme and I turned five in December 1966 and started school the following year, with Trevor in the grade ahead. He was six. Trevor was given a second-hand, sturdy red bike that we pushed and rode after school, falling off and grazing our knees.

On a weekday morning, we walked to school with polished school shoes and white socks, but the local kids taunted us. We found a hiding place in the bottom of an old gum tree, careful of the goanna who lived further up, and left our shoes and socks there for the day, walking the rest of the way to school in bare feet. We toughened up. Sometimes, we forgot to put them on again at the end of the school day and received a bashing from Joan.

On Sunday, we went to Sunday School and church – even Norm went on occasion. The church was a simple timber building with a peaked corrugated iron roof that trapped the heat. Utterly sweet to outsiders, Norm would be attentive and smilingly polite to the ladies congregating out front at the end of the service. Joan made sure we looked our best. I wore long white socks with a frill at the top, white gloves, a ribboned hat and shiny dress shoes in the fine crimson dirt that quickly left a layer over everything. Norm put on a show of being the doting dad. I wanted that picture to come true, but it was only ever that – a flat picture. Those smiles and that charm stopped at our front door. I was no longer his girl. That had ended in Brisbane, two years before.

Joan had given birth to a girl, Sarah, before we left Brisbane. In Broome, Joan was busy with Sarah and needed my help. I was a timid little person who knew to avoid attention and how to work instead. After I got up in the morning, I woke up my brothers and made all our beds. Then I got the boys ready for school.

One of my morning jobs was to find the green frogs huddled in the bathtub and carry them outside, where I carefully placed them on a patch of damp earth under the dripping tap. Joan refused to touch the frogs and instead hollered for me to take them away, if I hadn't been fast enough to move them. I was besotted with the frogs' compact presence and big, gleaming eyes and was often startled into laughter when they blinked.

I was desperate to belong and find a semblance of love. I had discovered my mother for the first time and tried to get her to like me. I did exactly what she told me, but even then, I'd be wrong. I couldn't work it out – from one day to the next her mood and what she wanted changed. It was only with my brothers in our little gang of three that I felt safe.

Trev, Graeme and I had clumped together. We had our private language. Joan demanded to know what we were saying, but we held a united silence. Then we bolted from the house, running through the dusty streets to the beach and its lukewarm tropical water.

Our favourite places were the rock pools and watching the waves break onto the headland, then playing hide and seek in the dunes among the tufted grasses. If we were lucky, we might spot a snubfin dolphin close to shore. And sometimes, when we wandered further away to the shallow lagoons, we saw placid dugongs feeding among the sea grass in the calm water.

Barefoot, with no adults, only my brothers, I felt free and one with the wild creatures, the lizards and snakes, the smooth green frogs, and even the old man goanna who guarded our shoes. And the dirt. I loved the red dirt that blended me into the rocks and stones and the land itself.

Chapter 5

A never-ending sea of pain

Joan was missing her parents. In Broome, with four children under seven and a husband who refused to help within the home, she often struggled. She wanted to return to Townsville and civilization. She hated the red dust that coated the surfaces no matter how hard she cleaned, and having to wait for the supply boat that came once a week from Perth, which provided fresh milk and produce.

Norm eventually gave in to Joan's pleading, or maybe he felt that enough time had passed that he wouldn't run the risk of bumping into his old mates if he returned to the east coast. Either way, towards the end of 1967, my parents packed up the house and fitted as much as they could into Norm's red Hillman, with us kids squashed in the back, and drove to Townsville. Plus the stray kitten who'd wandered in the week before. Shocked that they'd allowed us to keep him, we called him Cat and fought over who got to cuddle him. I loved his loud purr and wet nose against my skin.

It took six days to make the journey from the edge of the Indian Ocean on the west coast of Australia to the Pacific on the east coast. For miles and miles it was dirt but then the rain started, turning the land into an endless quagmire. We were bogged crossing a river and had to wait for a vehicle to pull us to the other bank. Norm rechecked the points in the engine distributor and then cranked up the front of the car using the starting handle to get it going again. I watched him avoid the vicious kickback of the metal rod as it suddenly spun around.

The rain stopped. The land dried out. The tall, distinctively striped stack of Mount Isa broke the monotony of never-ending scrub and dirt. Then, one evening, as dusk was deepening, we drove over the Great Dividing Range and Townsville was spread before us. The sea of lights seemed to go on and on, framed by the distant dark of the Coral Sea. Norm found his way through the streets and we pulled up out front of 1A Rowland Street.

Rowland was a short street of less than a dozen houses and sat at right angles with Redpath, an even shorter street that faced the Townsville Rugby League Grounds and Sports Reserve. These two streets formed a dogleg behind the main road into the city: Warburton Street. Castle Hill, an ever-silent watchful presence, loomed above.

I was awed by the hill after the flatness of Broome. It helped set my bearings in that new place. I could always work out where I was by staring up at its flat face or more gentle sloping sides and back. Later, as I continued to live with its changing moods and colours, I borrowed its solid presence by imagining it inside me.

That first night, when my father drove up, my grandparents appeared on the veranda that jutted out from the front of the stilt house. They waited together at the top of the front steps, backlit by the light from the house. They welcomed us in with wide, excited smiles. I didn't remember them.

My grandfather was slender and tanned a deep mahogany. He wore a plain-collared shirt tucked into khaki grey shorts that were belted tight at his waist. My grandmother was a small round shape at his side, in a simple floral dress that ended at her knees. She wore matt black shoes with a square heel, laced tight.

My mother was excited and wouldn't stop talking. After a mad scramble to make up beds and have toast and tea, we older children collapsed onto mattresses laid out in a line on the loungeroom floor. Joan and Sarah took the two single beds in the second bedroom, Norm took a single bed in the third. The smiles didn't last. Norm hated being dependent on Grandad and he and my grandfather clashed repeatedly during the next few days. Norm escaped to Broome, doing the return trip another two times to collect all our possessions.

Trevor, Graeme and I were enrolled at the local school: Central State Primary. Joan demanded that Graeme and I were separated into different classes, but I would find him in the breaks in the playground. This much larger school was too clean and there wasn't any red dirt, only prickly bindi eyes and spear grass that got caught in my socks. We were made to wear shoes.

I didn't know how to make friends. It didn't matter, because after two weeks of attending the school, Norm returned from Broome saying he'd bought a house in Currajong, a suburb on the plain behind Castle Hill. It was February 1968 and we were moving to Palmerston Street, our fifth move in six years. This time, the school was across the road from our house. I missed the hill's presence at my back.

In Currajong, my speech became one long stammer. I couldn't get any whole words out, no matter how hard I forced. Until I could say the words that were stuck in my throat, the ones that named what my father was doing, nothing would come out. School was silent misery. The other kids ganged up against me and mocked my inability to speak. Graeme was in another class. The school stepped in and arranged for a speech therapist to come.

Once a week, I was collected by a senior student and taken to a private room. I grew to dread the therapist's visits as she didn't understand what was going on.

The speech therapist, in her attempt to help, suggested we start with simple words. She used a Grade 1 book, *Dick and Jane*. I knew all the words. I could read, but I couldn't say them because I wasn't allowed to. Naming words had a different flavour to emotional words. Those identifying words had a heavy weight and a threatening presence that was greater than their sound. Even the idea of saying them would bind me stiff and silent and still. To force them out went against every survival instinct.

Speech therapy didn't help. It left me more lost and alone in the ocean of grinning children. I fell into a bottomless dark place. I kept falling until there was only a numb nothingness.

Into this, about eight months later, came Grandad with his perfect gifts. He gave Graeme and me a brand-new bicycle each for our seventh birthday in December 1968. Mine was shiny blue, the polished steel and crisp paintwork broken up by cool transfers. I didn't want to touch it at first in case I messed it up.

I stared at my bicycle until my grandfather helped me sit on the seat and pushed to start me off. I rode straight into the palm tree at the front of the house and fell off laughing. I climbed on again and this time he ran beside me, keeping me steady, as I wobbled my way along the footpath. I quickly found my balance. I took to the streets and rode and rode and rode, for hours at a time – all day if I could.

Nobody cared or knew where I went. I found an empty block. It had a wide dirt area full of large concrete pipes that I rode through, and mounds of compacted dirt that formed little hills. It was heaven: a playground with nobody else. Occasionally my brothers would join me, but they often grew bored and left. That was OK. The dirt held me and the pipes hid me when I needed a rest.

I found a private world of speed and wind and space where the words spoke inside of me. Ideas formed and pictures grew in my mind, but the minute anyone wanted me to speak my throat shut tight. The flowing movement deserted me. I became a blank wall. This happened whenever I was around people.

At least once a week, I stole coins from my mother's purse to buy a chocolate milkshake. It was my next favourite thing after my bike. But I couldn't risk asking for it at the milk bar, as I couldn't get the words out. I had to wait for Graeme. He did my speaking for me. In school, when my teacher needed to know what I couldn't say, she sent a pupil to Graeme's class to ask him to come and translate. Graeme was my voice.

One afternoon, after a lonely day at school, I decided to deal with my stammer. I hated it and wanted it gone. If I didn't have a tongue, people wouldn't expect me to talk. If I didn't talk, I wouldn't stammer.

I'd heard about people who had been enslaved and made mute by having their tongues cut out to stop them from divulging the secrets of their masters. This made sense to me on many levels, as I, too, was not allowed to disclose what was happening in our home.

I sat on the kitchen floor with the sharpest knife I could find and stuck out my tongue, gripping the tip with my other hand. I rested the edge of the blade against its bulk and tried to slice into its thickness. Time waited with me. I tried to find my courage, but I was useless. I couldn't do it.

*

Joan started throwing herself down the fourteen steps of the back stairs of the house we lived in. She was trying to lose the baby she was carrying. She didn't want another child. Every morning, she poured several powdered Bex from the small rectangles of folded paper onto her cornflakes along with sugar.

Bex, made up of aspirin, phenacetin and caffeine, was the go-to substance for housewives to manage their stress. It was made popular by advertisers and comedy shows. They claimed that all a housewife needed was a cup of tea, a Bex and a good lie down. Bex was later found to be addictive and cause kidney damage.

Joan's moods alternated between anger and crying. She blamed us kids for the mess of her life. We often got ourselves to school after finding some food.

Norm criticised what he called her big ugly shape. And then, when Joan was in the last trimester of the pregnancy, she went to the hospital to rest for the last months before giving birth. Sarah went to live with our grandparents, too young to be left without Joan. It was the boys and me again, alone in the house with our father.

I wasn't coping. I wanted out. To be gone.

I sat on the floor in the kitchen. It was always the kitchen I retreated to – my familiar place. The banana leaves were my friends. They shadowed the room. They leaned against the glass of the window and peered in at me. Then they drooped, saddened by what I was about to do. They knew.

I was seven, coming up to eight years old when I took the knife that I'd chosen from the kitchen drawer, and this time I sliced it across my wrist. The serrations lightly peeled the skin apart and a sharp red line seeped up into the air. The television said that this is what you do when you've had enough. The woman in the daytime soap opera had run a bath and stepped into it with her knife. The bath water had turned a brilliant red, masking her naked body.

I used the floor. The floor was my friend. I tried again and again to deepen that first cut. But I couldn't. I was pathetic. I couldn't do anything I longed to do. I wanted to have my wrists bleed out like the woman on TV, but that escape was beyond me. I was utterly trapped in a never-ending sea of pain.

Into this, a few weeks later, came Joan with a baby named James. My new brother lived in the bouncer on the fluffy yellow mat in the lounge room. A strange little thing that cried a lot. I looked at him as if from a distance. Nothing touched me.

It was on a Friday a month after this that my grandparents saved us from my parents' life together. That was the Friday my grandfather drove us to his home and the day that I forgot what had come before.

Chapter 6

Conflicting loyalties

We continued living with my grandparents, and in 1974, Graeme and I followed Trevor to Pimlico State High School. The school was on the south side of the city, not far from where we used to live at Currajong, but it was a three-mile bicycle ride from Rowland Street. It was a daily battle to beat the school bus and avoid being spat on by the students travelling on the bus. I would force Graeme to ride faster than he wanted.

We were enrolled in Grade 8; the first year of secondary school in Queensland. Pimlico bulged at its sides – Townsville didn't have enough state schools to deal with the rise in population. With more than 2,000 students and the school still growing, its rows of demountable classrooms invaded the playing fields.

It had taken me until Grade 7 to find my place at Central and become a semi-confident pupil, but any secure feelings deserted me the moment I entered the grounds of Pimlico High. I was confronted by hundreds of bikes that were already padlocked to racks in the school compound. It was too much. I shrunk inside myself.

I then struggled to find my class in the mass of bodies standing in the sun. I retreated further at the first recess when the students poured from the classrooms to find their friends. I stood alone and silent within the noise.

That first week, I couldn't orientate myself among the almost endless lines of silver seats and rows of buildings. I constantly lost my way. But I found the school library. I spent the recesses there, hidden on the floor in a corner behind a row of shelves. I escaped into stories.

*

During the first term, for the subject of Citizenship, I was told to give a speech. I stood in front of the class terrified of stammering. I couldn't speak. It was the same in English. I couldn't force any words out. The English teacher sent me back to my seat, but the young Citizenship teacher was determined to find a way to help.

He had kind eyes like Mrs McVane. I wanted to please him. I wrote my last speech of the year early and spent weeks standing privately at home practising the words. I spaced them out and made friends with the sounds. When it was my turn to speak, I stood in front of the class. This time my teacher nodded encouragement from the back of the room. I ignored the students and spoke to him with barely a stammer.

I was still attending weekly speech therapy sessions at the local hospital, but I couldn't get rid of my stammer. In a world of fluent speakers, my voice was a bottled-up lump that sat in my throat. It seethed with silent words. I had learnt to smile and nod and pretend to be interested, but inside I was desperate to escape attention. I'd rather stand unnoticed and hidden at the back, with an exit within easy reach. Yet in my imagination, I rehearsed the stories I longed to share and my side of the conversation.

I woke one morning to find blood staining my sheets and thighs. My stomach was a cramped mass of pain. I was terrified.

'I d-d-don't know ww-what's wrong with me,' I said to my mother.

Her face took on a gleeful shine with this opportunity to hurt me. Her eyes were vicious when she said, 'It's the curse. You're stuck with it now. It's what we have to put up with. It's called being a woman. It's all ahead of you: babies, men, drudgery. Get used to it.'

'Here. Use this.' She'd found one of James's old cloth nappies and threw it at me. 'Roll it up and stuff it in your pants. Wash it out tonight. I used them when your father wouldn't give me money for sanitary pads, so you can too.'

I used the nappies that day and overnight. Joan bought some pads and a special belt to tie the ends on to keep them in place.

'It's a shameful secret,' she said. 'Don't let the boys know.'

The bulky pad stuck out at the back and chafed when I ran. Blood often leaked out the sides. Every month at school, I was terrified of staining my skirt, which I sometimes did. I couldn't concentrate. Several years later, when I'd made some close girlfriends, one told me about tampons and showed me how to use them. Liberation came with my first box of 20.

My breasts developed too. My mother wanted to touch them to work out how big they were, but I evaded her hands. She took me to a department store and told the assistant that it was my first bra. They laughed together. The woman then measured and fitted me. I was grateful she was a stranger.

*

My father decided to claim visitation rights with his three eldest children. From then on, Norm would collect us on Sundays from 1 to 5 pm. I dreaded the first afternoon of this new routine, as we hadn't seen our father in several years.

Norm pulled up out front of our Rowland Street home in his red Hillman and waved us over. He looked the same: thick-set and swarthy, with the well-muscled, dark, hairy arms and legs that I remembered. His black hair was combed back in its familiar style, but he had shadows beneath his eyes and his clean-shaven face had lost its too-charming smile.

His grin seemed forced when he told us to climb into the back seat of his car. We didn't let him convince us it was fun. His smile slipped and he lapsed into a grim silence.

Our father now lived on Boundary Street, near the main railway line going south. His house was old, probably built in the early 1900s – one of the more modest houses known as a simple workers' dwelling. It sat about five feet above the ground on rounded wooden posts. It was fronted by a worn picket fence that was missing several slats.

The house seemed to be sleeping. Its shuttered front windows looked like closed eyes. Unsure, I walked up the front steps and through the front door. A well-worn central hall stretched in front of me, with rooms off to each side. The shutters kept the heat and sun out, but the gloom suggested a scary presence, waiting unseen. Norm took us through to the little bare kitchen at the back and boiled the electric kettle. A single, faded-red, Formica-topped table stood waiting. I remembered it from Palmerston Street and went on high alert. I didn't know why.

To break the silence, Norm asked, 'Do you want toast?' We nodded, even though we'd just eaten lunch. He let the toast burn.

'Eat it up. Burnt toast is good for you. Extra carbon.' He grinned and then made a pot of tea, but he didn't have any milk. I hated black tea.

He poured his tea into a saucer, which he drank with a slurp. The sound added to my sense of threat.

'Trevor, do you want to see the transistor I'm working on?' Norm took Trevor's arm and pulled him towards another room. Graeme and I weren't invited. We looked at each other and Graeme gestured to the back steps. We wandered down into the overgrown, narrow back garden. Norm must have spotted us there because he came down to speak to us.

'Here. You might as well be useful. Dig up the weeds. You do know what weeds are?' He glared at us. His smiles were only for Trevor.

'These – the tall ones.' He pointed out some plants and gave us a spade and trowel. We spent our first visit digging up weeds. It was hot, sweaty work in the afternoon sun, but we didn't dare stop. We went back into the house when Norm called us to leave.

Norm and Trevor had set up Morse keys at each end of an electrical wire that stretched the length of the hall. Trevor clutched a piece of paper with a list of dots and dashes next to each letter of the alphabet. Norm had written out the list of Morse codes for Trevor to learn. Trevor looked tense. He didn't smile but seemed relieved to see us.

Trevor was confused by Norm's attention. He didn't remember being belittled and ignored by Norm before the separation, but Trevor hadn't been able to form relationships with our grandparents and was desperate for affection. He was like a spare part that rattled around in the box that was meant to be his home. I needed my grandparents' silent presence, but Trevor needed something more, especially now when he was being bullied at high school.

With Norm's undivided attention each Sunday afternoon, Trevor believed Norm was the father he should be with and started idolising his dad. Norm would bad-mouth Joan, spouting a version of events that portrayed himself as the victim. He would blame Grandad for the change in his circumstances. Trevor swallowed Norm's poisoned words. He needed this one adult who seemed to care.

Trevor lived for the Sunday afternoon visits and started hating Grandad and his strict, old-fashioned ways. We weren't allowed to answer back because Grandad's word was law. Trevor would fight with Grandad, who refused to take it, slapping Trevor across the face. This fed Trevor's righteous fury on behalf of his misunderstood father.

One look at Trevor's sullen face was all it needed for Grandad to reach for the buckle of his belt. He twisted the leather belt in half, held the ends in one hand, and cornered Trevor near the bathroom. By then, Trevor knew what was coming. Trev hunched over, trying to protect his head and wait for it to start. Grandad didn't seem to care where he hit Trevor – across his shoulders, back or legs.

Grandad tried to bash Trevor's resistance out of him. It went on and on. My heart hurt for Trevor but I didn't know how to stop Grandad or speak up.

I couldn't comprehend this out-of-control man. He wasn't the Grandad I loved. I hated that he hit Trevor. Trevor was constantly in pain. *Please stop.* But no one stopped Grandad. I don't know where my mother was. Or my grandmother.

*

The area under the house was walled in with breeze blocks to provide a study room. We each had a second-hand desk to do our homework.

One night, after a visit to Norm, Trevor said, 'Wendy and Graeme, listen to me. It's important. We should be living with Dad.' Trevor stood in front of our desks, appealing to us. 'You know I'm right. Dad would look after us. We should be a real family, not like here. It's not right.'

'You're cr-crazy. That's th-th-the l-l-last thing I want.' I laughed at Trevor. I never called our father Dad.

'No, really. You've got it all wrong. It's Grandad. He's made up stories about Dad that aren't true. Don't you see? They're all lies.'

'Look Trev, it's different for Wendy and me,' Graeme said. 'Dad ignores us. He doesn't care about us like he does you. He only wants you.' He added, 'Maybe you should go live with him, if that's what you want. But I don't want you to—'

Trevor persisted. 'No, come on. Listen to me. It's for all of us. Dad really is good. It was all Grandad's fault. He caused the separation. Mum should go back to Dad. They should be together, with us.'

'Trev stop! You're wr-wrong. Leave us alone. I nnneed to do mmy h-h-home-wwork.' I'd raised my voice, hoping to get through to him. Graeme stood behind me. I wanted Trevor to shut up. It was too confusing. I could feel Trevor's pain but my own was screaming inside me to get him to stop.

'No, come on, listen,' Trevor reached for my arm but I pushed him away. He grabbed me by the shoulder. I stood up and shoved Trevor in the chest. Graeme joined in and within minutes, the three of us were wrestling on the floor.

I made it about Trevor, instead of Norm. I loved my grandfather and my home with my grandmother. I couldn't stand Trevor blaming Grandad, even though my heart broke for my brother. It was all too much. I was torn apart by my conflicting loyalties.

Trev, outnumbered, retreated to a corner where he buried his head in his arms and sobbed. He was alone in a house full of people, who couldn't and wouldn't see his distress. Norm had split our little gang.

*

Norm switched on the television at 5 pm on a Sunday to watch *Dr Who*, when we should have been back at Rowland Street. He and Trevor sat with their arms around each other on the sofa, Graeme forgotten at the other end. I hid behind, with my hands over my ears to block out the sounds. The images and noises of the aliens added to my nightmares. I hated the Daleks and couldn't shut out their mechanical voices.

My anxiety grew. It mixed up inside of me: the worry of being late, the tension of being with my father and the terror of the aliens. I imagined the shouting match when Norm dropped us off, as Grandad would be pacing on the footpath, fuming, ready for a fight. As regular as clockwork, we went to Norm's, and as regular as clockwork the fights erupted on our late return. I hated Sundays.

*

Norm decided his house needed raising with new concrete stilts so he could walk upright underneath it. Sundays were now spent making moulds out of old planks and mixing and pouring concrete. Then, one by one, using layers of bits of wood, we pushed each part of the house up and helped him fit the new stilt underneath.

It took us ages and Norm needed our help. Refusal wasn't an option. When the project was completed to his satisfaction, he took us down to a scrappy beach where Ross River opened to the sea. We didn't dare swim because sharks regularly swam in to feast on the outflow from processing plants further up the river.

Norm bought us each an ice cream. It was the only time he ever did. We were allowed to play in the sand, and then wipe our feet before driving back to his newly straightened and raised home.

*

Trevor was desperate to escape the school bullies and Rowland Street. At fifteen, he left school and signed on for a nine-year apprenticeship with the Royal Australian Air Force (RAAF) as an instrument fitter. In January 1976, we travelled to Sydney on the train to witness his swearing-in. With his right hand on his heart, Trevor was another shaved head in a room full of pale, shaved heads, as he said his oath of allegiance to the Queen and Australia.

The RAAF training base at Wagga Wagga became his new home. The word Wagga derives from the local Wiradjuri Aboriginal language and means 'crow', so Wagga Wagga translates as 'the place of many crows'. Trevor seemed happy in the letters he wrote to me. It helped us too, as Norm gave up the visits since Trevor was gone. Later that same year, Joan decided to divorce Norm. The Family Law Act, with no-fault divorce, had been introduced. I thought I was free of my father.

Chapter 7

Dreaming

In Grade 9, I stopped hiding in the pages of books and ventured into school life. I discovered netball and played in the school team, making some friends.

Then one day, a sign went up on the school board, advertising a volleyball tryout. The head of sports at the school, Randel Robertson, was running the session and wanted to start new teams. I was one of those he selected.

I asked my mother to drive me to training, but made sure my grandfather heard, so she wouldn't say no. When I arrived, the school was transformed, with overhead lights and volleyball nets set up on the parade ground. Several teams were training. I found the girls in my team and we were introduced to our coach. He asked us what we wanted our team to be called.

We decided on *Palanas* – our first group decision. Over the following weeks, our coach taught us how to set, dig and spike. We learned drills and match play, and won the C grade competition the first year we played, advancing to B grade.

The club grew and moved the training and games to the national fitness centre on the other side of town. With smooth wooden floors, we could now slide and roll without getting gravel-rashed knees from the school's bitumen courts.

Several of us were invited to play in the highest grade and started training twice a week with Randel as our coach. Within two years, I was representing Townsville at state competitions, with our team forming the base of the state team. Randel was also our Queensland coach. He was a powerhouse of a man, well-muscled and tanned from the hours he spent teaching outside. With his ready smile, he knew how to inspire without crushing our spirits. It was a line he found repeatedly with me, and I was able to rise to his expectations. I felt safe with that man.

I learned to jump, straight up, not fifteen or thirty times, but hundreds. My quadriceps, glutes and hamstrings screamed for me to stop. Then we ran sprints, followed by burpees, core and skill work. I built a wall between my body and mind. If Randel said jump, I jumped. 'No' did not exist; every command from Randel was obeyed. Did I love him or hate him? I couldn't decide. None of us could, but we reached exhaustion for him whenever we stepped onto a court. My life was full of physical pain, but it came with a high.

'Madness!' My mother said when I arrived home one night after another training session. I'd let my head collapse onto the dining room table. I was too tired to lift my fork to eat the warmed-up meal she'd dumped down in front of me.

'You'll kill yourself.' She said it almost like she cared.

I answered her back inside my head, not daring to speak out loud: *At least the team will win and you'll be happy without me here.*

I kept imagining my side of the conversation.

You'll have another chance to act proud of me with the other mothers, and another gold medal to show off. You'd rather have the gold medal than me – it won't answer you back or cost you anything to feed.

I lived for volleyball, doing hundreds of jumps against a mark on a beam at the side of the house. I wore out a patch of Grandad's lawn. Every week, I ran up and down The Strand with Graeme on his bike at my side for company. I could look into Randel's eyes and know I belonged. We won most of the competitions at local, state and national levels.

The next Australian Titles were to be played in Victoria. Our Queensland team flew south from the humidity to arrive in the crisp, cold air of a Geelong winter evening. On the first night of the competition, I stood with my team around a hire car. Eleven sweet young women were now screaming: 'Kill the Vics! Pulp the Vics! Smash the Vics!'

We rocked the car, almost lifting each end off the ground, to get ourselves pumped for the coming game. We raced onto the court minutes later, fired up and ready to play the team from Victoria. I loved wearing maroon and white.

Following a game and after the debrief when my teammates and I drank hot chocolate and ate Twisties, we settled down to sleep. We were bundled together in another strange motel. Before we dosed off, we gossiped about who was doing what with the boys from the men's team. Who was still a virgin? And how to cope with menstruation while playing. We talked about Randel, deciding we loved him, and then we moved on to comparing our mothers. I didn't say much.

Someone butted in and asked, 'Do you sleep with your volleyball?'

Half a dozen of us shouted: 'Yes, of course!' It helped improve our touch with the ball.

During one game, playing for Queensland against the dreaded New South Wales team, I was in the zone. It was the closest I'd come to moving perfection. At the end of the competition, the Australian squad for the upcoming Pacific Rim Volleyball tournament to be held in

Hawaii was announced. Janelle, a friend and one of my teammates, and I were selected. We were delighted and terrified in equal measure. It would mean a whole new bunch of girls from different state teams to train with and a new coach.

As a club, we were continually fundraising, doing bottle drives, chocolate sales, trivia nights and lamington drives – anything we could think of to raise money for flights. My mother complained about the money but would turn up at the local games and act proud of me, her daughter. She thrived on the publicity of my picture in the local paper.

Life was going well at school, too. James Cook University, who owned the buildings across the road from Pimlico High, moved to the outskirts of Townsville, giving the school its premises. Grades 11 and 12 moved across the road to have a separate senior campus. I wanted to go on to senior school, which was unheard of in our family. Graeme was leaving school at fifteen, as Trevor had. Grandad put pressure on me to leave too. He didn't want me to go to university – only long-haired layabouts did that.

It was the 1970s. Queensland was talked about as a police state with institutional corruption. It had been run for years by Premier Joh Bjelke-Petersen. He was later called the hillbilly dictator because of his conservatism and how he rigged the voting system through electoral malapportionment – the unequal distribution of the state's population within electorates. This allowed rural electorates, with their smaller numbers, to have as much voting power as the more populated areas. By doing this, he managed to keep the leadership for nineteen years.

University students in Brisbane were beginning to rebel. They were at the forefront of forcing change, holding sit-ins and protest marches, and blocking the steps of the Queensland Parliament. Young men with long hair became fair game for policemen to beat up and throw in the cells, especially in North Queensland.

My grandfather watched the ABC news on television at night. He grew increasingly agitated with seeing the university students fight the police.

He turned to me and said, 'You're never going to be one of them.'

I wanted to study veterinary science and was volunteering at a local veterinary clinic. I helped at reception and assisted during surgery. I tried to persuade my grandfather, but he wouldn't budge. He kept repeating, 'There'll be no bloody university for you!'

He allowed me to continue at school and when I moved across the road to the new senior campus, I excelled. In the 1970s, only dedicated students progressed to Grade 12. The staff loved teaching us and often chatted with us after class. I blossomed and my hopes were high. I was on a roll, feeling happy, even with a stammer, but my mother was waiting to see me fall.

'You're getting too bloody big for your boots,' she told me.

Janelle didn't make the final cut into the Australian team. I was the only player selected from Townsville and one of the youngest at sixteen in the under 20s women's team. It was mostly made up of confident eighteen- and nineteen-year-olds. I missed Janelle and flew alone for the first time to Canberra for the final coaching session before leaving.

On the first morning of being with the Australian team, when I walked into the Sports Academy cafeteria, I couldn't believe the wonderful food laid out in silver trays. I'd eaten bacon once before, at Christmas, but never pancakes, and here they were, stacked up high. My mouth was already watering in expectation. I indulged. I'd forgotten for a moment to be careful or watch my back.

The Australian coach, a fierce Eastern European man who looked to be in his early seventies, silently walked up behind me. He whispered in my ear, 'You'll get fat if you eat all that.'

I was frightened into a freeze response and instantly shut down, going mute. He had sounded like my mother and father rolled into one. The spite and blame and hate felt the same but dressed up in the shape of this overbearing man. A man who I was dependent on – who I was meant to please and play for.

I was yet to form a relationship with this coach. Instead, when hearing his confronting words, I went into shame. All of me was dirt beneath his shoes. And like dirt, I wanted to disappear into a crack in the floor. Highly sensitive to any form of criticism, I felt unsafe, with my newfound confidence shattering in the face of his harsh tone. It touched my young, traumatised child place – the part of me I was cut off from. With my low resilience to tolerating stress, I dissociated.

Dissociating was still my main defence system. I'd been doing it from a young age, and it had changed the structure and function of my brain. I lived mainly within the sympathetic autonomic nervous system – the part that stimulates the trauma response of fight, flight, freeze or flop. It was activated during any situation with a hint of threat, or with objects that reminded me, or my nervous system, of the trauma. While I wasn't conscious this was happening, my body was remembering and this is what caused the need to disengage from myself or reality.

To my unconscious mind, the external world was still a terrifying place, and in this way, I effectively severed contact between my body and my brain to survive. This was the downside of dissociation: it caused a disconnect from any sense of self and identity. With the option of escaping by fleeing or fighting never possible, I mostly used the third choice, freeze, although my body sometimes went to the fourth: flop. Flop was the last unconscious attempt to deal with threat. It caused my body to go 'floppy' and shut down. It's a natural instinct and the last choice available to try and survive: pretending to be dead. Within the freeze and the flop is this detachment. I had no control over it and couldn't see it coming.

Cut off from me and wary of him, I couldn't play when he was present. I became a sliver of myself. This fed his dislike of me. He made it known as he targeted me in front of the other players. My isolation grew. Perhaps he was frustrated with not being able to find that flowing, confident player he'd selected for the team. Maybe he was trying whatever he could to force it out of me. But force never worked.

He shouted at me, furious if I missed a set, and repeatedly threw the volleyball in my face. I couldn't raise my hands or voice to defend myself. All my energy seeped out of me when I was faced with this man – the flop response.

I'd been training hard. On top of my normal training, I joined my school's athletics team to do anaerobic sprints. I swam in my sister's squad to build lung capacity and endurance and endlessly jumped against the wall. I easily burned off all the food I was able to eat, but I couldn't stand up to this man. I didn't know how, or how to laugh him off as the other players did. I couldn't play or speak when he was present.

I couldn't make my body behave. My head and body hated each other. I gave up and retreated to a private place where nobody could reach me, not even myself. No one asked me what was wrong.

The night before we were due to leave, the coach took me to one side.

He said, 'If it was up to me, you wouldn't be going. I'd willingly leave you behind, but the others disagree. They've told me you've earned your place in the team so I'm being forced to take you. But remember, I don't want you.'

I flew to Hawaii in 1978 and played for Australia as part of the team. On the outside, I learned to smile and performed well enough to get court time, but I couldn't find that person I'd been. I couldn't find that zone of bliss, of perfection. That and all my dreams had deserted me.

Chapter 8

Escaping

I returned to Townsville from the volleyball competition in Hawaii a different person. My body was still shut down and my mind was in despair. From dreaming of being an athlete, I now watched myself as if from a distance. I was distraught yet powerless to change it. I didn't know how.

I finished school, went through the graduation and farewell speech night, and received my awards, but nothing touched me. I wasn't there, even as my face smiled and my body made the right responses. I played in the Queensland team again but I'd lost my sense of connection with Randel. I needed him to grab me and shake me awake, but the world went on around me.

No one noticed I wasn't there or asked me what was wrong. No one tried to find me.

This proved that age-old message that I wasn't worthy. It woke the chaotic crazy-like place within me.

My mind kept running an internal commentary: No one cares. It's all a pretence. It wasn't true. It didn't happen. I'm nothing – a useless creature, just as my mother says. Better I just disappear.

My mother now watched and smirked as I stopped visiting my volleyball friends. She enjoyed my fall. She noticed how the veneer of a smile slipped off my face at home. She gloated over my isolation. She'd won again and was proven right. I was a waste of space.

Underneath the constant self-blaming thoughts, I was trapped in a deep, dark hole of utter silence. I had no words. My lips were stuck together. My arms limp at my sides – silly creatures that hung there. One part of me couldn't understand why I couldn't change it, yet most of me had given up. What was the point?

I left volleyball the way I left my body, without consciously choosing, but with numb desperation cloaked in shame. I needed to run, but to where? And what was I going to do now I'd left school? I looked ahead into nothing as I'd given up my hope of going to university. Dreams were not for someone like me. I'd graduated in the top 5% of Year 12 students in Queensland, but I was dirt.

My grandfather said I could be a teacher or a nurse. They were my choices. I couldn't be a teacher because I stammered. That left nursing. I applied to the local hospital, the largest in North Queensland, where I'd been going for speech therapy for years.

When I walked in for my interview, the woman across the desk introduced herself as the matron. She started to ask me questions without a smile or nod of encouragement. My throat squeezed shut. I tried to answer by pushing through my stammer. She stopped after a few minutes.

'You're wasting my time. You will never be a nurse because you can't speak properly.' The matron looked me in the eye. She waited for a moment, then continued.

'How will you cope if there's an emergency, a cardiac arrest? You'd have to telephone the arrest team and tell them what was happening. You wouldn't be able to get the words out. So, no, you'll never be a nurse.' And with that, she told me to leave.

I rode my bike home. Shame was now a constant blanket wrapped around me. I needed to hit out at someone.

'Yes, Mother. Of course, Mother.' I said the words in a sarcastic voice when my mother told me to wash up. I was clearing the table after dinner that night.

My grandfather heard me. 'Don't speak to your mother in that tone.'

'I'll sp-speak any way I-I wwant!' I stood up to my grandfather for the first time. He took two strides across the room and slapped me hard across the face. I crashed into the wall. He'd never hit me before.

I struggled to my feet. 'It's nn-not fair! You don't ask the b-b-boys to ww-wash up.' Then the words that I needed to say bubbled out. 'I can't be a nn-nurse. Don't you un-und-d-d-erstand? I c-c-can't speak. You're nnnot being fair by only g-g-giv-giving me those t-t-two choices.'

He raised his hand again. I saw it coming and braced myself. His hand was like a plank of wood. This time I stayed down.

'You will do as you're damn well told! You bloody hussy. It's about time you bloody kids learned your place.' He stood over me but I refused to be cowered or let the tears spill. We were meant to be friends.

*

My speech therapist told me about a new program – a three-week intensive teaching a new technique called smooth speech. I signed up, dreading it. I didn't expect it to help, but I always hoped to find a magical cure to make me fluent.

My great aunt in Sydney had sent Grandma a cutting from her newspaper, advertising for a new intake of nurses for the brand-new hospital, Westmead. It was almost finished being built out in the west, near Parramatta. I thought what the hell and signed up. I wanted to escape Townsville and the shame of bumping into my volleyball mates. I needed to make this work.

In the smooth speech course, I was one of several people with a speech impediment. The idea was to slow our speech down and extend the sounds, merging the end of one word with the beginning of the next. The sounds were flattened and drawn out and we took minutes to get to the end of a single sentence. I practised at night, speaking into a tape recorder. I cringed internally when I heard my voice played back. My mother laughed when she heard my attempts, so Graeme and I hid under the house and he helped me practice. I was barely speaking to Joan.

We sped up the sounds, lengthening and joining the words. It sounded strange to my ears. My speech was stilted, lacking life, but I could get whole sentences out. I flew to Sydney for my interview, feeling hopeful that this time I could hide my stammer. I did. I became one of 187 students for the first intake of nurses at the new hospital – the largest in the southern hemisphere. Over half the intake was from country and rural areas, with some from interstate like me. I didn't think past the interview.

*

A few years earlier, Graeme had shot up, surpassing me in height. From a chubby boy, he had grown lean, wiry muscles and a strong, determined chin. I'd stopped winning our physical fights and was secretly delighted he was beating me. He was having fun, making friends and carving out a life. I marvelled at the confident young man who had emerged from my quiet, timid twin.

Graeme had left school at fifteen and was working as a storeman with the Aherns at the collection of shops around the block from us. The older ladies loved him. He was kind, funny and helpful. The shop owner's family encouraged him to learn the trade. Once he passed his driving test, Graeme drove the truck delivering the groceries, meeting and getting to know many of the locals.

He bought a second-hand Thorpe – a twelve-foot sailing dingy. He named it *Wave Dancer* and painted the name on the side. He then bought a car to tow it – a yellow Corolla van. He invited me to crew with him and we became 'the twins' at the local yacht club. We entered the races on weekends and in any local competitions. We didn't do a lot of wave dancing – mostly capsizing in the erratic swell off Townsville as we learned to sail.

One time, we turned turtle and had to swim under the hull to take the mast and sail down. The rescue boat towed us in once we righted the boat, but we were a team.

I was happy to be his crew with our old positions reversed. As I watched him take charge in the boat, I softened into his side, protected by my now tall twin brother. It settled the ache I'd carried since childhood, as we were now able to be together whenever we chose. I came alive when he was next to me, but I couldn't find the words to share my distress around stammering and losing my volleyball dreams. I was so good at pretending I was coping that I hid it even from myself. Because I didn't understand what was wrong with me, I turned away and abandoned myself – the system I'd learned at the hands of my mother. I was repeating to myself what she had done to me.

We celebrated our seventeenth birthday together, sharing a single cake as usual. Grandma made us her special four-egg sponge with mock cream and icing. We blew out the candles in synchronised breaths. Grandad shared a bottle of beer. A typical birthday.

*

I left home in January 1979, a month after that birthday, leaving behind Graeme, my siblings and grandparents – the people who loved me – and flew alone to Sydney. My anxiety was so extreme that my menstrual cycle stopped for the next year.

After I left, Graeme left too. He wanted some freedom from our strict grandparents and moved in with Norm. I was horrified, although I couldn't tell him why, but the arrangement seemed to work. Graeme had a girlfriend, Christine, and started going to parties. His hard work at the store was rewarded with a pay rise. He wrote me long, newsy letters, telling me he was happy, that he was growing up. His confidence fizzed and bubbled through his written words.

When I moved into the nurses' quarters at the back of Westmead Hospital, I was unsure of how to behave. I escaped to my little box of a room and listened through the thin wall to the conversations in the common room.

Neither my mother nor grandparents had prepared me for managing alone. I'd never set up a bank account or received a pay packet. I didn't know about tax or doing a tax return. I didn't realise I'd have to register to vote – all those grownup things. I was naive, but so were half my class who'd also left home for the first time. We worked it out together.

Spooked and excited by all the freedom, with cash in my pocket and space once classes were finished, I bought new sheets and a bicycle. I made some friends. Jannette taught me how to play squash and we joined a local gym. Tanya showed me how to make real Italian food, using her family's recipes. Until then, I'd only eaten spaghetti out of a can. I learned how to use chopsticks and fell in love with the foreign spices and strange new vegetables of the Chinese and Lebanese restaurants around Parramatta.

The first nursing skill we were taught was how to make a bed, sheets pulled tight and smooth, at right angles into the perfect corner – something I was already good at. I washed my first adult man. I let him do his privates, but then I put his pyjamas on back to front in my haste to avoid looking. He laughed at me. It was manageable, if a little scary, but so far, I was doing well.

We were the final intake of nurses to train fully on the wards as nurse training was changing to a university degree. After our initial six-week block, we did our learning as we worked shifts with real patients on the wards. Nurse educators first took us through each new skill. I coped until I had to give the handover of my patients to the next shift of nurses and the charge nurse. My smooth speech broke down under the stress of saying the list of naming words: each patient's name, medical history, current medications and nursing care. The next one was worse than the last, until, red-cheeked in shame, I wanted to hide in the pan room.

After a week of torment, I found the speech therapy department in the bowels of the building and signed on with a therapist. It was another round of trying to get my dreaded voice to behave. I discovered evenings and nights were more relaxed without the scary charge nurse watching. I started binging, eating whole loaves of bread and then throwing it up. I yoyoed in weight, gorging and starving, going on extreme diets, having my uniforms taken in then having to ask to have them taken out.

Somehow, I got through. We moved from the dormitory into more permanent accommodation half a mile away from the hospital. My three flatmates – Yvonne, Jules and Judy – and I went out as a group. Jules introduced me to bush dancing and we joined the Bush Music Society. Jannette joined too, and we danced whenever we could, at the colonial-built town halls in the older suburbs of inner Sydney. Drinking only water from eight to midnight, we danced solidly, not missing a set, and made friends with the bands. Dancing helped.

I received top marks for my assignments and tests and mostly coped with the handover reports. I learned to ski, getting the overnight bus to Thredbo with my new friends. Jannette took me home to her parents and introduced me to her horse, Sorrette. She taught me to ride.

Jannette and I went on a month-long trip exploring the wilds of Papua New Guinea to celebrate passing our first-year exams. We ended up hitching on single-engine aeroplanes through the highlands, sitting with pigs on our laps and having our breasts grabbed by the locals to check if we were women. Many had not seen a white-skinned woman before. Near Goroka, we were caught in a tribal war and tear-gassed by the police. After the battle, I collected the blood-stained arrows and managed to get them through customs and into Australia.

Trevor visited me whenever he could. He would sleep on a blow-up on the floor next to my bed. We repaired our past and rediscovered our friendship. He often turned up with a carful of mates – young men who dated my friends. We single-handedly improved Air Force–nurse relations.

Trevor wrote off three cars, but each time he escaped with only minor injuries. His V8 red Leyland P76 was my favourite – a hoon's car, ramped up at the back. I could hear it coming down the road. He let me drive it on the M4 from Parramatta to Penrith, urging me to go faster, as music blasted out of the stereo.

Chapter 9

Rape and love and being on the ceiling

I decided it was time to try dating and asked a patient out – one who'd let me know he liked me. My first date. It was a disaster. I tried to be a real woman and wore high-heeled shoes. They were way too high and I could barely walk, especially on the cobbled street where the man took me to eat. I was too embarrassed to see him again.

Jannette and I trained at a gym in Parramatta. A German bodybuilder suggested different exercises. I liked him and was flattered when he asked me out. I was nervous over dinner, trying to act grown up. He drove me home after our meal and parked at the front of my unit. He asked, all smiles, 'Are you going to invite me in?'

I wanted to do it right. 'Yes, sure. WW-Would you like c-co-coffee?' He grinned and followed me as I let us into my flat. I tried to remember the actions of the women I'd watched in films. It was unusual that nobody else was home. I made him coffee and we sat together in the lounge room. We chatted a little but then he reached across to kiss me. I tentatively kissed him back.

He pressed his lips harder against mine and reached under my top. I moved a little away, not able to speak, hoping my actions would give him the hint. I didn't want his hands on my chest, but it only seemed to make him more urgent. I tried to speak.

'Hey, I only wwwant to kiss.'

'What are you? A tease?'

'P-P-Please … I'm nn-not. You're g-g-going too fast.'

He didn't listen. He didn't want to listen.

I tried again. 'I want you to st-stop. N-No I don't want …'

He grabbed me.

'Please stop! No. I d-don't want this.'

He'd planned this all along. 'You've been asking for it all night. So shut the fuck up.' With that, he pushed me to the floor and straddled me. He was big. His weight flattened my hips and his hands gripped my wrists as I pushed to escape his hold. I couldn't free myself.

Something seemed to deflate inside of me. When he felt me go limp he leaned down and whispered in my face, 'I've got you now.'

He flipped me over and pressed my face into the carpet. He used one hand to keep me pinned to the floor as he pulled my underwear off with the other. I went very still and retreated deep within myself.

I could see us. I was sitting safely in a corner on the ceiling. I looked down and felt it as he penetrated me. I watched, coldly uncaring, cut off as if I were watching a movie.

After he shuddered to a stop, he briefly collapsed on top, then got up, did up his jeans and left.

I watched my body for a long time. It was a polluted shell. I felt a detached sadness, almost as if I was miles away. She was nothing. She was useless. She never protected me. She never screamed or fought or yelled.

I stayed on the ceiling, looking at my unmoving body lying on the floor. I didn't want to join her, but I needed to come back inside as someone would soon come home. I didn't want anyone to see her like that.

I got up off the bottle-green carpet and stumbled my way to the shower. I tried to wash him away – the pain and hurt and shame. The water boiled my skin. I wanted to burn it off. I stood there for hours, weeks, years. I never wanted to move again. I wanted time to stop.

I heard the front door opening. It jarred me back into my skin. I didn't want anyone to see me. I crept to my room. I knew there was something wrong with me. It was an old, familiar feeling.

I never spoke of the rape and in the following days, the pain and soreness was a constant reminder of how useless I was. I swallowed it down. I stopped going to the gym. I'd bought a year's membership, but I couldn't ask for my money back. Jannette shook her head at me, baffled by my behaviour, but I couldn't tell her. The shame kept me silent.

*

A few months later, I took the train to Cronulla. I worked my way along the coast, exploring the Sydney beaches. I left my bag, towel and shoes on the sand close to where I swam, so I could watch them, and body-surfed in the waves. A young man chatted me up while he paddled next to me, but I smiled politely and didn't lead him on.

When I came out of the water, I couldn't find my belongings. Shocked and feeling exposed, I made my way to the police station wearing only my swimmers.

'Yes, can I help you?' the young policeman asked.

'Hi. All mmy b-b-bel-ongings have b-been stolen from the b-b-beach. I live in WWWestmead. I'm a nn-nurse. Could you pl-please help me get hh-home?'

'We don't assist with thefts. You can report the crime but that's all.'

'I nneed to g-g-get the train home and I d-don't have any mm-money for the fare. Is there any way I can b-b-borrow some? I'll p-pay you back.'

'Look, I can't help you.'

'P-Please, I d-d-don't know anyone here. Just a few d-d-dollars. Please …' I was crying now.

'You're wasting my time. If you're not here to report a crime, please leave.'

I pleaded with my eyes, hoping to sway him, but he turned away and retreated to a desk.

I left, confused. Why wouldn't he help? I was miles from home.

I returned to sit on the beach. The guy who'd chatted earlier came up and asked, 'What's wrong?'

I explained what had happened.

'Look, you're welcome to come back to my place. I've got some old clothes and I'll give you some money for your fare.' I stared at him, grateful. Once we got to his flat, he suggested a snack. After we ate, he reached across and kissed me. I froze, but I couldn't refuse because I needed his money and clothes. Numb and shut down, still in shock, I wondered, *Is this how women get into prostitution? Because they need something?*

He didn't stop. I let him do whatever he wanted. I wasn't there. I was on the ceiling. I was safe up there. Let him have my body. My body didn't matter. I was gone.

The next morning I got up, collected the money and clothes, and left. I was 17 but felt old and worn-down by this business called life. I didn't know how to do it or stay safe.

Why didn't I go into some shops and explain my situation? Beg for money? My one attempt at asking for help at the police station was all I could manage. I didn't go to a beach for a long time after that, and then only with a friend.

*

It took me ages to venture out again with anything like confidence. I kept passing a West Indian man on my way to work. He started chatting and told me his name was Henry. He was a paediatric registered nurse who was more interested in psychiatric nursing. He was in his late thirties – twenty years older than me. Henry was sweet, with a wide-open smile and soft hands. He said I was pretty and I laughed. He told me I was wrong and to prove it he invited me to do a photoshoot.

He took me to the banks of the Parramatta River where the weeping willows brushed the edges of the water and arranged me in the dappled light. He took a series of photos. I giggled. Later that week, I stared at the developed pictures. Henry had made me look beautiful against the strands of the sweeping tree.

Henry cooked amazing West Indian curries using green bananas and chillies. My throat burned. He laughingly gave me milk to drink. He was easy to chat with. He knew things and helped me make sense of events happening around me. I looked forward to his company and spent more time in his flat than my own. After a long, slow, old-fashioned courtship, I went to bed with him. He went gently, stopping when I needed to.

Taking his time. Making sure I was enjoying myself. It was different. It felt like love, not sex.

My friends told me Henry was too old but his kind, rich, chestnut eyes looked patiently into mine. I loved his tight curly hair and dark skin and how it contrasted strongly with mine. We looked like yin and yang. He was widely travelled and told stories to put me to sleep, as sleep was difficult for me. I felt safe, sleeping in his arms.

Henry said he was in love with me and asked me to marry him. I panicked, too scared to speak. I ran away because I didn't know how to say no or to be kind – the way he was with me. I hurt him, I know. I'm sorry. Please forgive me. I couldn't find the words.

Then one Sunday, returning with Jules from Lithgow, I found a note stuck to my door, asking me to report to the weekend nurse manager. I walked across to the hospital in the last of the autumn heat, wondering the entire way. I'd never been summoned before. I found her room at the top of a stairwell at the front of the hospital. She sat me down and told me she'd received a telephone call from Townsville … from my mother.

My twin brother had been killed. Graeme.

Chapter 10

A life without Graeme

Everything stopped. I went quiet, disbelieving, still. The nurse manager told me to call home. I went downstairs to use one of the public telephones in the main foyer of the hospital. Dozens of people were walking past in both directions, some pushing prams or wheelchairs. Kids were being told to behave. The noise and busyness were overwhelming.

My grandmother answered my call. She started crying. In between sobs, Grandma said Graeme was in an accident. He was driving to Airlie Beach for the Easter sailing regatta, towing his beloved boat *Wave Dancer*, with his girlfriend, Christine, at his side. The story came out in pieces wrapped by her tears. Grandma stopped for breaths. I listened, not able to say a word. I felt my Grandma close but I was far away, already distant from the body I stood in. I pressed the phone hard against my ear, scared to miss any of her words.

The police said Graeme and Christine had been hit head-on by a drunk driver, who'd left his side of the road after failing to navigate a curve. Graeme didn't have a chance, the policeman said. Graeme's car was mashed in half lengthways. Grandma couldn't stop crying. She managed to get out that Christine, shocked and lacerated beside him, was still alive. She'd been cut from the wreckage after being trapped for hours.

The nurse manager arranged a week's compassionate leave. Somehow, I booked a flight and got myself home. I walked into a nightmare. Numb, I hugged my grandparents, letting them talk, but I didn't want to touch my mother when she came at me with her arms outstretched. She demanded I hug her. She was crying in a loud-pitched wail. I hated her touching me, but I gave in. She clung to me. Feeling her hot, sweaty flesh pressed hard against mine was too much. Panicked, I pulled away and made an excuse to leave the room.

All that day, and the following days, a constant stream of subdued visitors came to the house to express their condolences. I made endless cups of tea as Joan retold the story, soaking up the attention, of the one suffering the worst. Her recounting of the story grew to include me – how I was a terrible daughter, not looking after her. The visitors stared at me in various states of disbelief or accusation. I wanted to run. Instead, I stood, silently absent, staring back. They didn't understand. The more Joan talked, the more cut off I became. In the face of her grief, a mother's grief, mine was invisible.

A few days later, Joan grabbed me by the arm. 'You're coming with me, you bloody bitch.' I let her drag me into her bedroom where she thrust me up against her cupboard.

'It's your fault. It's all your fault that Graeme is dead. It should be you!' She shoved me hard against the doors in time to her words. With each push, she repeatedly said, 'You should be dead, not him. He's the good one. You are a monster. You should be dead.'

Fine spit landed on my face as she continued to scream the words. 'You're a horrible daughter. I never wanted you.' She'd finally admitted out loud what I'd always known.

'You should take his place and be dead, not him!' Joan yelled these words as she continued to shove me in a relentless pattern. I let her because, sadly, I believed her. I was the bad one. Over the years, her words had soaked in and done their work. They were true. The world would be better if I changed places with Graeme. He was always the better half.

I allowed her mishandling of me and refused to react. My lack of words was my only defence. It gave me a focus and a way to withstand her onslaught, and a place to put my frozen rage.

*

The service took place at the crematorium south of Townsville. There wasn't enough space or seating for the people wanting to attend. They spilled outside, filling the entrances and walkways – a mass of grieving bodies come to honour my brother. When the coffin was receding from view, I stood up with my sister and together we threw red and white carnations on top of the coffin. It was my symbolic statement that Graeme was mine.

Trevor had flown home for the funeral from Amberly RAAF Base where he'd been working. The following day, Trev, Sarah, James and I took the ferry to Magnetic Island where we tried to deflect our grief. I'd hired a Mini Moke. We found a back road and showed James how to drive. It took our minds off Graeme for a bit as we shouted at his near crashes, and then we tried to wash our pain away in the surf at Arcadia Bay.

It was weird to be four, not five. My eyes couldn't take in the space that should have held Graeme. Graeme was gone. He'd always been there, even though we were separated, I'd fought to stay connected. From the beginning, I'd started as two, not one. I'd never lived without him. How was I going to manage? A life without Graeme?

I floated free. I didn't cry. Nothing touched me.

My right to exist was through Graeme. I accessed this through our twinship. He was my primary attachment figure, as I hadn't been able to form an attachment with our mother because of her need to make me bad. She'd saved all her attention for Graeme, the good one, so I found my belonging through him. This also informed my identity, which was based on being one of two and never singular.

When he died, my link to the planet was cut. I was up there in the sky, looking down. I didn't know how to find my way back.

*

I returned to Sydney via Amberly RAAF Base with Trevor. He and I huddled together in the back of a Hercules transport plane, the last of our little gang. He'd arranged the lift south. We were strapped into a harness along one wall of the plane, feeling the wind blow through the gaps where the rear ramp fitted into the side. The immense roar of the plane was muffled by an ear-protecting headset. I glimpsed thin slices of blue sky and puffed-up clouds. The temperature dropped the higher we flew. I clung to Trevor's presence beside me.

Trevor showed me around the base, his room, and his immaculate cupboards and drawers. His shoes were polished to a high gloss by an old pair of my tights. Nylon tights were the best cloth to use he said, as he proudly showed off the shine. I flashed back to the two of us with Graeme, cleaning our shoes after we came home from school. Grandma always made us polish them before our snack. We'd jostled each other as we'd fought for a space at the bottom of the back steps. Emptiness threatened to swallow me whole.

Trev took me to his work area. He'd received permission to let me fly the F1-11 simulator that he was operating. I flew the fighter jet into the ground on my first attempt to land it. Trevor encouraged me to fly it again and on my third go, I brought it in perfectly. Trevor was proud. We didn't speak about Graeme.

I returned to Westmead and a new ward for my next nursing placement – the orthopaedic ward. On my first shift, I was confronted by mostly young men from motor vehicle or motorbike accidents. They were alive when Graeme was dead. I was face to face with my pain. It tore me apart to remember the feel of Graeme's skin and know that I'd never touch him again, as I bandaged and tended to the flesh of these hurt young men.

One teenager looked like Graeme, with the same sinewy, long frame. I sat with him at the end of my work, letting him talk. I felt like I existed when I sat beside him. At the end of the placement, the charge nurse took me into her office.

'Here's your ward report. You'll see my comments but I also want to tell you to your face. You're a disgusting nurse, but I couldn't write that. You have favourites and you neglect your other patients. I'll be glad to see the back of you. Now go.'

I sat for a moment, stunned. I couldn't remember if I did have favourites. I'd tried my best to divide my time fairly and do my work. I wanted to be a good nurse.

I couldn't stand up for myself or ask why she'd waited until the end of the placement to tell me. This was my first negative ward report. It destroyed something in me. That, and the lack of acknowledgement of my grief, cut loose the last fragile strand of belonging and any loyalty to the training.

We'd recently finished a classroom block on death and dying, learning Dr Kübler-Ross's ground-breaking work on the stages of grief. I knew the theory. A distant part of me recognised it in myself. I'd sat in class listening as our tutors told us how to be aware of our patients' pain. Yet it didn't apply to me, eighteen years old, back from cremating her twin brother. How could they put me in the orthopaedic ward? And how could I go from being at the top of my class to performing so miserably without anybody noticing?

It was the repeating pattern of my life: crashing into being nothing again, yet unable to ask for help.

Graeme's six-foot-two frame was cremated in a five-foot-five coffin. The many pieces of him had been collected by a stranger and made ready for burning. I hadn't been allowed to see him. I'd wanted to and asked but had been told no.

I kept imagining how his blood would have been left on the road of that bend. It would have seeped through the flattened metal of his yellow Corolla van, his dinghy smashed up against it. I don't know what happened to the pieces of his boat, but I pictured the crash. And the red ants drinking his blood, unperturbed by the black crows agitated by the smell of death they couldn't reach.

Whenever I passed a curve in a road, marked by somebody else's flowers to remember the death of their loved one, I would whisper hello to Graeme. While staring at the flowers wilting and sweating in their plastic wrap, I remembered his long, skinny body, tanned toes pushed out in front, his sure hands with the clearly defined muscles of his arms relaxed at his side. What stays with me, frozen in time, is his grin – his fine, red lips and the sweep of his dark hair falling into his eyes.

I never thought to check on Christine. None of my family mentioned her. I hope that, somehow, she found the help she needed.

*

The flat I shared with the other student nurses was one floor up. I sometimes sat on the wall of the balcony, leaning out, daring myself to fall, to let go. Jules watched me. She couldn't relax when I was around. I rode my bicycle for endless miles – up Great Western Road, from Westmead into the city, weaving in and out of the trucks and cars and buses. Hit me, I wanted to scream, but the words were silent, screamed internally into my mind. Then on to Coogee Beach where I swam far out. I wanted to drown.

I gave up on nursing and asked friendly doctors to write me sick notes when I ran out of leave. I stopped studying and wandered late at night, sleeping on a bench at Central Railway Station when I missed the last train back. I knew my friends were worried but nothing touched me. With Graeme dead, I struggled to be alive. I belonged with Graeme but he was gone.

I went through my days like a puppet, smiling and nodding in what I hoped were the proper places. I avoided words. I spent most of my spare time alone. I saw Graeme from the corner of my eye and turned around, only to discover it was another stranger.

All alternative things started to attract me, like the festivals held regularly on land north of Sydney. They offered Tai Chi, yoga and whale watching, with stalls and workshops on massage, herbs, tarot and vegan and vegetarian food. People camped between the eucalyptus trees or the dunes behind the beach.

One morning, after an early swim, I walked along the sandy track back to my tent. A stranger stepped in front of me. He asked, 'Can I read your palms? It's important.' He smiled at me. He waited another moment, then added, 'I've been drawn to you. Will you let me?'

I nodded and he gently held both my hands in his, turning each over to study the lines. He looked at me and said, 'You're on a journey – a painful and terrifying one. You're lost and alone, but you'll learn and get through. Your life will continue to be a struggle, but in your early thirties, you'll start writing a book. That will be the start of your healing. From then on, you'll free yourself and begin to understand. And you'll find the love you desperately need. I wish you well. You're going to do this.'

He smiled at me, a full-faced smile that crinkled the skin around his eyes, nodded once and left.

I stood and watched him walk away. A voiceless, hidden piece of me wanted to believe him. I tucked his words into my heart to keep them safe, even as another more brash part of me dismissed them. I'd given up any sense of hope. Hope was not for me. Hope only hurt. I'd chucked it away.

At this time, the memories of my earlier traumas were still buried, but their unconscious impact continued to control my behaviour. They left me with a sense of wrongness – there was something different and ugly inside of me. And it was all my fault.

*

At one of the festivals, I listened to a talk by the group BUGAUP (Billboard Utilising Graffitists Against Unhealthy Promotions). I approached the speaker and after we chatted he invited me to go out with one of their teams. I became a willing participant. Late at night, we spray-painted the tobacco advertising signs at the edges of the railway tracks that trailed into central Sydney. We were often chased. Hyped up and anxious, I loved the adrenaline rush.

One night, alone, I spray-painted a sign at the end of a block of warehouses in inner Sydney. I finished and rode my bike along the dead-end street. It was hemmed in by buildings. A truck driver leaving one of the sites saw me and took offence. He drove straight at me.

I dodged him but he turned around and chased me. With no sideways escape, I cycled to outrace him, coming to the maze of buildings that were the nurses' quarters at Camperdown Children's Hospital. Jules's friend Joanne lived there. I pedalled down a walkway and bashed on her door. It was late but she let me in. I collapsed on her floor, laughing hysterically. My pulse was racing. It was the closest I came to being alive.

*

On my days off, in between my nursing shifts, Hoyts, the cinema in George Street in Sydney, became my favourite place to go. I would sit in an under-lit back-row seat watching whatever film was on. In early May 1981, *Ordinary People* was being shown. It was almost a year to the day since Graeme had been killed. My tears were still locked within me.

I watched the two brothers play in the rowing boat far out on the lake. One boy fell in the water and his brother dived in to save him. He couldn't and his brother died. I started crying and couldn't stop. I didn't save my brother. It was my job to look after Graeme and I hadn't, like the boy in the film. I stumbled out of the picture theatre and made my way to the train station. The tears refused to stop now they'd started. I stood for long moments imagining stepping in front of the oncoming train, but defeated, I got on instead.

I found myself at Henry's door rather than my own. It was nearly midnight. I knocked and knocked until he let me in. Still sobbing, not able to find any words, Henry held me. It was the first time I'd seen him in more than a year, but he let me cry, stroking my head and back.

After I explained my brother's death and my guilt, Henry suggested, 'You need to talk to Graeme. You need to say the words so Graeme can forgive you.'

He explained the gestalt therapy technique of chair work, where I imagined Graeme sitting in the chair in front of me and I would say all the words I needed to say to him.

With Henry's encouragement, I pictured Graeme in front of me and I spoke to him, telling him I was sorry. It was real. Graeme was there. I felt him when I thought I'd lost him forever. Graeme was on the chair in front of me. I stared at his gorgeous face, his blue, sparkly eyes, and his easy smile. He grinned at me and called me sis, the way he always did.

I cried and cried and spoke. I told him how much I loved him and missed him. He laughed and told me I'd always be with him. We were two who were one. All the separation was gone. We would always be together. I would never lose him – never again. He was mine. He was in me and by my side, forever.

Then Henry said, 'Now you need to switch chairs and be Graeme.'

'No, I c-can't.'

'You need to feel what Graeme feels. You need to feel his forgiveness.'

I swapped chairs and became Graeme, and I felt like Graeme. I looked at Wendy and my heart broke. She was sad and lost and alone. I wanted to take her in my arms because I loved her. She was mine as much as I was hers. It was sad to have lost her. I made a promise to her that I'd never leave her but always watch over her, forever and always. We were one now – two halves made whole. A whole one.

I told her there was nothing to forgive. It was OK she'd gone to Sydney while I stayed behind in Townsville. I'd been having fun. It was sad I'd died, I knew, but it happened and we needed to let it go. I asked her to start living again, to feel my love wrapped around her, keeping her warm and safe.

I switched back and became Wendy. I looked at Graeme one more time, making sure I remembered the planes of his face, and said goodbye. I wished him well wherever he went and he went inside of me. He disappeared into my flesh and the essence of my being.

Graeme lives along my left side. If I think of him or say his name, I feel him there, particularly in my left arm. He is with me. I occupy the right and we are left and right together. People assume I am a single person but I'm not. I'm a twin, one of two, with the two of us now permanently inside.

Henry validated my grief, and I reclaimed my brother, but the longing for absolute joining with a physical person, one who was alive, lived on within me.

Henry and I talked about him and me, and he forgave me too. We stayed friends but not lovers. I was too lost and needed to work out who I was. The idea of claiming my individuality denied my being a twin. This paradox is at the heart of a twin relationship.

I was alive but not living. I didn't know how.

Chapter 11

A perfect finish

Disillusioned with the hierarchy of nursing, not the job itself, I hid within the blue stripes of my nurse's uniform and silently fought to hang on to the appearance of normality. I learned Chinese massage and Shiatsu and earned a diploma in Swedish massage, embracing these alternative healing practices. I used my new skills with my patients. During the night shift, I would offer a massage instead of sleeping pills. My patients often said it was their best night's sleep in years.

My next placement was in the operating suite. I thrived on the stress of being on alert. I started as the runner, getting various instruments from the sterilised stores that the surgeons needed, and flourished, learning their ways. I'd spent my childhood trying to get it right with my parents and then fitted myself into my grandparents' world. I was the perfect assistant: leaving myself out and thinking only of the other person.

I progressed to assisting in the operations themselves – simple stuff but enough to see into people's cavities and how a body works. It helped answer the call of that long-ago dream of being a vet. Plus, the charge nurse wanted me – she asked me to come back once I graduated. I'd seamlessly slipped into her team.

My last year of nursing was spent dancing whenever I could. Jannette, Jules and I often busked. Wearing early settler dress, with Sydney

Harbour Bridge behind us or in Martin Place, we drew large crowds. Australian bush dancing was growing popular with major bands like The Bushwhackers and Red Gum attracting attention.

The Bushwhackers held an outdoor dance at Circular Quay in Sydney. Thousands of people came, surrounded by the city and harbour lights. The set steps of the dances were called as the band played. It was easy to notice those who could dance and knew how to spin in a controlled way. The competent dancers found each other and Michael found me. His sure hands were suddenly around my waist and then he swung me off the ground during a turn. Delighted, I laughed and looked at this stranger who so easily matched my steps. I stared up into his eyes and that was it – I didn't want to dance with anybody else.

When he leaned in close, his ragged beard brushed my face. 'Hey, I'm Michael from Boston. And you can dance!' He grinned. His slightly crooked teeth added a vulnerability to his confident stare. He was tall and slender yet somehow floppy in his movements. This was a man who didn't play by the rules, with his hitched-up lungi – a tube of cloth worn by men in India – and martial arts black-cloth shoes. We danced until my feet ached from pounding on the road. I invited Michael to the next dance at Glebe Town Hall and he asked me to visit him at his place in Marrickville.

Michael was seven years older than me. He'd been travelling with his bicycle for six years and was newly arrived in Australia. He confronted my narrow view of the world – one that had grown from my sheltered North Queensland existence. He busked to earn money, playing a tin whistle and hammered dulcimer, and worked as a vegetarian cook in Kings Cross. He'd set up a food co-op in his neighbourhood where people could exchange services for food.

Michael questioned my assumptions. It became acute. I was too scared to say a word. Instead, I watched, listened and learned. I would sit in his overcrowded house and look in wonder at this strange new world: people walking around naked and talking about scraping their tongues, juicing carrots and growing cannabis. It helped focus my attention outside myself, away from the pain of my grief. I didn't speak of it. It was eighteen months since Graeme had died. *I should be over it.*

Michael's world was a magical one that I didn't know how to join. I sat on the edge, never daring to sing yet loving the feeling of community as different people took up the beat, singing Joni Mitchell's 'Circle Game' or the latest Bob Dylan release.

One evening, we lay wrapped around each other on a mattress on the floor of Michael's room. Filtered light slipped past the curtain from the single street light outside his ground-floor window. I lightly traced the patterned lines on his skin.

Michael faced me and said: 'You're a lesbian. Do you realise that?'

'What? What d-d-do you mm-mean?' I heard the words but I didn't understand what he was saying.

He laughed. 'You're a dyke and you don't even know it. I always fall in love with lesbians. You're not the first.'

He'd hit me with two startling words, love and lesbian, in one sentence. He grinned at my bewilderment and told me to read *The Women's Room* by Marilyn French. He bought me a copy. It overturned all I knew about women and my place in the world. French's words were a mirror of those stuck inside me, which I didn't know until I read her words.

I was submissive, like French's character Mira, who felt trapped by the choices of wife and mother. I didn't know what I wanted. I only knew

I didn't want to be like my mother. And that I carried my grief like an invisible shroud of loneliness. I couldn't find the words to share the pain, not even with Michael.

Michael encouraged my education by buying me a copy of *Ruby Fruit Jungle* by Rita Mae Brown. I lost myself in her world of lesbian love. Her story permitted me to define myself, instead of struggling to fit in. Brown's book suggested that I, too, could find my path. But my path was confusing. I was not a singleton like my friends. I was a twin endlessly seeking what I would never find in another person – a perfect joining. Somehow, relationships always fell short of what I needed and I didn't know how to ask or make it happen.

My grief and unacknowledged trauma left me slightly removed – always an observer. I feared yet wanted closeness, swinging from an over-intensity to a cutting-off. There was no middle ground.

Ruby Fruit Jungle celebrated female genitalia. That was too much for me, but in a secret part of myself, I wondered if I could reach the point of celebrating my body instead of hating it. Michael talked about Sappho, the ancient Greek lyric poet, and her island of Lesbos. His telling started me dreaming. Maybe I could visit there. He encouraged me by saying, 'You need to have a love affair with a woman.'

Michael urged me to experiment with different ways of being intimate. Our conversations opened me to the idea of exploring my own needs and boundaries.

Jules's friend Joanne stayed over at my flat in Westmead. She'd been on exchange in Germany, where she'd lived with a lesbian host and been introduced to feminist ideas. She was struggling to cope in backward Australia and missed the politically progressive scene she'd grown to love. Jo would talk about women's power. I became her spellbound audience.

I'd never heard another woman speak like this.

Jo looked at me and I felt the pull in her eyes. I felt her energy and her need. With Michael's knowing grin still strong in my mind, I plunged into this brand-new world of women's energy. Women without men. Womyn. What a revelation. I started seeing Jo while keeping my relationship with Michael separate. When I told him, he was delighted.

It quickly became intense with Jo. I would spend different days with each of them then escape back to my flat to work out how I was feeling. I felt pulled apart by their dissimilar needs and aware of how I became a different person with each of them, like a chameleon. I couldn't hold myself steady or settle into the core of me. I didn't know what I was: straight or lesbian. I loved them both, but I couldn't do what each of them was able to do: climax. I stopped myself short, detaching, and gave what I thought the other person wanted.

A few months later, I met Peter, another friend of Jules's and a different sort of man. He was an artist, working as a cartoonist. He looked into my eyes and made my body his canvas. He stroked and caressed my skin, waiting for me to fully show up. He created an intimacy I'd never known.

His presence seemed to sing to me – somehow, he called me awake. All of me felt alive and uncovered in front of him. I had nowhere to hide. Tender and utterly tantalised, I looked over the edge into what I knew would be an explosion. I didn't know what to do to safely release such unbearable feelings. Panicked, I ran.

Peter had somehow got behind my defences and into the very core of me. This deeper connection terrified me. I was frightened of letting go and losing control. I wouldn't and couldn't do it. When I got close I'd shut down. I didn't know why, but I'd leave my body and find myself once more on the ceiling, looking down, the self-blaming stories jamming my head. I wasn't woman enough; there was something wrong with me. In my confusion, I left Peter and his clear blue eyes.

I never told Jo or Michael what was going on with me. I pretended I was happy. And I was, with the physical touch, just not going near the orgasm. I felt content in Jo's arms but I couldn't make her happy in the way she needed. She wanted all of me, but I kept a part of me removed, watching rather than being present. I was constantly thinking rather than feeling.

Michael fell in love with Martina, a Swiss woman he shared a house with. I was his project though. He still stopped me mid-sentence, demanding to know if I thought what I said or if I was parroting someone else's words. And was that all of it or was there more?

With him, it was my mind that was turned inside out. He didn't let me get away with anything. I learned to consider my words before I voiced them, and even then they came out hesitantly – a hesitancy separate from my stammer. I was scared to expose my thoughts in case they were laughed at. They were too tender to risk being pulled apart – better to keep them hidden and try out lesser ones.

One morning, Michael and I sat together at the well-worn kitchen table, a French press of freshly made coffee in front of us. He said, 'Hey, my Australian visa is running out.'

I waited for him to continue but Michael left the statement hanging between us, watching my face. I played along.

'WW-What are you g-g-go-going to do?'

'I was thinking of riding up through Southeast Asia. Do you want to come with me?'

'Me?' He nodded. I scrambled to organise my thoughts. I hadn't seen this coming.

'But wwhat about Mar-Martina? Don't you ww-want her?'

'She doesn't want to leave. She's too involved here …'

'I d-don't know … d-do you really wwant me …'

Michael smiled. 'Of course, I want you. Who else would I ride with? You're fit and strong and we dance so well together.' He finished with a laugh, attempting to mask his sadness.

'B-But you d-don't love me. Not really. You love M-Mar-Martina …'

He turned away to stare into the overgrown backyard. The sunlight flickered through the grey-green leaves of the paperbarks and played on his face. The moisture in his eyes was like tiny sparkles. I waited for him to answer. I needed to know why he was asking me.

'Will you come? We can wait till you've finished your training. What do you think? Do you want to?'

I didn't press him further, but imagined it: a way out. Riding with Michael. Leaving Australia. Could I do it? It opened up a space. I looked into the future and found it stretching into the distance – a distance I now envisioned myself riding towards. I smiled. Decided.

'Yes.' And with that simple word, we planned a bicycle trip up through Malaysia, Thailand, into Burma, as it was known then, making our way to a kibbutz in Israel where Michael had previously lived and longed to return.

I bought a gleaming red touring bike, panniers, spare tubes, tyres and tools. Bicycle parts took up one pannier, leaving me the other one for a single change of clothes, sarong, towel, swimmers and not much else.

Michael demanded I travel light, as I needed to be able to lift my bicycle by myself. It left me without luxuries, no face cream, no camera. To prepare for the trip, we cycled for hours to build up our stamina.

My mother surprised me by making me a simple, royal-blue colonial dress. It was edged with white lace. I wore it to the ball held at the Sydney Town Hall in George Street. We waltzed the night away, working through the list of dances on a card hanging from a cream ribbon at my wrist. The men claimed what dance they wanted, and Jo claimed some too. I finished the night by doing cartwheels in the middle of George Street at midnight. Jannette joined in, in her shiny sateen gown. The hoops under her dress fell around her shoulders with each wheel then bounced back into place.

Jannette and I often talked into the early morning. She was sure of her opinions and invited mine. With her, my words flowed. I stammered but she didn't care. I leaned into her steadiness.

On other nights, our group piled into the back of a Kombi and drove to a beach. I'd get dropped off before my morning shift, shove my third-year nurse's cap on my head – not bothering to straighten the crumpled cloth – and run to work. Later, I'd find sand in my ears and holes in my tights, but I didn't care what people thought.

I questioned the idea of healing as I continued training as a nurse. I was taught practical skills of how to care for and tend to an ill person, but something was missing. If I was invisible in my grief, what did it say about accepting the whole person? Here, a person was divided into physiological systems, with different wards and their associated medical teams attending to each disorder or condition. What about the person's essence? Their spirit? Their soul? There was more to healing, but I wasn't finding what I needed within the tight confines of the hospital.

A month before I was due to leave, Joanne confronted me. 'You can't leave with Michael. You can't go. He doesn't love you like I do.'

I looked away from her. I'd been waiting for her to say words like these.

'You can't leave what we have. Look at me. Don't you care?' She sat up next to me, pulling the sheet to cover her body.

'Look at me! Don't you care about me at all? About us? About what we have together?'

I couldn't meet her eyes so I gave her my arms, but she was having none of it. She cried out, shoving me away. Any words were silent within me.

Jo's voice softened as she continued: 'I love you. How can you leave me? You're breaking my heart.' She sobbed, curling into a ball at my side. She let me pull her close.

I held her as she cried, but my heart was barricaded before her hurt. I had nothing to offer her, even as a few tears slipped down my cheeks, called to join her own. A distant part of me questioned myself. I didn't feel the way Jo felt. And yes, I was choosing to leave, so I couldn't be sad. I was causing this pain. I was a horrible person. Had I used her? I didn't know.

How could she love me when I was unlovable? That's why I was leaving. I was running away from Australia to find out. I was a cardboard cut-out next to Jo's flushed skin and raw pain. I couldn't find the words to describe myself to her. She didn't get me. I was too embarrassed to even try.

I attempted to offer her something. 'I'm ss-sor-ry. I'm so sss-sorry but I c-c-can't stay. I have to leave. I d-d-don't know if I can explain it to you, but I am ssorry. All I know is that I need to g-g-go.' I couldn't say the words she wanted: that I loved her. What was love? I didn't know. In my quiet way, I cared about her, but it was never enough. The intensity of her feelings often overwhelmed me.

Joanne sent me RD Laing poems, the lines giving form to her distress. Had I mistaken sex for love? I'd gone through the actions, copying what Michael or Joanne did, but somehow I didn't go to the places they went. I pretended instead, and now it all crashed around me on the eve of leaving.

I was still mourning the loss of Graeme and couldn't tell Jo that nothing touched me. Inside, I still keened for him. The pain of never again being able to see or hold Graeme kept me separate. I'd claimed him mentally, but I would never hear his voice or see him laugh at me, his strong hands on the tiller, his joy when tacking into the wind, swearing when we capsized and stood on the centreboard hauling the sail out of the water, his clothes plastered to his skin.

Graeme had been my anchor and with him dead, even two years later, I continued floating, disjointed from myself. I needed to run. I needed to leave Australia. It was too painful to stay still.

*

I refused to study and didn't open a textbook. I sat my final nursing examinations cold. I'd panicked a few weeks earlier and approached one of the large tomes that lay on the floor of my room, but one look and I was overwhelmed. It was too late. Jannette felt the same. The night before our big exams we drove for miles, up into the Blue Mountains and home again, trying to drown out our panic with music from her car stereo.

I thought I was free when I walked out of the examination room the next day, but I hadn't factored in the amount of time I'd taken off after Graeme's death. I'd passed the exams but I needed to make up the missed shifts before I received my nursing registration. I was the last student of our initial 187-strong class to finish their time and leave the hospital, the first graduating class of West Metropolitan Group School of Nursing.

It was a big event for the hospital. The head of nursing, Mrs Noone, arranged the graduation and celebration dance. I'd been planning for weeks what I was going to wear, having been inspired during my time in the operating rooms. I'd borrowed a set of scrubs, a mellow shade of blue, baggy and loose – the type of clothes I loved to wear. I spent hours sewing beads and pieces of fine leather onto the cloth, painting an eagle flying freely across its front. Its wings outstretched, soaring through the pure blue of the welcoming sky.

I walked in with women wearing evening gowns, glittering, the men in swish suits and me in scrubs. It caused a ripple of stares and shocked faces but one by one they turned their backs. I was dismissed. Only my friends danced with me.

My mother had come down for the graduation. I'd felt pressured to invite her. If I'd thought about it more, I should have invited my grandparents. She was horrified. She wanted me to wear a lovely dress. I'd stopped wearing anything soft and girly in front of her when Graeme died.

I spent the evening avoiding my mother, but she managed to corner me with Mrs Noone at one point in the night. She complained to the head of nursing about how horrible a daughter I was – her same old consistent rant but this time public. My mother berated me to this powerful woman, who couldn't get a word in and gave up trying. Joan went on and on about how I was not a good daughter.

I stood listening until finally, without speaking, I left the room and didn't come back. I was done. A perfect finish. My mother.

Part II

Searching

Chapter 12

Another beginning

I walked out of Westmead Hospital as a registered nurse in early 1982, aged 20, yet I couldn't embrace it. The accomplishment was tainted by the struggle of growing up without my twin. I'd proved the Townsville Matron wrong regarding my stammer, but my defiant words sat there – empty sounds floating on the winds of a life skewered sideways.

I'd packed up my belongings in a single tea chest and shipped them back to Townsville, after arranging to fly home for a few days to say goodbye to my family. Trevor was in Binghamton in New York State, USA, learning about a new simulator the RAAF was buying. The flight simulator was invented in the city, and he'd fallen in love with an American woman and wanted to bring her home.

For my last week in Sydney, I moved into Michael's shared house. For dinner most nights, an extra twenty or more people came to celebrate our leaving. The 16th National Folk Festival was being held in Sydney and helped fill our days with music and dancing. Most of us cycled to the events, commandeering a lane from the cars on Anzac Parade with the power of numbers. We spilled with laughter and mad pedalling, stopping for gelato on our ride home. It was a week full of movement, food, people and noise.

On our last evening together we congregated in the lounge room. Martina sobbed. She couldn't bear that Michael was leaving. She sat, cradled in his lap, his arms tight around her. His cheek was pressed to her tear-streaked one. Before long all of us were crying and saying similar words. I love you. I'll miss you. What will we do without you?

To ease the pain, we stood in a circle and took turns to be lifted horizontally. The individual was supported by hands, passed around the circle high in the air, and then gently propped back up on their feet. For those moments of being held, I loved it so much I imagined I was a cloud floating in the night sky.

We followed with massage, where I found the ends of myself again. Candles softened the light in the communal room. The essential oils of camomile, lavender and bergamot soothed the pain. More tears followed, gentler this time, then exhaustion as I slept.

The day of our departure arrived, after weeks of planning and saying goodbyes. I woke before the rest of the house began to stir. In the raw space, between sleep and being fully awake, I faced the stark truth: I was kidding myself. Michael and me? I'd never be able to satisfy him. Why was I going? It was selfish, I knew. But could I make it work? And then the elation hit me. I was leaving Australia.

I turned my face to the wide-open sky and imagined the new horizon waiting for me. It reminded me of being in my grandfather's car when I was eight years old. This was a chance to reinvent myself. It felt appropriate that today was the 13th too, not a Friday but a Tuesday. Somehow, this fact alone signified positive change.

After loading up our bikes, Michael and I rode in a group of nine to Sydney Airport where we were met by a dozen of our friends. We held an impromptu bush dance, taking over one of the aisles, much to the amusement of the check-in staff. We danced for half an hour to fiddle and guitar, backed up by bodhran beats, and finished with a wild, swinging 'Strip the Willow'. Joanne hid behind a pillar, where I bid her a teary, heart-wrenching goodbye.

I left with Michael and my bicycle on my first touring adventure. I was a novice. I'd barely changed a tyre. I'd bought a one-way ticket to Singapore and sat next to Michael, expectant, but he didn't want to leave Martina or tour again. He'd been cycling the world for six years, whereas I was at the beginning. During the flight, he only cried.

Michael did love me, but in a big brother, know-it-all, teaching-me-the-ropes sort of way. We were friends, but seeing his tears plunged me into self-doubt. I wondered what I'd gotten myself into.

We arrived in Singapore late at night and collected our bikes and belongings, but the central nut was missing from the stem of my handlebars. I couldn't lock them into place. The airport cleaning staff took pity on us and brought us a trolley to take apart. We found a nut that fitted and rode out in the early morning. Within minutes, I was side-swiped by a speeding car and thrown into a ditch. Unhurt but shaken, it didn't help my confidence or Michael's mood. I climbed back on my bike and rode on in a bubble of silence.

It was a long ride into central Singapore. We found a fenced-in park and set up our tent for what remained of the night. I climbed into my sleeping bag, but woke not long after, covered in large biting ants.

'What the hell!' I said to Michael, waking him up. 'They hhurt.'

'Come on … move it.'

We packed up and rode to the waterfront. We arrived in time to catch the beginning flare of the sunrise. It claimed the still sea and turned the flat blues of the water into a sparkling wash of reds and oranges and glinting golds. The brilliant colours tugged me out of my dullness.

I called Michael, 'Hey, it's b-b-beautiful here.' I wanted him to join me. Maybe we could start again. Make this our first day and forget about last night, but his eyes purposely avoided mine.

I made myself as small as possible and became a silhouette at his side. It was my fault, this terrible start. When Michael leaned his bike against a fig tree and found a park bench to sit on, I wandered close. He took out his tin whistle and started playing. Within a few minutes, his foot was tapping in time to the music.

My pleasure of the dawn slipped into sorrow. His tune brought a wave of melancholy. I buried a few glints of gold within my chest, to remember later on my own. It was what I did when the land, sky or moon spoke to me – my secret world.

It was quiet between us, the whistle music a thread of connection and a sharp contrast to the bustle and noise of our previous week. I didn't have a buffer of people between us or a way to dilute my presence. I'd never been alone for long periods with Michael before. He needed more than me – an entire group to fill him up. I failed before I'd even started, but that was nothing new.

Dozens of elderly people were practising Tai Chi on the strip of grass next to the water. I watched them. They gave me a sense of calm. I joined their line and borrowed their quiet strength as I attempted to follow their lead, making it mine.

We fixed up my bicycle and rode towards Malaysia, but a sudden tropical downpour drenched us in minutes. We huddled in a shop entrance and waited it out, eating coconut pastries. Once it eased, we rode towards the border. The trucks splashed us when they passed. The sun came out, steaming up the tarmac. The moisture lifted off the surface in waves. Michael complained of the high humidity but it felt like home. We crossed the long bridge marking the boundary from Singapore to Malaysia and turned to each other. Our first smile and high five.

We rode up the less-populated east coast to avoid as much traffic as possible. We cycled for three or four hours in the morning, stopped for lunch and a rest, and then rode again for another couple of hours before setting up camp for the night.

Michael continued to brood. Then one day, he cheered up and started talking and singing as we cycled. I joined in.

'Shut it, Wendy. You're spoiling my song. You know you can't carry a tune.'

I'd forgotten to be careful. I should have told him to shut the fuck up, that I could sing if I wanted, but I went silent instead and withdrew into myself. On the odd nights when it felt safe to do so, I stopped sleeping in the tent and started lying under the stars. He complained one night but I ignored him.

I bought an unlined notepad and my diary became my best friend. My confidante. I poured my heart out to it and faced up to the truth. I was second best to Martina. Michael looked down on me – my inexperience and lack of worldliness. The age gap between us was too much, and I lacked Martina's bolshy grace. Next to her, I was nothing. It confirmed what I believed about myself.

We rode mostly through towns or smaller fishing villages. The smell of drying fish was constantly in the air. I learned about the special Friday night trains heading north into Thailand, full of men going north for sex. The women usually ignored me whereas men followed me, but one day I sat down on a wooden bench next to two elderly women. Within minutes, a dozen women and children surrounded me, asking questions.

'What are you? A girl or a boy?' I'd shaved my hair off before leaving Sydney, to prevent lice and make it easier to manage.

I smiled, 'I'm a g-g-girl.'

'Are you married? Where is your husband? Why are you alone?'

'No, he's my fr-friend, and he's mminding the b-b-bikes.'

'But you can't be with a man unless you're married.'

I didn't answer. Instead, I said, 'We're rriding to Ban-Bangkok.'

A few of the younger women looked at me, startled, but then a group of men butted in. They demanded my attention and shoved the women aside. I left, waving goodbye to the women. The children followed me back to our bikes where Michael played them a tune on his whistle.

It was difficult to find a private place to pee, as men congregated around us as soon as we stopped. They were usually there at dawn when I woke, already squatting and watching me, or outside on those mornings when I emerged from our tent. I became an expert at peeing under a lungi or we'd set up the fly sheet for some privacy.

When I was cooling off in the sea, young men and boys swam under the water and attempted to grab me. They made rude signs with their fingers when I shouted at them. It was a relief to find isolated fields, stretches of uninhabited coast or rubber plantations to camp in. Mostly, though, the people were kind, curious and questioning. We joined in badminton games that were played in the dirt over a rope stretched between two palms, and in soccer matches with chairs marking the goalposts. I did handstands and cartwheels with the kids, playing games of leapfrog and brandy on the beach. When we stopped, people gathered around.

'Where are you going?' their voices asked. 'Come home with me.'

We slept on people's floors, in half-built houses and run-down building sites, happy to find a dry area and a cover for the night. I learned that girls did a stint in the army alongside the boys, and the grandmothers loved smoking from a shisha. It was an intricate water pipe, first heating then vaporising some kind of tobacco and sometimes cannabis, hashish or opium, often flavoured with mint. Or else they chewed a soft leaf spread with white paste. After a taste, I felt high and learned to smile and wave it away.

Most villages were arranged around a central well, which sat in an open square. When I asked if I could wash at their well, it turned into a performance. The villagers scrutinised my every movement. I washed under one lungi then slipped a dry one over my head before letting the wet one fall. The men watched with hungry eyes. It was a relief to get through without a mishap and ride away, after saying thank you and pegging my wet clothes to my brake cables to dry.

We raced with the wind ahead of the dry dust storms, taking turns to pull each other along – one long passing-each-other game often going for miles. Michael and I sometimes talked as we rode. In the hot sun and thick humidity, the breeze dried our sweat as our legs worked in rhythm. With time to think, I imagined fantasy worlds, keeping one going for days, just as I'd done as a kid.

We took turns talking during our rest periods, unpacking our last few weeks and examining our lives. Michael shared his love for Martina, and his dreams for building a community of like-minded people. I questioned my schooling, playing volleyball and nursing. I reflected on the repeating pattern of striving, being defeated and starting again.

I often swam at night when the men were gone and I marvelled at the sea's display of bioluminescence. I played with the swirling patterns of sparkling light. It cascaded like a curtain over my skin. Until, like magic, wearing only my glittering sea-grown gown, I was going to a ball. The smiling moon and brilliant stars were my dance partners.

Later, I'd lay in my sleeping bag, watching flashes of lightning over the distant hills and hearing peels of thunder but never any rain. Soothed by my night-time performance, I drifted off to sleep. We'd learned to avoid setting up camp under the coconut trees after nearly being hit by a falling coconut. We watched out for water buffalos, which were often curious in the night, attempting to poke their noses into our tent or getting tangled in the guy ropes.

Our usual breakfast was rotis with fish curry for dipping. I would have eaten them three times a day but Michael rationed our food purchases from our combined kitty. I deferred to him. He did the speaking, negotiating with the locals for our meals: rotis in the morning and vegetarian stir-fries at lunch and night. We used wooden chopsticks to avoid the thin aluminium cutlery. I struggled to make myself understood when I did speak; my stammer alienated me and messed up my words. I ended up with meals I didn't ask for.

Michael was impatient with me. 'Do you think you could get your inside wish and your vocal statement together? How else are they going to understand you? You're not helping them.' He stomped off.

He couldn't comprehend my struggle with foreign words and accents. I was agitated before I even attempted to speak. I jumped on my bike and sped off, channelling my frustration into cycling. That was a movement I could control. Sometimes I did attempt a conversation, with an Irish couple we met or the odd Australian tourist, but I was usually too tired after cycling to string any words together. Instead, we entertained the villagers with juggling. We carried clubs and balls. It brought the laughter we were hoping to find.

*

We made it to the border with Thailand, but the Malaysian police refused to let us pass. They demanded a bribe. Once paid, they waved us through without a smile. Entering Thailand was like entering another world. The people were bubbly and curious with open grinning faces, demanding to sit on our bikes and asking to learn how to juggle.

We stayed in monasteries if we were stuck for a place to camp. The monks and novices were demure and sedate outside the compound but erupted into movement and noise the moment they were back. They carried their large silver alms bowls, heavy with food, into the kitchen for the nuns to arrange and dish out. The nuns served the monks, cleaned up and swept out the hall, only then sitting down and eating, always at the back of the room.

One part of me wished to join their order but another part refused the subservient life of a woman contemplative. I didn't understand that it was a spiritual calling. It woke a longing though – hearing the early morning peels of gongs calling all to meditation and prayers.

We made our way further north, hearing rounds of gunfire. Muslim freedom fighters were rebelling against discrimination by the country's mostly Buddhist majority. The rebels shot at government buildings and passing trains. One night, we tried to hide our tent and dropped off to sleep, but were woken by the police. They demanded we follow them to the police station where a local teacher was waiting. She explained we could sleep in her home. They didn't want us shot.

Westerners riding bicycles in Asia in 1982 were rare. Other travellers told us of two cyclists who were riding through India. Backpackers would often walk up to us, grinning and wanting to talk. The travellers' grapevine was surprisingly efficient. Whenever we met, information was shared – an important source before the internet and mobile phones. We learned about the best places to stay, where to exchange currency at the cheapest rates and where to buy low-priced airfares. We heard about Khaosan Road – the main place where travellers congregated in Bangkok. People crisscrossing the world from all directions would meet there. I heard about Nepal, Kashmir, India and Europe, and dreamt of the places I would cycle, keeping detailed notes.

Travellers prided themselves on how far they could go on how little and never missed a chance to ask how long the other person had been on the road. Less than a month was nothing. It didn't count. Three months in and you were getting started.

Life was simple. I didn't wear a watch, which created a sense of timelessness and, as cyclists, we were free to get off the usual backpacker's route. We carved out our own. It was liberating and slow-moving. I felt the change in the land gradient with the extra effort needed, often before I could see it, and could smell the monsoon rains coming. I acclimatised to the everchanging conditions a pedal push at a time.

Michael and I got to know each other's states of mind. He could tell when my period was coming. I'd bought sea sponges before I left Australia and sewn catgut – the strong thread used for stitching skin – into each sponge, which allowed me to pull it out. I rinsed out the blood and reinserted the sponge: cheap, efficient and reusable.

I used American Express Travellers Cheques, with their offices functioning as mini post offices. Communication back home was through lightweight aerograms, with a poste restante section at major post offices dealing with travellers' mail. I crammed tiny words onto each aerogram. It helped ease the isolation of always moving, meeting strangers and continually saying the same opening words.

My mosquito bites became infected in the humid heat and refused to heal, with the bugs a constant irritation. It was a relief to get into the tent and behind the netting. We made it to Bangkok after six weeks of cycling.

Michael surprised me when we found our way to Khaosan Road.

'I've had enough. I'm tired. I'm sorry, Wendy.' Michael looked at me from across the flimsy table at a restaurant in the busy Bangkok lane. We'd finished a meal of noodles laced with tofu and vegetables. He waited for me to understand but I didn't.

'WW-What are you sssaying?'

'I'm over it. This travelling lark. I've been doing it for years and my time in Sydney has spoiled me. I want home comforts again … it's been hard, riding every day … the mosquitoes, sleeping on the ground. It's not like cycling in Europe.'

'Spit it out M-Michael. What are you s-su-suggesting?'

'I can't keep doing it, meeting strangers. I don't want it anymore. It's not you. You know I've been missing the group, especially Martina. I know I promised you, but … I want to go directly to Israel. I want my second family – the life I know I'll find on the kibbutz. It was always our plan to end up there, you know that.'

'Yes I know, b-b-but we were g-g-going to ride first, not only to B-Bangkok but further … up through Asia.'

'I know, I'm sorry, but I'm leaving. I've decided, I have to. I know I've not been much fun. Hey, it's been good.' He attempted to lighten the atmosphere, but I was having none of it. He'd worked it out in his head, privately, without giving me any clues that this was how he was thinking. I was pissed off but couldn't say.

'Come on, talk to me. Please tell me how you're feeling.'

I shook my head and left him sitting at the table. How could he? After all his promises? His lofty words?

I wrote to Jannette, asking if she'd like to join me, and waited for her reply. I'd written dozens of letters home but this was my first opportunity to collect any back. I picked up a bundle of mail and found one from my mother. She told me to stop with the emotions – she didn't want to hear. I don't know why I expected something different from her. I longed to be close but didn't know how. If I was honest with myself, did I want to be friends with my mother? No.

I should have known by now to protect my heart, but I always left myself open to her criticism. I lost myself in long newsy letters from my grandmother and siblings and felt homesick for the first time – for something familiar and comforting, in the face of Michael turning away.

We talked again over dinner. I was being selfish and not considering Michael. I plunged back into where we'd left off.

'WWe've shared so mmuch … I h-hate to see you go. I t-tell you things I've never t-told anybody else. D-D-Do you realise that? How will I be without you?'

'You'll be fine. I love you—'

'Like a ss-sister.' I butted in. He grinned. Our relationship was stronger without the sex. I could be myself, sleeping next to him, cuddling, the occasional massage. But mostly talking. Our time was woven together by being side by side, spinning pedals and buffeting words.

'You're m-my bro-brother, my special b-big brother.' I could let him go. It terrified me, but I didn't have a claim on Michael.

To celebrate our time together, we rode through Thailand to a small island, Koh Samet. To get there, I made my first outrigger canoe crossing with a bicycle. We lived in a grass hut on the beach and listened to waves lapping the almost white sand as we drifted off to sleep.

Returning to Bangkok, I embraced the place, playing games on my bike with the tuk-tuk drivers. They joined in, encouraging me. Michael and I helped the bicycle rickshaws in turn, pushing them up any hills.

On my last day with Michael, I stayed close by his side, fixing his smile in my mind. He left. I cried myself to sleep, then fell into a void waiting for Jannette to answer my letter. I played games with myself: *today I am strong. Today I love myself and won't get hassled.* Then I'd get hassled and fall into a grim space, anxiety stiffening my movements. *It's only emotion*, I tried telling myself. *I'm getting experience by feeling uncomfortable*, as Michael would say. I rehashed our last conversations, taking comfort from his words. *I can do this. He believed in me, so why can't I?*

I wandered the crowded lanes, watching the monks and street life, and slowly enjoyed my space, stopping and eating whenever I wanted. I pigged out on rotis and luscious tropical fruits, indulging in rambutans, mangosteens and mangoes, loving the strange new textures alongside familiar tastes.

Jannette wrote, telling me she was coming with a brand-new touring bike and panniers. She was ready for adventure.

Chapter 13

Jannette

Jannette waved to me from the arrivals entrance at Bangkok International Airport. She wheeled a silver bicycle loaded with rear panniers. She looked tired and dishevelled but had a big smile on her face. She brought a wave of freshness with her weary body. I gave her a fierce hug.

Everything about Jannette was a contrast to Michael. Where he was over six foot in height, with a long, lean body topped by an untidy mop of hair and a straggly beard – Jannette was a compact five foot five inches. She had a smooth, open, tanned face framed by sun-lightened, wavy brown hair. Michael always seemed ready to break into sideways movement: into dance, juggling or preparing the next meal. Jannette was more contained – a muscled bundle of controlled excitement. This very different person now stood solidly in front of me. I was a satellite, spun out of one orbit and into another. I needed to orientate to a new energy.

'OK, which way?' Jannette asked. She let me take charge. It was a noticeable change from Michael's maleness. I led Jannette to where my bike was padlocked. I'd planned a low-key route into Bangkok to avoid the busy roads. I didn't want her to have the same terrible start I'd had when I first arrived in Singapore.

Jannette expected fun, not the naval gazing she accused Michael of. I watched her as I introduced her to Bangkok. She was eager to explore and swept away my carefulness from being with Michael. I could say what I wanted without first doing the internal checks.

We talked into the night, as we shared a double room, and caught each other up on our last few months. It was simple sharing – girl stuff. I struggled to adapt to this new lightness. There was something about the depth of Michael's curiosity that met the shutdown, unknown place within me. It was at least alluded to. With Jannette, life was outward facing; the internal didn't matter, or rather, it was ignored. She didn't question what I said or explore any of the underlying layers. I was a bit lost for the first few days.

I was now the expert on all things bicycle. It went to my head. I found myself being mean and Jannette told me to back off. She told me bluntly, to my face.

I'd swallowed Michael whole. It took me time to discover myself and to stop repeating his ideas. I learned to appreciate Jannette's very different attitude as we explored Bangkok. I looked at the city with fresh eyes as her delight allowed me my own. She played tourist and was relaxed about spending money and time. She wanted a little luxury and moved us into a better room.

We planned to ride through Thailand and into Burma but we discovered the land border was closed; we had to fly in. We found a 'bucket shop' in the backstreets of Bangkok and bought discounted air tickets: Bangkok to Rangoon, then to Dacca and Calcutta. We also bought our flight out of India, dated for a year from then: Bombay to Athens.

In Burma (Myanmar) our bikes were confiscated for a week by the Soviet-influenced socialist government that wanted to control the movement of any travellers within their country. We were required to keep a record of any money exchanged and prove that it matched our outgoings; all travel and accommodation details were first written and then stamped in a special booklet that we carried with us. We learned to avoid the official stamps as we negotiated with the alternative economy. The locals helped us, happy to exchange money at a higher rate and get one up on the government.

Bangladesh was starkly poor, with large billboards stating: 'See Bangladesh before the tourists arrive'. The only westerners we met were foreign aid workers. It was distressing to see some of the living conditions next to the highly fenced-in compounds of the wealthy.

Both of us suffered from recurring diarrhoea and vomiting, so we holed up at a hotel in the mountains. My illness came with terrifying nightmares and high fevers. We took turns going out to buy water, yoghurt and flatbread. After a week, we recovered enough to make our way to Dacca airport and flew to Calcutta (Kolkata).

Jannette and I rode into the overwhelming maze of noise, colour and laughter that was the city of Calcutta. We dodged motorised and pulled rickshaws; bicycles; old-fashioned, mostly black cars; pedestrians; the odd camel and even an elephant.

That night we wandered the streets. At a crossing, I watched well-dressed Indians feeding small animals in an enclosure. It took me a moment to realise they were rats. I looked across the road to where a row of beggars sprawled at the edge of the gutter. Most of them had a limb missing. *Welcome to India.*

The next morning, we queued at the ticket window at Howrah Station to book our seats and bicycles on the train to Jammu. Two young boys approached us. They offered to hold our place if we paid them, but I laughed. It wouldn't take long. But it did. It took hours for us to reach the single window.

We were the only women in the queue and drew the eyes of the men around us. The Indian men who seemed poorer, in threadbare clothes and worn sandals, stared blankly at us, but the men who seemed wealthier – more educated or higher up the caste system, with more flesh on their bones and better dressed – demanded our attention.

One of these Indian men called out, 'Come here!'

Jannette and I looked at each other and silently agreed to ignore him. The man left his place and pushed in front to block our way.

'What are you doing? Do you need my help?' His voice was commanding. He leaned closer and demanded, 'Where are you from?' He took another step towards us.

'We're f-fine and we d-don't need your help.' I stepped back to make some room but he stepped in again, almost against me.

'Where are you going? Answer me!'

'Look, we're Australian and we don't want to talk. Do you mind? Give us some space.' Jannette was getting annoyed.

'Are you married? Why don't you have a man to protect you?'

Jannette had reached her limit. She stepped up to him and looked into his face. 'This is not how you have a conversation. Go away!' She firmly shoved him and turned her back. The man stumbled back and then stood for a moment, uncertain. He stalked away.

I was conscious I couldn't deal with the men's unasked-for attention like Jannette could. My strength seemed to leak away. I hated the way we weren't given any private space, especially with their eyes. Somehow, it was worse in India, with its mass of sullen, constantly staring maleness. I wasn't a person. I was a sex object, waiting to be used. I couldn't relax. I'd been living in a state of low-level fear for several months, like background noise.

I compared myself to Jannette's self-sufficiency and her ease at speaking up. I watched her and learned how to push the men away, but my actions lacked intent, as my first impulse was always to freeze. Jannette shouted and punched when they refused to budge.

Long periods passed when we didn't talk. I wanted a hug, for reassurance, but I knew she wouldn't understand my need. I'd never told her about being raped and she wasn't part of Michael's crowd – the hippy types who welcomed comforting touch from both sexes. I left her in peace, respecting her clearly defined gender lines, and smiled; I pretended I was OK.

The journey to Jammu was 1,981 kilometres with eighty stops. It would take two days, so we stocked up with non-perishable food, bottled water and toilet paper. We arrived at the station as dawn lightened the sky. The train was waiting: a long trail of seemingly endless carriages, with families and individuals already finding their seats. We padlocked our bikes to the metal side of the luggage compartment, after being reassured it went the whole way.

Order arose out of confusion, as the carriages pulled out from the station. The train's couplings creaked and groaned, almost as if they grumbled about starting the journey. Nothing happened in the allocated time, but it happened if I could learn to be patient.

Vendors selling different foods got on at each station. They shouted their wares to the passengers as they walked the length of the train, getting off at the next stop. Chai was sold in small china cups, which were later collected, but the yoghurt was served in unfired clay bowls. These were thrown out the windows.

We watched the other passengers as they watched us. Several children peeked from behind the next seat. The women gave us little smiles as the hours passed. A person dressed in threadbare clothes came onto the train at one of the stops. He crawled the length of the carriage on his knees, cleaning the floor before him with a handheld brush. He begged for coins from the passengers. My neighbour explained that he was one of the Dalits, the 'untouchable caste', who were not allowed to stand up on a train.

In the evening, orderlies came with bundles of pressed, white sheets and a small pillow. They showed us how the sleepers worked. The carriage settled down for the night. Jannette and I padlocked our belongings to our bench, having heard too many stories of bags stolen overnight. A curtain pulled across the opening gave a semblance of privacy and I was rocked to sleep by the swaying of the train.

In Jammu, we found the coach to Srinagar and loaded our bikes onto the roof, then squashed together on slender seats through 260 kilometres of winding curves and hairpin turns. It was a relief to emerge from the tunnel into the Kashmir Valley. The valley appeared like a curving rug of lush greens edged by the jagged grey of the mountains towering above. In the middle of the valley sat the city of Srinagar, spread out on the banks of the Jhelum River. The city was a patchwork of washed-out red, orange and yellow-faced buildings, outlined by the browns and whites of the twisting streets. Further in the distance, on the placid flat blues of the Dal and Anchor lakes, houseboats crammed the water's edges. Colourful boats called shikaras crisscrossed the waters.

Jannette and I rode around Dal Lake until we found an enticing houseboat and negotiated a price. We sat on its deck and watched the light change to pink and muted gold as passing ginger-haired Kashmiri men tried to tempt us with shawls, pashminas and rugs. The children begged for money. They demanded "baksheesh" and held out their hands. With the lack of electricity and heating, people of all ages carried around a small clay bowl of hot glowing coals tucked under their phiran – a long robe commonly worn in Kashmir. The children's bellies were often scarred by burns.

Jannette struck up a conversation with two young men who drove a jeep. She wanted a drive and flirted with one of them, who willingly joined in. She took him on, joking and teasing. His friend looked at me but I hung back. We were the audience.

They suggested a weekend trip into the hills. With a single look at each other, we decided to go. We booked a separate room in a traditional Kashmiri hotel, full of old-world charm. It stood three stories high, built with stone and brick, with wooden balconies and eaves edged by delicate fretwork. Walnut trees with mature walnuts lined the road and swept against the windows of the rooms. The men helped us gather some before dinner.

The atmosphere added to the men's long glances as we shared a meal and wine. I couldn't play like Jannette. I became quieter as she stepped up. She enjoyed their maleness. I kept avoiding their direct looks, eventually saying I was going to bed. Jannette joined me soon after, high on the energy of their attention.

I was terrified to join the sexual game. During the day I was fine – the light gave me courage. Jannette loved men and wanted to meet these different cultures head-on. I'd been protected from male attention by being with Michael, as people assumed I was his wife. Now I was exposed, as Jannette invited it, but I didn't want this heterosexual dance.

We left our bikes in Srinagar and went by bus to Sonamarg – a hill station 80 kilometres to the northeast. Historically it was the gateway to the Silk Road and into Tibet, but now it was mostly visited by wealthy Indians who came north to escape the heat in the south. There were few westerners in the village. We camped by the curve of the mountain river. The slate-blue, icy water rushed through the narrow valley, framed by tall pines against the backdrop of snow-covered Himalayas. For dinner, we feasted on paneer and spinach, dahl and freshly baked naan.

We found a local, Rashid, who was willing to be our guide on the seven-day trek to Naranag. He explained it was a dangerous trail with the risk of altitude sickness, but we were in time before the mountain became inaccessible during the winter months. We needed to be self-sufficient and prepared for changes in the weather. Rashid suggested we take porters with mules to carry our belongings, food, water, fuel for fires plus the tents we would need, to allow us to walk freely.

On the trek, we walked past mirror-like alpine lakes, snow-clad mountain peaks, bare rocky gorges and meadows awash with wildflowers. We trekked up and over a creaking glacier and cleared the highest mountain pass, Harmuk, at 13,800 feet. We'd walked up into the snow by then. It was icy underfoot with a strong wind blowing. It cut through my clothes and froze my toes.

We came to a narrow ice bridge straddling a break in the trail around the edge of the mountain. It was barely wide enough for a single person to navigate. I wondered how the mules would manage but they plodded behind us, calmly stepping in our tracks.

Rashid went first to set the pace, Jannette next, then the porters and one mule. I came last with the second mule. The weight of multiple people and animals was too much for the bridge. I felt it shift under my feet. With a metre to go, I pulled the mule closer to me, terrified I'd lose her, and hurried to reach the other side. The ice crumbled and fell away as I made my last lunge, hauling the struggling mule with me. She panicked and rushed to push past me. We collapsed on the other side, trembling but alive.

The sharp, too-cold mountain air, the brilliant blues and whites blinding me, and now this – the ice falling away beneath my feet. Life and death. I was here again, like when Graeme died. Somehow, this was the only time I felt alive. Sex didn't do it for me, but I lived for this knife edge, never knowing when it would come. But when it did, I came fully into my skin.

Jannette hugged me tight, not saying a word, but she kept hold of my hand as we walked on around the mountain. Rashid checked the mules and then found a sheltered place to set up camp. The group was unnerved by our close escape. After dinner and warming tea, I lay in my sleeping bag and listened to the storm growing around me. I watched the tent change shape. The wind lashed it almost flat, sometimes hard against me, but each time it sprung back. I snuggled close to Jannette.

Our pleasure of being together blossomed in the mountains. She now let me physically close. We hugged, for comfort and warmth. I gazed at her face and knew that I loved her. I imagined tracing her cheekbones with my fingertips. She glanced at me, leaned closer and whispered that she was falling in love with Rashid but was scared to let him know. We talked it through. She smiled and wished me good night. I was content.

The storm passed in the night and we came out to a perfect mountain morning – crystal-clear sky, weak sun, crisp snow and utter silence. Jannette and I escaped the group, stripping off and washing in a secluded bend of an icy stream, careful not to get caught in its racing current. It left us both giggling. We thawed out over several cups of tea.

The wind returned, blowing swirling patterns of snow around our feet. We made our way down to the lower altitudes, crossing from stark whites and greys into greens and glimmering blacks. We walked through tall forests of spruce, fir and pine, and scrambled over slippery moss-covered boulders. Our time of solitude was past.

Jannette decided to stay with Rashid and I left her in the mountains, getting the train south to Rajasthan and a ten-day vipassana retreat with the world-famous teacher Satya Narayan Goenka, affectionately called Goenkaji by his devotees. Vipassana is an ancient meditation technique, its name meaning 'to see things as they are'. It promised me a look into my mind and a way out of my internal turmoil. I'd booked this retreat before leaving Australia.

I struggled with my mind. It bullied me. I couldn't control my self-destructive thoughts. Every day was an unknown ride. I was never satisfied with myself and always wondered what the other person thought.

It was my first silent retreat. Ten days of quiet, waking up at 4 am, meditating for ten hours a day, collapsing into bed at ten at night, for it all to start again the next day. We meditated in a large hall filled with more than 300 people: Indians and westerners, men and women separated on different sides of the room. The Indian women jangled their bracelets and chatted in secluded corners. I was irritated by the rustling and noise and wanted quiet. I couldn't settle or keep my mind still or focused. I was being mean to myself, but I didn't know how to stop it.

Our main meal was lunch with a light fruit platter at 5 pm, then nothing until 7 am the next day when we were served porridge with dried fruit and nuts. I never felt satisfied. The serving staff frowned each time I returned to the queue. I was fixated on food, needing that escape. Day three was still, quiet torture.

Then, on day seven, I felt it – the calm abiding place of stillness, of ease. I wanted to rest in it forever. Never move again. And like most beginners, I grabbed it too tightly and lost it. I finished the retreat with a taste of what could be accomplished, even as my body fought the physical practice.

*

I rode my bike into the busyness of Jaipur, struggling to hold on to the calm of the retreat. A flat tyre forced me to walk the last kilometre – first to the main post office and then to the strange, cave-like room where I'd arranged to stay. I'd received a letter from Jannette, telling me her love affair with Rashid was over. She'd felt claustrophobic and left, planning to join me after the retreat. I left her a note telling her where I was.

I gave up trying to fix the puncture, padlocked my bike to the gate and fell into bed in tears, spiking a temperature. I was delirious, burning up with a fever and semi-conscious when Jannette found me. She took one look at the dismal space and arranged to have me, my bike and belongings, carried to an upmarket hotel. I woke up two days later, clean, in fresh pyjamas, in a sunlit, airy room, but still very ill.

I'd heard stories of westerners dying alone in rooms. This was the second time I'd felt like this and worked out it was recurring malaria, but I didn't want to see a doctor.

I had received several aerograms from Michael. He explored our relationship:

> *I'm writing this from the Vatican City. I've woken up to fever and chills. The last time I had the chills, you held me and were just wonderful. I wish you were here … I hope you and Jannette are getting on. Your*

energy never ceases to amaze me. I'm finding this writing extremely frustrating ... we used to talk so openly. I don't have the energy to put all the words down ... I've reread your letter and have tears in my eyes, just feeling you there.

I'm afraid that I've given you too much negative energy with respect to travelling. It wasn't right for me and I was clear about that. I should have gone directly to Israel. You, on the other hand, are growing in leaps and bounds, and seem to graciously accept the lifestyle. I do miss the sense of endless time from our trip. Here I am ruled by the clock and must finish up. Be strong and discover new aspects of yourself. I love you heaps, respect you and enjoy you. Kisses all over your body!

My brother Trevor also wrote, saying he was back at Richmond RAAF base in Sydney with his American girlfriend. He couldn't get going on the simulator project as the 'bloody Yanks who were supposed to ship it, dropped it, causing some damage. It's delayed by a year.'

I'd tentatively communicated with my father when I was nursing, trying to be my idea of a good daughter by sending him my photograph as a first-year nurse. I blamed myself for my difficult relationship with my father, believing the flaw was mine.

My father replied to my recent letter, starting it by saying: 'Hi daughter, it's time you knew a few things.' He then continued:

My home and family were destroyed by the dumb stupidity of your mother and the wounded self-righteous, domineering, possessive vanity of your grandparents. I had not known they considered your mother 'backward', having been sent home by the headmaster who'd said there was no point keeping her at school, as it was impossible to teach her anything. I could kick the stupid bastard ... they kept her home, working in the boarding house, then got her a dull job with a dressmaker ... where she spent all day picking up pins with a magnet.

Your mother said she married me 'to not get left on the shelf' and 'to get away from her father'. I did my best ... I never came home drunk or abused her. I devoted my life to your mother. I saved and scraped and planned ahead, then gave away a promotion so your mother could be near her parents. I was one of the fastest and best Morse code operators ever known in Australia. My voice and my Morse were known around the world. In London, I was doing a top job with a security clearance. I've been through the bloody blitz and fought around the world in a stinking, bloody war. I'm a quiet bloke and have been shit on for no good reason.

His words prompted me to remember some of Joan's stories: of her love of dressmaking and working as an apprentice to an experienced dressmaker. She'd told of sewing hundreds of beads onto a wedding dress by hand, making fine linen suits and pleated skirts. The only time I heard passion and love in her words was when she talked about sewing.

When I read my father's letter in India, I didn't understand what fuelled his hatred.

*

Jannette and I booked into a Rajasthani tourist bungalow, dotted with graceful cane lounging chairs, placed where we could watch the sun dropping down the sky. The rapidly changing light caused the sandstone buildings of the old city of Jaipur to radiate a luscious pink – hence its name, the Pink City, which was my favourite so far.

We ordered fried eggs for breakfast after discovering most of the menu was unavailable – a regular occurrence. We turned to each other and smiled, as we both said simultaneously, 'What to do?' That expression was part of most travellers' vocabulary in India. Why stress? If we don't do it today, there is tomorrow.

Jannette asked me to read the poems she had written. One was a fantasy: how she imagined herself to be after two years of travelling. She'd portrayed herself as a modern-day Amazon, daring and confident. I laughed out loud.

Maybe if I embraced myself more, like Jannette, and welcomed my crooked toes, my lazy eye that turned inward when I was tired, and my stammer, I'd let go of my frustration and the moodiness that consumed me. To trust it all and accept the world for how it was, as Jannette had said in her poem, rather than how I wished it to be.

We rode to Ajmer, then on to the mystical village of Pushkar. Ajmer is known as the heart of Rajasthan and is thought to have the oldest fort in India: Taragarh Fort. Pushkar, eleven kilometres further on, draws visitors and pilgrims to its lake and the important 14th-century Brahma Temple. Brahma, a Hindu God, is referred to as the God of Creation and forms a divine trinity with Vishnu and Shiva.

The men stared at us as we easily rode the long rise into the town of Pushkar with our Western-geared bicycles. Our bikes attracted attention everywhere we went. Whenever we stopped, men would play with the gear and brake levers, and the children would plead for rides.

We found a room in a building made of stone and white marble that butted up to the edge of the lake. Our balcony extended over the water. It felt like heaven with its white and dark blue chequered tiles. The perfect place to meditate. I listened to the lap of the small wash on the rocks below and attempted to find that peaceful place I'd fleetingly caught at the retreat.

On each side of us, stone steps tiered down to the lake's edge. Each morning, as dawn broke, the locals bathed and washed their clothes on the steps. They trampled the cloth with their feet and then beat it on the stones. I copied the women, enjoying the whack of wet washing.

Late one afternoon, a curving line of nomads walked in from the dunes that stretched away from Pushkar. A string of camels plodded behind them. The erect, fierce-looking men were dressed in brilliant white trousers and tunics, with the softest pink turbans wrapped around their heads. Their faces were burnt to a dark mahogany, with eyes that sparkled above glistening moustaches that jutted out sideways above their mouths. The women were a mass of swirling skirts, mirrored waistcoats and jingling bangles that caught the last rays of the sun – a kaleidoscope of colour.

The nomads quickly erected a Ferris wheel, made by a cross of wooden beams with chairs at each end, about 10 metres high. It was operated by a single man who stood in the centre and walked the cross bars around.

Jannette and I both fell in love with the women's clothes and had a set made. My skirt was purple with blue trim; hers, the opposite. We celebrated by doing a wild polka along the dirt street, to the laughter of the watching locals, and reminisced about our dancing days.

From Pushkar, we cycled to Udaipur, the City of Lakes, affectionately known as the Venice of the East, and booked into a sprawling, farmhouse-type hotel outside the city, which catered to westerners. Jannette came into our shared room with a bounce in her step, saying she'd been talking to the brother of the Maharana of Udaipur, Naranda, who owned the hotel. His brother was the highest ranked of the Rajasthan rulers, like a local king, and Naranda had shown her the photographs of himself with the British Queen, the Shah of Iran and the Kennedys. He'd asked us to stay and lead the morning trail ride for the guests and help in the kitchen. He would give us free board and lodging in return.

It was easy to work with the kitchen staff and house boys. I made banana cakes, Australian dampers and big fruit salads to add to that day's curries, rice and chapatis. About a dozen other travellers were staying. We arranged a barbeque with dancing afterwards, the music provided by a visiting group of tribal musicians. The night was a success, bringing us closer together. One of the women suggested doing Tai Chi at dusk the following night before dinner, the flat rooftop being the perfect space, and a yoga class in the early morning before the horse ride.

A section of the Maharana's palace in the city was being converted into a hotel for the James Bond film crew that had arrived from Britain. They were filming *Octopussy* around the lake and through the streets of Udaipur, using Naranda's horses. Jannette and I sneaked past the guards at the gate and onto the set. We acted as if we belonged there.

We spotted Roger Moore being pulled tightly into a corset, with pads pushed up inside his cheeks to help define his cheekbones, and with a last check of makeup, he was on.

We left to find the food tent. It was a long space filled with rows of tables, all piled high with an amazing variety of food: fresh loaves of bread and barbequed meats on platters, masses of different cheeses, and fresh strawberries next to bowls of whipped cream. The food arrived daily on flights from England. We stuffed ourselves discreetly and planned to come again.

Life took on our first routine for a long time, starting the day with a morning Tai Chi or yoga class. We then saddled the horses and Jannette led us through the lanes to a nearby lake with a waterfall at one end. We watered the horses, easing their saddles, and plunged in for a swim. Children, minding a small herd of goats, squatted and watched us. They laughed at our white skin. Then it was a wild gallop home, with the horses more eager to return than we were.

A Dutch woman, Billie, arrived at the farm and joined our team and the international community of people. She was twenty-three and travelled alone. I was immediately drawn to her and listened to her conversation through dinner that night. Her English was excellent. She explained that it was because Holland is a small country and they need to get on with other much bigger countries. Plus, they grow up with a lot of American and English television shows and learn English from a young age.

Afterwards, I watched Billie from a sofa across the cosy sitting room, entranced by her easy confidence. She travelled with a battered guitar. She gently strummed the strings and quietly sang. The others soon joined in.

Billie looked up and met my eyes. I knew that look. It was the knowing look of one lesbian recognising another. At that moment, I admitted to myself that maybe Michael was right. Maybe I was a dyke.

Chapter 14

Navigating love and connection

Billie approached me, as I was all nervous energy, like a startled fawn held still in her eyes. She sat next to me on the sofa, near but not touching. She said a little about herself – that she'd had several girlfriends from a young age and was involved with the women's movement in Holland. I told her about Joanne. That first night we came close with words – a careful, tentative sharing. We agreed to meet at yoga in the morning.

As dawn broke, we did the yoga poses side by side, then swapped our yoga mats for horses. I rode Mary, a bad-tempered horse who constantly turned her head around to try and bite me. Jannette yelled, 'Don't let her do that. Take charge!' Billie grinned. She was riding a placid chestnut mare.

That afternoon we found a secluded spot in the lounge and continued talking. We missed dinner but begged for a plate of dahl and rice from the kitchen staff. We pinched pieces of chapati from each other's plates. Billie asked, 'Hey, do you want to go for a walk?'

It was late, but I nodded yes. I followed her through the house to the dirt lane outside. It was a ribbon of paleness threading through the night shadows. The sky was lit with a sprinkle of stars and a quarter moon, enough to illuminate our way. The air felt dry. A light breeze rustled the corn stalks in the fields that edged the lane. A dog barked.

Billie took my hand and smiled. Her hand felt equal to mine: a broad, warm, enveloping surface. We walked for several minutes in silence then I sneaked a look into her eyes. Billie noticed and turned to face me. She waited. We were even in height. I didn't speak, but took in her oval face, her short wavy hair and her relaxed gaze. She leaned in, and like a whisper of air, briefly touched her lips to mine.

'Tomorrow night, do you want to sleep on the rooftop? It will give us some privacy to get to know each other. What do you think?'

I imagined it. My spine tingled. 'Yeah, ss-sounds g-g-good,' were all the words I managed to find. Billie walked me back to the room I was sharing with Jannette. She left me without another word, just a nod that was filled with promises.

*

The next night, we took our sleeping bags up to the flat roof. Under the smattering of stars, we talked through the night, sharing our histories, or 'her-stories' as Billie suggested. We took turns. In between, Billie pointed out the constellations in the sky above. I alluded to my internal struggle but glossed over it. I didn't want to tarnish the magic.

Over the next week, I let her in close. I'd never been able to feel much in my body before. I could be real here with her, in this romantic place that almost seemed apart from normal time. I was free in a way I'd never felt in Australia and could expand, since only Jannette knew me. Jannette watched on, happy but distant. The rules I knew from the West didn't apply. I could push boundaries and act out, and nobody would lock me up. It allowed me to loosen the tight control I kept on myself.

Billie was a psychiatric nurse and encouraged the exploration that I'd started with Michael and put on hold with Jannette. She questioned me, hearing what I wasn't saying. She wanted more and prodded until I opened up, voicing feelings I'd never dared find the words for. Being intimate with this woman unleashed a layer within me.

The closeness with Billie touched and woke up my longing for an absolute joining that had sat in my heart from birth. That knowing had never left me and secretly I craved it. It beckoned for Billie to fill it.

Jannette felt abandoned but I didn't want to hurt her; I loved her too much to see her in pain. We talked it through. Jannette didn't understand my attraction to women; she was securely heterosexual. We chased different dreams. The gathered community was gradually breaking up as people left in ones and twos. Jannette decided to go to Nepal and meet me later in Puri, south of Calcutta, for our birthdays in December. They were a day apart.

Billie and I moved into a room in Udaipur and continued our enchanted romance, walking hand in hand around the lake, dancing and making up songs that she later sang to me.

*

We found an elephant chained by a single foot, alone in a large enclosure by a river leading to the lake. The elephant was docile and welcomed our attention, letting us stroke its trunk as it reached for us. It could easily pull free of the stake that was keeping it captive. I thought about myself and my chains. What kept me trapped?

We travelled to Jaipur, where my skin and the whites of my eyes turned a profound yellow, with vomiting and fever that left me exhausted. I had contracted hepatitis A from contaminated food or water – a common occurrence among long-term travellers. Billie caught it too and we compared symptoms. We lived on single chapatis, crushed garlic and yoghurt. Once well, we travelled by bus to Pushkar. We squashed together with my bike and panniers, and her pack and guitar, on the roof with dozens of others.

Billie wanted all of me: the struggle, the sadness, the delight. She decided to initiate me into the worldwide sisterhood of witches and lesbians. I stood in a secluded angle of a park. A cooling breeze stroked my skin. She wrapped a pink ribbon around my forehead and tucked single daisies into its folds. She chanted the ritual words and sprinkled me with water as she turned me three times.

'You're in. You're now one of us – a sister.' It sunk into my skin. It went deeper than I expected.

Billie mentioned her long-term relationship with Rosa, who hadn't wanted to come travelling so they were spending time apart. Billie said we could still be friends if I came to Holland. It left me unsure but planted the idea of a future beyond India.

I came out the next morning to find my bicycle had been stolen. Distraught, we went to the local police station to report the theft and ask for a police statement to send to the insurance company. The policeman behind the desk referred us to his highest-ranked officer – a large Sikh man who looked at me suspiciously.

'You're lying,' he said. 'You've sold your bicycle on the black market. That's what foreigners do. I'm not writing your report.'

'I hh-haven't. P-P-Please b-believe me. It's b-been s-st-stolen.' I pleaded with him, but he wasn't budging.

It went on for hours, back and forth. When Billie left to find some food, his manner changed. He said, 'If you have sex with me, I'll write the report.' He smirked. 'You're a loose Western woman. You're all the same.'

I'd seen it coming. I shouted at him, 'You bastard! Why d-don't you do your job?'

He stood on his side, sneering, secure in knowing he would get his way. He continued taunting me with sexual comments. I kept swearing.

A slim, middle-aged man suddenly stood up from the pool of men trying to work at the back. He walked through to the desk and calmly cut through the noise. 'Enough! Enough of the swearing and shouting.' He turned to me and quietly said, 'I can write the report. Come.' He opened the side door and invited me through.

'I'm visiting from another station and have the authority to do so.' He wrote the statement, first in Hindi and then in English, and sighted my passport details.

'You'll need to have the statement verified at the Australian Embassy in Delhi.' It was completed in twenty minutes. I thanked him but he waved me away. Nothing was said to the other officer. I spent the next day recovering and making my panniers into a backpack.

Who was I without my bicycle? It was an extension of my arms and legs. The loss sent cracks through my idea of myself. I'd prided myself on being a cyclist and different from backpackers, but now I was reduced to their ranks.

We left the day after for Delhi. Mid-trip, we waited for two days for a connecting bus. The locals camping out with us assured me it was coming. They'd come prepared with bundles of food they shared with us, the unrealistic westerners. To them, we seemed so impatient. Billie played her guitar and taught me the words to 'The House of the Rising Sun' and 'Summertime'. I fell in love with her all over again as I lay on the concrete floor of the simple bare room where we sheltered, waiting for the bus.

*

Delhi was a deluge of noise, smog and humanity, but we didn't stay long. We hired two Indian bikes, rode to the Australian Embassy and had my form verified. Billie introduced me to chewing paan and the cheap Indian cigarettes called bidis. I left her to it. She looked cool, standing with the men, offering her packet of bidis around. She mimicked the male stance, her weight evenly balanced over both feet. She loved playing with the confusion as men assumed she was my husband. It took them time to realise she was a woman.

We went to Srinagar, where my passport, ID papers, airline ticket and money were stolen. I don't know how it happened. This shock plunged me further into chaos. It felt personal and threatening.

I was being stripped away – of money, health, identity. I had nothing to prove who I was. The cutting loose that started with Graeme's death was continuing. I was a wide-open expanse without boundaries. Pushed in all directions, I was unable to centre myself in my skin.

I imagined looking down at myself from space: a single dot in India, among millions of dots, all scrambling to make a living. What's another dot on this land? I didn't matter or belong. Who was I? And if I wasn't a twin, what was I? I didn't have Graeme to ground me and wasn't able to find any security in myself, as an individual. I floated free even when I squatted in the dirt.

It left me feeling split in two – the surface parts of me having a mad love affair with Billie yet deep inside lurked this grief, waiting to grab me. It destroyed any romantic love. I see-sawed between the layers, hating the struggle but unable to explain to Billie why I suddenly cut off and distanced myself from her.

I didn't know that I'd disassociated from my childhood trauma and that it still defined me. I was living in the top layers of myself, but any new ordeal sent shockwaves through my system, threatening it. To cope, I pushed outward, hoping the next place, the next person, would give me the answers. I looked to Billie, but the relationship was too new, too unknown. I was caught between wanting and running, spinning further away from myself with this new loss. I pretended I was coping.

*

Billie and I decided to hitch to Puri to save her money. We approached the truck stop on the outskirts of Srinagar and asked around. The men stared at us in confusion. Western women didn't travel in trucks. We found one driver willing to take us.

Snow and ice lined the road and a heavy overnight frost had frozen the diesel in most of the trucks. Our driver beckoned us to help him. He showed me how to pump the button in the cab to get the diesel flowing as he crouched under the truck, holding an open container of burning coals to heat the pipes. I later heard stories of trucks blowing up – a reminder of how precarious life was there, and how I continually skirted this line of life and death.

We discovered a different India: truck-only stopping places full of cane-woven bed frames lined up in rows for the drivers to sleep, pots of dahl and rice continually heating, stacks of freshly cooked chapatis and bottles of Limca and Thums Up.

Once we went south, it warmed up. We sat in the small wooden enclosure above the cab to avoid the men, but one night I woke to find a man looming over me. Then Billie sat up and punched him. She'd caught him trying to fondle her breasts.

'We go,' she said. With that, we grabbed our stuff and jumped out, to find another truck. It set the pattern for our trip.

The men travelled in groups of two or three. We watched them begin to discuss us. It took them a day to work up the courage to grab us. We lived in a state of tension, taking turns to sleep. To make things easier, Billie played the man, telling the new driver we were married. To keep the charade working, Billie went with the men into the chai shop, sharing her packet of bidis. I was left, the lone woman, sitting in the box on top of the cab.

At one stop, several men clustered around Billie, gesturing and pointing at me, then at their chests. Billie was shaking her head, trying to calm them down. I found out later they wanted to have me for the night – fair payment for giving us a lift.

We crossed the continent and made it to Calcutta, exhausted but unharmed. We found a clean room and holed up, feeling safe for the first time in more than a week.

Jannette arrived and we made our way to Puri – a coastal city 400 kilometres south of Calcutta situated on the Bay of Bengal – a pilgrimage site for Hindus. It was soothing to see the sparkling blues of the ocean and hear the waves thundering onto the golden sand. The beach stretched as far as I could see in both directions. About a dozen wooden fishing boats were pulled up to the edge of the dunes just outside of the city. Nets were stretched out and being repaired. I could smell fish and dung – a mixture of human and animal – then the wind would blow and I tasted salt air.

Adjacent to the beach was a large, open square, lined by temples and shops. The broad stone steps of the buildings provided convenient places to sit. Carts selling produce were scattered haphazardly around. Hindi and Western rock music took turns blaring through loudspeakers. It didn't stop until late at night and then started again first thing in the morning. Sleek, well-nourished cows with distinctive humps and swishing tails wandered through, unbothered by the noise.

*

Our visit together started well. Jannette had loved Nepal and its mountains, especially its Western food; peanut butter and chocolate cake were her favourites.

The day before my birthday I stepped aside on a narrow street to allow a funeral procession to proceed. A body was wrapped in white cloth and lay on a wooden frame held on the shoulders of several men. Orange and yellow chrysanthemums, with a splattering of red rose petals, were thrown on top. Some fell to the ground as the body was bumped – a silent trail to mark the funeral's passing.

They reminded me of a blood trail and prompted thoughts of my brother. Visions flooded me: of his flattened yellow Corolla van, his blood dripping through the tortured metal, the red ants and agitated crows.

The mourners pulled me to them and I found myself surrounded by chanting. Hand drums kept the rhythm as the beat was softened by bells. Tomorrow we would be twenty-one – a coming of age. My mother should give us each a wooden key – the traditional image in my family to mark this point of growing up, with a single cake baked by my grandmother and my grandfather opening a beer.

I should be in Australia, enjoying being a nurse, not in India mourning my brother. How can he be dead? It was nearly three years but it still felt raw, like an exposed wound that refused to heal. Memories surfaced as the huddle of mourners dragged me along.

Graeme's face, his hands, his voice. I no longer looked for him on the street, especially here in India. I clutched him close and sang my silent chant as I stood and watched the funeral pyre being lit. I stood for hours as it burned, turning away as it was dying down. I longed to feel my twin against me and went to sleep not speaking to Billie or Jannette. I lost myself in dreams of Graeme.

When I returned to the still-smouldering mound of ash and half-burned wood the next day, a single hand had fallen from the pyre. It lay stark and alone on the soot-coloured sand. The person's hand was unburned, the flesh untouched … all that was left of a life, apart from some charred bones that protruded from the ash.

I imagined the hand was still reaching for life – that it was Graeme's hand reaching for mine, for our birthday. We turned twenty-one that day. I reached out to hold his hand one more time … I couldn't find him. My tightly held control, loosened over the previous months, now broke and I splintered apart. I didn't exist in skin and bone. I wasn't encased in flesh. I lost my lines. I was shards of pain, of hurt, flung out like chips of stone.

My mind started running an internal commentary, almost like I was another person watching me. I later tracked the words in my diary:

I splinter and splinter further out.

I view the horizon and see a single line: of how the sky meets the sea, how one passes into the other and gives birth to the clouds that rise and give shadows to the sand. Lines, more lines, that I refuse to honour. I'm a tiny shard. I deny the lines their life.

The lines are limits and boundaries but mine are gone. I'm crazy. I know it now. This line I've crossed. But why be scared? I've been chaotic all my life. I've tried so hard to play the game but the game is now laid bare for me to see. I've crossed the line: I've set the crazy chaos free.

I wanted to hit out. I didn't know at what. I returned to our room where Billie, a psychiatric nurse, recognised my distressed state and met me head-on, pulling me onto our bed. She encouraged me.

'Fight with me! Come on gentle lady, let yourself go.' Billie grabbed my hands and pushed against me. We struggled. I silently screamed the words but I couldn't say them. In my frustration, I became distraught with not finding what I needed.

I attempted to find myself in my diary:

I no longer exist. I touch nothing, yet I'm raw. My skin jumps and twitches and my legs don't belong. I'm light, yet I'm heavy. I sink into the ground. I walk faster and faster – I run. I'm so tired, everything's hazy. I don't know what's real. I want to stop this stupid crying, stop feeling so damn open, stop screwing my mind. Why is it so important? What do I want?

I wanted an absolute joining with another; what I'd experienced in the womb was the perfect beauty of being with my brother. I needed to be merged whole, and not this empty, seeking half that constantly cried out to be soothed.

I was trying to find myself in Billie – the system I'd used with Graeme. Attachment is at the heart of a healthy sense of self but my attachment was based on being a pair, challenging the idea of being an individual. Graeme's dying confronted this paradox, sending me into this spiral of despair. To claim my individuality required denying him, which I refused. Instead, I sought to recreate it in another. Sex, the usual method to connect as an adult, wasn't enough of a joining. It needed to be total.

Flooded and overcome, I lashed out, pushing both Billie and Jannette physically. I didn't understand that I needed to look in – to a quiet mending of the shattered pieces. Instead, I looked to these two people who both loved me in their way. Somehow, sex and love and wanting all meshed together. I yearned to be in their skin. I didn't want mine; I wanted theirs – to be pressed up tight in them. I was overcome by pain and hurt and heartache. I pushed Jannette as much as Billie.

'I hate this tri-triangle. I want you b-b-both. Jannette d-do you l-l-love me? I need you to love me too.' The words burst out. Jannette stared, saying nothing.

'I pr-pre-tend all the time. I try to d-do it right, but I love you.' I'd finally said it. She had no answer, but I didn't see fear in her eyes and she didn't move away. I rested my head against hers and stroked her face. She let me. I knew she loved me but why wouldn't she say?

'I nn-needed to say it to you and f-for you to know.' I was calm by then ... shivery and light.

'Do you love me?'

'It's your mind I want, not your body.' Jannette grimaced, then whispered, 'I'm sorry.'

'I've always known that. It's OK.' Billie got up and left the room.

I feel nothing ... I'm a jerky old film that splatters and jumps. I'm in the back row watching myself.

I didn't want Jannette. Not really. Somehow, she'd become Graeme – a past life. But Billie was the now. What had I done to us? Billie pushed me to be honest, so why did she run away? *Damn you.*

Billie came back and held me like a baby. She rocked me.

'You g-give me so much. Billie, you're my warm, safe place. I know I've used you b-b-between Jan-Jannette and me. I'm sorry.'

She nodded a quiet acceptance. But now that I was unleashed, I couldn't stop. Another layer reared up.

I'm rotten to the bone. Smell that smell? That's me. I don't need people. I just feed off them until they turn against each other and then I kill them both and they don't even know.

My pushing went on for days and destroyed our birthdays. Jannette was done. She was worn thin. She cornered me and said, 'I'm disgusted with you. I don't get it. I don't know what you want. I can't take it anymore.'

I stared up at her from the floor as she stood over me. 'I'll meet you in Greece in a few months. Hopefully, you'll be over whatever it is that is going on.'

Jannette packed, left and didn't look back. I stood at the door and watched her grow smaller. At the last moment, she turned and shouted, 'I still want to be friends, OK? But you … crazy like this … it scares me.'

Fuck, where do I go from here?

I'd talked and talked and left nothing out. I'd thrown myself open – I'd turned myself inside out.

Billie stayed but I became more distraught after Jannette's abandonment. It released another layer of pain. I was lost and trapped within my disordered mind and I couldn't find my way. Billie was exhausted too, as

I wasn't sleeping or eating so neither was she. She didn't know how to treat me; she tried what she knew, but nothing worked.

Billie calls me her gentle storm, but there's nothing gentle about me. I'm a destroyer. I hate me I hate me I hate me.

Too lost to care about Billie but still pushing and wanting her to save me, I swam far out into the sea. I waited for it to settle my fragmented soul, as I treaded water behind the wave line, but it didn't help. Nothing helped. At first, Billie was worried and swam after me.

Save me, Billie, please save me. I need saving – you're the one, please, Billie.

But she swam back in. She left me alone in the ocean swell.

I swam further out, this time for real, to finish what I'd started in Coogee. This time I would drown, or something would eat me – a shark swimming up from the depths – and it would be over. I would find my way to Graeme.

I swam into the midnight water until I couldn't lift my arms for another stroke. The stars watched as I breathed fully out. My final breath. My body sank, but the sea fought me. She buoyed me up. I dived down deep, taking great gulps of water. The boy in the film *Ordinary People* drowned easily, but I couldn't force myself to stay under. My body struggled for air and pushed me to the surface. It ganged up against me and demanded I breathe.

I can't live, I can't die … a crazy no man's land; I hang suspended in the middle.

I gave in as a new day nudged the night sky, and started the long swim back. When I got closer to shore, Billie emerged as a contour from the lines of sand. She was walking up and down the rose-tinted beach, shouting my name.

Sorry, sorry, sorry. I'm a shameful creature – only the waves understand.

I wanted to stay in the water – my replacement womb. I didn't know how to face Billie. I couldn't make relationships work.

In even more pieces, I knew I needed Billie's help, but I now knew she couldn't save me. I was unsavable and utterly separate from any hope. When I stood up from the waves, she took one long look and stalked away, furious. I trailed her back to our room, but she refused to talk to me.

Billie told me the next day, 'I've had enough. I can't do this anymore. I'm leaving. We need some time apart.' She looked hard at me. 'You're doing me in. I'm losing myself. For my sanity, I need to separate from you. Please understand.'

Billie, you've lost yourself in my darkness and now you need to run. I get it, but please don't go.

Billie left on the bus with her pack and her battered guitar, taking her music with her. Her love, her arms and her smiles. They all left.

The dogs cry tears of blood. I love you, Billie, I hate you, but where's the line? I draw it in the sand. It reaches up and grabs me, but the sea attempts to claim me, it tugs and pulls and says, 'Come, you're mine.'

I've killed me and Jan, and me and Billie. There's nothing left. I let the sea claim me.

What did I do wrong? I did as you asked. I opened up and followed my feelings and they led me here. I fucked up but I don't know how. I trusted you to hold me but I've destroyed you instead.

I've gone too far – you told me that I had no right to act like this. But don't you see? I was following a lead into myself and this is where it led me, to this. You invited me and now you tell me off.

I joined with the sea and sand and sky and stars. One star came down to twinkle between my feet. I moved slowly over the grains of sand to float in the waves, but the star was too gentle for my evilness. I needed harsh scratching. I buried myself in the sand but the sand tried to choke me. The sky reached down to free me. She was wet and cold. I hung between three worlds, suspended in the dark. It was so cold, it was beautiful. The shadows passed me, silent and staring. I laughed and waved. But it got so cold I ran and ran and ran. I lived every race I've ever run. My power denied my pain. I would never stop. It was a race between my body and mind, always so at odds with each other and now, finally, we were having it out.

My heart reached out and demanded, 'Stop! I've had enough.' I felt me for the first time.

Stuff you, Jannette, stuff you, Billie. There's only ever me. I'm in love with the evil beautiful monster that is me, that eats people and spits them out.

The show is over. Everyone goes home but this actress still has lines she needs to say. I'm not finished. You say I push boundaries but I haven't even got there yet. This has been the rehearsal. There is going to be an explosion. I feel it rising.

Through all this crazy, a small part of me watched and knew.

I know something is in me, something big. Something scary. I'll leave it for now. I've nearly looked it in its face, but I need to find a better way.

I play at playing me and show you this me, yet you've not seen the real me behind the playing me. The real me is lost. I call out to her and look for her. But she is hiding. Which me is me? You will never know. This is one game I'm good at.

That me exists in pain. If you fail to hurt me, I'll make you. It's easier this way.

I sliced Billie's name deep into my thigh. I used the big blade of the Swiss army knife (I'd managed not to lose) to curve the individual letters. I cut over the same lines until they fully opened and bled freely. Only pain made sense. The stark red letters shone against the white of my skin. My tears smudged their line.

My fire has burnt you. I played too far and I've lost … you've flown away. My fire dies without your air. Alone I'm nothing … only ash, I blow away as the wind picks up.

I hear footsteps and imagine it is you. I search every shadow. I stare at every footprint but it's getting dark … I'm tired. I try to sleep but I start at every voice and every figure. I cannot rest. Have I lost you forever?

Billie had loaned me some money before leaving, but I didn't have enough to stay in our room. The man at the local chai shop was kind. I asked if I could sit there and he nodded yes. I sat and watched him make chapatis, rolling them out, slapping them down. He handed them to his blind father, who squatted at the edge of the hot plate above the oven.

The son allowed me to sit there all day as my already splintered mind kept splitting further. At night, when it was time for him and his father to sleep, he nodded for me to stretch out on the dirt floor. He fed me cups of chai the next morning, and plates of dahl and rice through that day and the next. I sat or laid there, never saying a word. I lost track of the week.

My mind was a broken thing, still spilling in all directions – tiny pieces that I sat and watched, while wondering how far they would travel. They crossed galaxies. The sharp points and sweeps of light swept through the unlit spaces surrounding the stars. The dense, infinite expanse sucked in the points, until they too disappeared. I was a useless waste – better that I vanished into that endless space.

I was allowed to sit without any demands. The chai man kept me alive and gave me refuge, but I wanted my mind wiped clean. When Graeme was killed, I wanted another self. But none came. Even the people who said they loved me walked away. Michael, Jannette and now Billie. How many more people would I destroy?

I didn't dream of a knight charging in on a white stallion – that was a fantasy from a book – but I wanted to be saved. When I saw how starkly I hung on to this wanting, I realised it was never going to happen. No one else could do it for me. I only had myself and my mind. I was responsible. The choice was mine. These thoughts chased each other in quick succession.

They made me pause and sit up straight. I saw the line – a different kind of line – a line of choice. I wavered on one side of it, knowing that if I dared to cross this line, there was no going back. I would have to find all the different pieces of my mind and put them back together. Did I want to do it? Could I do it?

I was nearly defeated, but I knew I needed to retrieve them all – find each delicate shard and cautiously find a way to slot them into the puzzle that was now my mind.

Once I saw there was a choice, I couldn't turn away. I dreaded it but knew I had to do it. It started with my next inhale. Only I could save myself. Resigned, I faced up to the meticulous work. In the chai shop in Puri, I took the first step towards finding all the splintered pieces and calling them back.

I left the shop for the first time in more than a week, eternally grateful to the son and his father. I wandered out into the square, weak from mostly sitting. I went out at dawn, as the sun was peeking at me over the sea. I sat on the stone steps of the temple and watched the light change, brightening the sky. In the square, the music was starting. The Beatles were singing their famous song, 'Here Comes the Sun'.

The sun's rising woke something in me as the words from The Beatles song sang to my broken, fragmented heart.

It was a sign saying it's time, time to start again, time to be all right.

I want to tell myself it's over, but is it?

'It hasn't even begun,' that small knowing part of me whispers in my ear. 'You haven't got close yet. Trust the crazy. There's more.'

I want to run from this voice but there are no signs to mark my way.

I saw a line and took it apart, but I was too scared to look beyond the bad and ugly. It crept out and filled every space. I tried to deny it life, but it killed those around me.

The crazy butts in and shouts at me, 'See what is going on here! See the real story.'

I let it speak. 'You need to close a little. Find your lines and be a container once more. You need to shut yourself down. It's not yet time.'

I listen. Everything fades away. I find a little peace.

Chapter 15

Do I matter?

I kept tight control of my mind, but still, I struggled. It was a daily fight to stay contained as I called the splintered pieces of myself home. I was an insignificant person on this land, not bound to any place. There were many lives. Why did I value mine? What was another life in this sea of lives? Did it matter if I let go of this fight?

I felt distant from my family and Australia. I looked up at the stars at night and imagined I was a single star in a mass of stars. What did it matter if I winked out? Permanently. Twinkled for a brilliant moment and then died. Our little human lives are fleeting when compared to the stars. What's one more life gone from this planet?

I drifted, often going days without speaking. The locals somehow knew to leave me alone. I sat on the beach, swam sometimes, walked and rested in the temples. I kept working as a container and shutting myself down. At one temple, I read a sign advertising a silent retreat in Bodhgaya, led by an Englishman, and decided to go. My Christmas present to myself. I needed to do something different to break this endless curving spiral.

After taking the overnight bus to Bodhgaya, 770 kilometres north of Puri, I stepped out into the sacred city. I was accosted by boys and men wanting me to go with them in their rickshaws and stay in their hotels. I waved them away, smiling, and wandered through the holy Buddhist site. It was comforting to see pilgrims of many nationalities, intent and introspective, among the normal Indian life. Sadhus and Bhutanese people in colourful clothes circumambulated the great stupas and temples alongside Buddhist monks and nuns in various maroon or saffron robes, depending on their order.

I came to the Bodhi tree. Its branches spread wide – leafy and sheltering. It invited me in from the hot sun, offering rest and something more. An embrace. It was the tree under which the wandering Prince Siddhartha sat and meditated for three days, determined to achieve enlightenment, 2,500 years ago. It was here that he fought all the demons, the maras, confronting them and not allowing them to pierce or confuse his mind, reaching the ultimate state – full enlightenment. Maybe I could take a small step.

My mind needed all the help it could get. I felt fragile and fragmented. The risk of shattering sat close, often on the edge of my consciousness. I guarded my mind, holding it as softly as I could; I smiled, nodded, and pretended I was OK. My health was poor. With only enough money to buy a single meal of dahl and rice each day, my clothes were hanging off me.

I signed on at the retreat centre, relieved to be given one of the sponsored places. The retreat was going to be small, maybe sixty people, mostly westerners. They joked about how we'd receive extra good karma by doing this retreat in Bodhgaya. I was sharing a room with several other women; it would be my home for the next two weeks. The room had a bed, a shower and even hot water. Vegetarian food was provided three times a day. What a blessing.

Christopher Titmuss, one of Britain's senior Dharma teachers, led the retreat. He was offering insight meditation, like Satya Narayan Goenka, only here he was planning to use sitting, standing and walking meditation techniques to push us towards wisdom. Christopher had been a Theravadan Buddhist monk in Thailand for several years, later disrobing. It was a much gentler teaching, and with his understanding of the Western mind, its distractions and the fragility of westerners in terms of self-esteem, he spoke directly to my heart. His light touch was the balm I needed.

At the previous retreat, relieved to get through each hour of sitting, I broke into movement as soon as the hour finished. Any stillness was left behind on the cushion. Here, we were taught how to carry the meditative state into our standing, then step-by-step into walking until we sat to eat, and then to eat mindfully. Cleaning up, showering and lying down to sleep became an extension of holding our minds in meditation.

It was breathtaking in its simplicity. More difficult to keep it going, but at least I understood and had a direction to follow. And it worked. I could feel it nourishing and feeding my body and mind. My thoughts settled, coming together. The frame of quiet contemplation and silence, with healthy food, was exactly what I needed to keep collecting the shattered pieces of my mind.

My physical body was deteriorating, even with the nutritious food. The bites I'd originally scratched in Thailand, which turned into sores, continued to plague me. They'd never healed. The dozen sores continually formed a layer of pus under the scabs. The one on the flesh over the bone that I needed to sit on to meditate burst when I sat. The pus then dried and glued the cloth to my skin. When I stood up, the cloth was pulled off, the sore bled and so the cycle repeated.

After the retreat, I found a cheap room in a local village. My home was now a small, square, clay-lined room with a dirt floor and no electricity. I washed in another room, luckily with a door, which held a rectangular tub of water filled by a bucket from a central well. Another wooden bucket and scoop were used to pour water over my head. It was simple but efficient. My bed was a wooden frame with cloth straps woven across it, slightly off the floor.

Even though I was elevated, I fought a nightly battle with the rats. By lighting a ring of candles around my bed, I created a circle of light that kept them at its edge. I dreaded the time when the candles went out as the rats then roamed freely. Often, I woke when one ran across my limbs, sometimes my face. I hated that.

A large boil was growing on my left thigh. It was hot and throbbing and continued to grow until it was about 10 centimetres in diameter and raised high. My whole thigh became swollen, red and sore. I developed a fever and struggled into town to find a homeopath-type doctor. He gave me some powders to take and I stocked up with clean gauze and bandages. I was planning to lance and drain the boil, to relieve the tension. It was straining against my skin, whatever was underneath. I didn't want to wait until it erupted. That scared me.

I sterilised my knife, passing the blade through a candle flame a few times, with a bowl ready to catch whatever the fluid was, and sliced into the boil from one side to the other. It split like a yellow tomato and mustard-coloured pus poured out, filling the bowl to its brim. One part of me was interested. I was impressed, never having seen so much pus pour from a wound.

I cleaned and packed the gaping hole that now appeared. I could see the edges of my muscles in the deep crater. I was feverish and dissociated, and looked at myself quite dispassionately. The skin at the top needed time to join after first healing from the bottom up.

I cleaned and repacked the wound daily, and covered it with a sterile dressing. My fever broke, leaving me weak. I found red lines trailing up my legs to my groin, to the lymph nodes, now solid lumps. My white cells were fighting. I wished them well and watched the lines daily, to see if they changed.

Another three boils erupted, one on each of my other limbs – skyscrapers of throbbing heat and straining skin, like the first, with fever each time. I lanced them as they reached that bursting stage and each formed a crater. None were as deep or wide as the original one but each needed packing. It took me over an hour to unwrap, wash and repack them.

*

I'd let Billie know I was at Bodhgaya and received an aerogram from her inviting me to Kathmandu, in Nepal. She wanted to repair our relationship.

Jannette sent me several letters, the first angry. The next saying she'd found perspective on why my storm of emotion had happened. She said my pushing was a big deal for her, too. She'd received a hard-to-read letter from another woman she knew, detailing a disturbing experience with her Turkish lover. That also made Jannette think. She didn't know about my childhood suffering as it was still buried in my unconscious, but my grief around Graeme made sense to her. She finished by wishing me a happy 1983.

In her third letter, she wrote of her love affair with an American, Bob. They went to Pakistan and the Afghanistan border to find a friend of his. She told of the heavily armed police and army presence, the Afghan refugees and freedom fighters. They'd tried to enter Afghanistan with the mujahideen fighters, to set up a radio station and for her to work as a nurse. But their contact was arrested and deported, leaving Jannette and Bob under suspicion from the military. After a night spent sitting in a room with a dozen Muslim freedom fighters, smoking and getting stoned, Jannette the only female for miles, they'd made a hasty run from the border.

She finished by saying I'd laugh, that she, so fucking tough, had finally bitten the dust. She'd felt passion and pain and confusion, like me, and understood me better because of it. Jannette told me that she felt closer to me than any other person. I was too special to lose. She ended by saying she loved me.

A love letter and forgiveness from Jannette. Now I needed to mend the damage I'd done to Billie. But first I needed to go back to Srinagar and get my passport, airline ticket and traveller's cheques, which were waiting at the police station. They'd been found, minus the cash, by a kind stranger, who'd handed them in. Another traveller heard the police message over the radio in a café one day, asking for my whereabouts. She'd approached me in Calcutta, on the other side of the continent, guessing somehow that it might be me.

I arrived in Kathmandu, fever-free, but with both legs bandaged to protect the sores, and took my first breath of fresh mountain air. I found Billie waiting at a café. It was heart-stopping to see her face. I sat down across from her and searched her eyes for any hesitancy; I found love and acceptance.

'Hey, relax gentle lady.'

'C-C-Can you still call me that af-after all that's h-happened?'

'Yeah, I can.' Billie laughed. 'I've thought a lot about what happened in Puri and I'm beginning to understand. It's OK. I forgive you.' She leaned across the table and gently kissed me, then reached for my hand.

'I still love you. And I want more time together. What do you think?'

'You sure? I d-d-didn't know h-h-how you wwould be … I'm so sorry …'

'You've already said sorry. And I had my part too. I'm sorry I pushed you to open up … so that's what's underneath everything, hey? Maybe I should call you scary lady.' She laughed. 'That's why you kept shutting down?'

I nodded, too fragile to risk any words.

'It makes sense. I should have trusted you … to find your own way.'

After a long pause, Billie said, 'Enough! Let's go exploring.'

Billie's presence lessened my fears. I fell in love with the city, its temples and cafés. I found real cheese, fresh white and heavy dense brown loaves that tasted like bread, and Cadbury's chocolate imported from Australia. I spotted food I'd forgotten even existed, like apple pie and fresh cream buns.

I heard of a Tibetan woman practising traditional Tibetan medicine. When I walked to her clinic on the outskirts of the city, I found a long, snaky queue of people waiting patiently to see her. I stood in line, the only westerner, and towered above the shorter, smiling Nepalese.

The doctor nodded at me when I walked into the small hut and gestured for me to sit down. I wanted to tell her about the sores but she shushed me – no English. Instead, she took my wrist and started feeling my pulse. She wasn't counting it like a nurse and I didn't understand what she was doing. I was handed a small jar of cream to rub on my sores, not the craters, and a paper bag full of round, pitch-like balls, to be taken twice a day.

The sores healed a little, the pus going, but the craters would take months to grow new flesh. I needed to be patient. We travelled to Pokhara – seven hours perched on top of the bus. We found a room in a lodge at the end of a dirt track leading away from a collection of chai shops. Snow-capped mountains hugged the edges of the calm blue lake. The lake shimmered in the soft light from the setting sun. It added a tranquil presence to the jagged grey rock.

It was our last few weeks together since we'd met in Udaipur more than five months before. I was going south, to Bombay and Goa, then flying out to meet Jannette in Greece. Billie planned to trek in the mountains. We said a sorrowful goodbye. I was too uncertain to ask if she still wanted to see me in Holland. Besides, she was returning to Rosa.

I'd been tentative this time with Billie, keeping a part of me contained. I'd longed for her but couldn't trust myself not to hurt her. I was still putting myself together, conscious of my fragile mind. It was painful to separate, but I'd already done it once. I'd hoped she'd be my ultimate love, but I wasn't good enough. I struggled with the aftermath of Puri. It was probably better this way. Better she let me go.

I felt at home in India and was anxious about leaving. I would never cope with the plastic and shiny surfaces of the West, the food in neat rows. Here I squatted for nearly an hour, bargaining with the banana sellers, to talk them down to the local price. I'd been in the East for a year. I thought I'd stay and become one of those hippy westerners, never daring to deal with the West again.

But then, in the special train compartment for women travelling alone, I wanted out and away from the constant harassment of Indian men. I'd taken care to lock the compartment door early because the big Sikh guard who checked the tickets looked at me too long – the sole woman in the compartment. During the night, I woke suddenly after hearing a noise and managed to jump down and barricade the door just in time, pushing him out. Being the guard, he had the key to get in, but I'd found my voice. I screamed and he left.

*

I had a culture shock in Goa when I saw the westerners I thought I'd wanted to join, emaciated, in Indian clothing like me, who'd been living there for years in a constant drug-induced high. Big balls of hashish and opium were easy to buy and it was cheap to live in the caves surrounding the bays of Goa. One man invited me back to his space. I was curious, so we climbed up using the creepers of a large fig tree. The trees edged the surrounding cliff face and provided easy access to the caves. When he tried it on, he was too stoned to be a threat. I shimmied down the vines, content and relaxed in my strength.

A German woman approached me, a knowing look in her eye. 'You're new here,' she stated. I was feeling lonely, missing Billie, so I chatted.

'Yes, just came from N-Nepal. And y-you?' It was always easier if I encouraged the other person to talk.

'I've been here for about three months. Do you want to walk on the beach?'

I enjoyed having another woman's presence – it stopped the men from approaching me.

'Let's sleep on the beach tonight.' She looked at me.

I couldn't decipher her look so I said clearly, 'To sleep. I have a g-girlfriend, so no sex. I'm not in-interested.' I stared at her, making sure she understood.

She nodded, 'Sure.'

I believed her. It was a beautiful night. The water sparkled under the crescent moon.

I was jarred awake to find her on me. She was pushing inside me with one hand, her long nails sharp and piercing. She used her weight to expertly pin me to the sand. Her other forearm was crushing my throat. I couldn't breathe. In my waking terror and the dark of night, I panicked and went instantly to my survival place. I froze and then flopped, shutting myself down.

I abandoned my body, giving it over to her. It was hers to use. Her nails, cutting into my intimate places, woke my previous trauma, even though I didn't remember the content. I was a child again. Alone. Powerless, under the stars. I watched my body and the woman do what she wanted, and how she then got up and left.

I stared at my body, hollow and removed. I noticed the haphazard spread of my limbs, somehow knowing I was not her first. She was too practised. Too strong and sure in her holds.

I woke hours later, to find water lapping my feet and legs. The tide was coming in. I hadn't thought to sleep above the high tide mark. Maybe it wouldn't have happened if I had. My shocked mind was grasping at anything to understand it.

I was a useless shell of nothing. I hated myself for not pushing her off. Why could I never fight? I hadn't believed a woman would do that. I thought it was only men who did, and that I was safe saying no to a woman.

What is it about me that attracts these people? How do they know? Do I have a sign above my head? 'Hey, you! I'm here. Come and rape me.'

Jannette would never have laid there. She would have fought, her nails slicing the woman's cheek, her hands throwing the woman off, her fist punching her face.

I lay on the sand in the early morning light, trying not to feel the growing soreness between my legs and in my throat, or the jagged cuts stinging my breasts. I focused instead on the cool stroking of the incoming tide. My newly grown belief in myself was now trodden into the sand.

I couldn't recover.

I found a single room with a thin reed mat on the floor. I lay on it for hours, feeling the harshness of the concrete underneath, staring at the naked lightbulb hanging above. The pain was what mattered. Only the pain felt real. I retreated deep inside, almost giving up. What did it matter? Let me be another statistic, another body found.

I didn't understand why I couldn't keep myself safe, spend money, or indulge and buy nice things. Stay in a cosy room. Or even a room with a bed. I lay on the thin mat and compared myself to my friends. I was flawed. I'd run out of answers as to how to fix myself.

Maybe I needed to get out of India, or I was going to end up dying here. I had to get on that plane and get to Greece. Start again. I couldn't trust women either. Being raped by a woman and being raped by a man. How was that possible?

I could trust no one. Neither parent protected me – I had a shadowy awareness of that, even as I didn't remember the details. I knew my mother was as bad as my father, just different in what she did. The strange symmetry of the present trauma to my earlier life pushed me further into an exhausted bleakness.

Both sexes were abusive. Both of them blamed me. It was always my fault. This was the pattern I'd learned young. I'd swallowed it down, swallowed and swallowed until I'd made it mine. I believed it was me – I was to blame. The classic victim.

In that harsh room in Goa, I drifted in the middle, disowning both genders, wanting nothing to do with either of them: male or female. Overcome with shame, my now constant and consistent companion, I put a wall around my heart and got a bus to Bombay and the flight to Athens. I left India.

Although I was blessed with an optimistic nature, at least on the surface, deep down it was another story. There, it was a pessimistic, hollowed-out centre of absolute despair. I wasn't worth saving – I knew that– but boy could I learn. I could pick myself up and start again. Start. Nothing more.

I trotted out my now familiar mantra, repeating it again and again to myself in the hope it would provide some relief, some insight: what's the learning in this?

I first realised that this is what I did at the last meditation retreat in Bodhgaya. The teacher encouraged us to notice our thoughts and to be aware of what was driving our actions. This mindfulness technique slotted neatly into my system of always trying to work out what I'd done wrong. I'd grown it, flipping my thoughts away from being wrong – although that feeling of self-blame stayed deep within me – and to this more conscious idea of learning: looking to the future and how I could do it differently.

I racked my brains, as my brother, Trevor, would have said – his favourite saying.

I racked my brains and came up empty. I went back to repeating my mantra, again and again. What's the learning in this?

Years later, when my children hit their teenage years, they used to get angry with me. When they were having a hard time with something in their young lives, I would trot out this now familiar question, asking them to learn how they could do it differently; how to not repeat the same mistake, or feel the same pain.

'Mum, do you have to?' they would reply. 'Why do you always have to say that? I want to be angry!'

I'd never had the luxury of being angry. To be angry means you have some agency. I was too busy surviving, and my survival was rooted in passiveness and being frozen still. The learning came after, with that distant, always-watching part of me trying to work out what I'd done wrong. There was always a lesson to be learned from the latest trauma.

My children could be angry. I looked at them in wonder.

Chapter 16

Starting again

Athens was the perfect bridge between India and Europe. Not too clean in parts, a little haphazard, with ancient architecture among modern life and glorious food. Feta and spinach pastries, tzatziki and fresh pita bread, Greek salads, with baklava to finish. I couldn't get enough and stuffed myself silly. I'd written to my mother asking her to send some of my money to the American Express office in Athens, but it was delayed. With only a few cheques left from my original bundle, I needed to be careful.

Many of the men hanging around central Athens were big – much bigger than the slight Indian men I'd grown used to. They scared me, trying to sell me handbags, wallets and belts I didn't need. I was an obvious target in my cheap Indian clothes. I'd made it through customs without being stopped but on the streets, I was hassled. Jannette later told me the immigration officials assumed she was a drug smuggler. They pulled her aside and took apart her luggage, breaking her bars of chocolate and pulling open her tampons.

A Greek family had lived next to us on Rowland Street and our families had supported each other through floods and cyclones. When the father, Christos, had learned I was going travelling, he'd encouraged me to contact his sister who still lived in Athens. I'd written to her, and at the main post office in Athens, I found a letter in reply. She'd invited me to stay and gave instructions on how to get the bus to their apartment in an outer suburb of Athens. I anxiously arrived at their door, unsure of my reception.

Momma, as she asked me to call her, was reassuring, enveloping me in a big hug. She lived with her four daughters and her husband, who was away, in the small two-bedroom apartment. I was to sleep in the lounge room. I met thirteen-year-old Eleftheria. She and I instantly hit it off and she took me under her wing. Momma, with only a smattering of English, needed Eleftheria to translate. Eleftheria told me her mother thought I was too skinny and needed fattening up. She then produced the most amazing homemade dinners and puddings, all designed to do exactly that.

What would I be like if I had a mother like Momma? One who cared? Who wanted to nourish me instead of hurting me? It was bittersweet to be made a part of this loving family. I couldn't help but compare them to my own. I stayed for several days, luxuriating in the comforts, before getting the boat to Crete to meet Jannette.

The ferry pulled into Heraklion. I rushed, relieved, into Jannette's welcoming arms. I'd been unsure of her greeting. We talked as we sat drinking local coffee in an outdoor café, tucked neatly out of the wind. We decided to hire a bicycle for me. She still had her silver bike.

We left most of our luggage at the cycle hire shop and rode the coast road, pedalling the hills and mountains of Crete. It was delightful to have Jannette at my side and to be on wheels. I'd forgotten how freeing it was. The steep climbs and mountain passes tested my muscles as I was unused to cycling, but we freewheeled the long downhills on the other side.

Jannette told me the story of almost being gang raped by a group of African men. They'd snuck up to surround her tent as she camped alone just outside of Athens, but she'd fought and screamed until others came. The men fled. I couldn't speak of my rape. Once again, I was too ashamed of my inability to fight.

We slept in caves dotting the coast, or in olive groves, stealing oranges from the many trees laden with fruit. We lived on pots of jam and sticks of bread, avoiding the restaurants that overcharged tourists. It was cold, with snow on the high passes. We slept huddled together. The waters surrounding the island were brilliantly clear. I managed quick dips, and even quicker washes in the icy mountain streams. Jannette left me in Chania after a week of renewing our friendship.

Within hours, I felt the familiar chills of another bout of malaria. I knew I was in for a week of high fevers and nightmares. I needed help and care. I asked a woman to help me find a hospital. This kind French woman paid for a taxi to take us and waited with me as I progressed in the queue to be seen.

She left once the admitting staff led me into a room. The nurse pulled an old woman from a bed and pointed for me to get in. I felt sorry for the woman but I wasn't getting into the bed until the sheets were changed. A used bedpan, full of strong-smelling dark urine, was lying on the stained bedding. The nurse went to find clean linen.

The fever hit me and the nurses came every few hours with glass syringes full of unknown medication. I fought them, refusing to let them inject me when I didn't know the drug. They brought in male orderlies and held me down. I explained it was malaria but they didn't speak English.

A doctor came – a large Greek man.

'Stop fighting! You are a disgrace. Do what you are told.'

'It's m-malaria. I d-d-don't know what dr-drug you're g-g-giving me. You need to take b-blood first.' He detested me on sight. His gaze traced the length of my body, noticing the sores on my legs.

'Greece doesn't have malaria. You're a prostitute. I'm going to do an internal examination to get a vaginal swab. It's a sexually transmitted disease. We need to determine which one. Just look at you.'

I was silenced by his words, but then I started swearing and fighting back. He forced the internal on me, with the same orderlies holding me down. It was rough and invasive.

'You fucking bastard!' I kept shouting it. I'd never sworn at a doctor before. In my distress, I was fighting for my life.

I continued running daily high temperatures, waking from terrifying nightmares feeling alone and panicked. During the week I was there, I wasn't offered any nursing care, only the ongoing fight with the syringes. It was the relatives of patients who brought in food for their loved ones and who did the washing and feeding. I asked for water and begged the staff for something to eat. They brought in oranges, then after a few days, when they saw I wasn't being fed, thin soups and bread. I washed over the sink when I was lucid enough to stand up.

I went out to the nurse's station and asked if they could help me change the dressings on my sores. The nurse took me to their treatment room and showed me their single dressing tin. It was empty. She shrugged. There was nothing – no bandages, no gauze, no packs. It made me aware of the privilege of working at Westmead Hospital, as I pictured its well-stocked shelves.

The first boil that had erupted on my thigh was still a deep hole but was now coated with a layer of green slime on the inside of what should be reddish flesh. Worried, I decided to find the outpatient department and ask for help. I wandered through the small hospital, finding a clinic and the same doctor who'd done the internal.

Resigned, I explained that the wound didn't look healthy and needed to be cleaned. He told the nurse to hold me down as he used gauze-wrapped metal forceps to scrape the walls of the crater clean, back to raw bleeding pink. He didn't offer any anaesthesia to help with the pain. I swore and kicked but in my weakened state, I wasn't a match for her. The doctor did a good job. I left, disorientated and even more distressed.

The next afternoon, a slim, well-dressed man arrived and asked to speak to me. The same doctor was with him.

The man smiled and said, 'You have malaria – a Southeast-Asian strain. I've come from Athens to tell you personally. The blood tests were repeated and confirmed the result. And even better, this strain is treatable.' He handed me a bottle of chloroquine – an antiparasitic medicine. 'It works by killing the malaria-causing parasite. You're the first case of malaria in Greece in twenty years.' He smiled, excited.

'Thank you so much.' I looked at the doctor, but he didn't apologise. I didn't expect him to. I was grateful and could thank him too, plus the staff of the hospital.

The doctor then told me, 'Go!'

I packed my bag and left, getting the first ferry back to Athens. I collected my money from the American Express office, plus letters from Michael and Billie, and planned my trip to Holland.

I was going to see Billie. She'd invited me to stay.

*

After catching the overnight ferry from Patras to Brindisi, then the train to Milano, I luxuriated in the comfort and silence of the ultra-modern train to Switzerland. I'd treated myself.

Zurich confronted all my senses: the smell of chocolate hung in the air, the clean cobbled streets like little pads underfoot, and in the open squares of the old town, the elegant and opulent shops sparkled at me. Every quarter-hour, as the bells in the arching church spires released their different voices, I was brought to a standstill by the clamouring of different melodies rising above and around me. I felt young and enchanted as I walked the streets, amazed that a girl from the humid heat, dirt and sweat of North Queensland was strolling in Switzerland. It was almost like I'd stepped into a Disney film.

I couldn't resist trying the Kalberwurst and Cervelat and broke my no meat rule. It was grilled on open-air stands, the sausage ends cut and curling back. They beckoned me personally, demanding I eat them.

To save my funds, I decided to hitch from Zurich, taking a bus to the outer area and the beginning of the major highway going north through Germany to the Netherlands. I stood with my sign held out at the side of the highway, feeling exposed and a little silly. Within fifteen minutes a lovely old Mercedes pulled over, the driver leaning out to say he could take me as far as Dusseldorf.

Zurich to Dusseldorf was 600 kilometres, approximately six hours driving, the man said. I got in, enjoying the pale red leather seat that moulded itself to my body. Simple pleasures, a ride with a likeable, older man, content to chat. He talked about his family and his grownup daughters, and bought me lunch and coffee when we stopped. I compared him to my father. It woke my longing for a father's care – similar to my need for a mother.

The man dropped me on the other side of Dusseldorf. I stuck out my sign. A truck stopped. The driver said he was going to the Amsterdam Marine Terminal. He said he expected to get there later that night and that I could jump in. This man was middle-aged, asked me lots of questions about what I was doing and seemed OK, but I doubted it. Two drivers in two goes was always going to stretch my luck.

About three hours later, he pulled into the truck bay at the terminal, then turned to me and asked, 'Will you have sex with me? As payment like, you know, for my driving.'

I pressed myself hard against the truck door, ready to leap out. 'No. I aa-asked you for a lift, not sex, and you s-said yes.' I stared him down.

He grinned and said, 'OK, it was worth a try. I had to ask, just in case … you know … I won't touch you and I won't force you, don't worry. You can sleep in the back.'

He was true to his word and left me alone, but it took me hours to trust him enough to sleep. I said goodbye as dawn broke and made my way into central Amsterdam, crossing the slightly curved bridges over the canals and down dozens of lanes. The early morning noises – of passing trams and people with clear destinations – were growing louder as the city woke up. Lush, red oriental rugs sat under glass on top of the tables in several cafés. I smiled – it was magical – and breathed in the smell of freshly made coffee. It masked the stale faint whiff of last night's dope. I'd made it to Amsterdam.

*

When I did phone Billie, she invited me to Haarlem. It was 20 kilometres by road from the centre of Amsterdam – an easy bike ride. But I didn't have a bike. I bought a sturdy, second-hand, sit-up-and-beg-style cycle, with a Dutch lock built into the back frame and a heavy-duty chain.

Haarlem, on the river Spaarne, was situated on a thin strip of land above sea level. It was near long, windswept beaches and forests that lined the coast – the historic centre for tulip bulb growing. Billie met me in the cobble-stoned, open town square. The market was on. I shyly let her hold my hand as we wandered past the uniquely Dutch sights. There were stands full of hundreds of varieties of liquorice, salty or sweet; various chocolate spreads; young and old cheeses, offering thin slices to taste; and hot, thin-cut chips served with mayonnaise.

We walked and cycled through the town then stopped by a canal and let our legs dangle over the edge. Billie told me about her shared house, her relationship with Rosa and how Rosa felt threatened. It would be better if I stayed in Amsterdam. She wasn't saying no to me. I needed to be patient.

Billie then told me about the Tropical Disease Institute in Amsterdam, where returned travellers could request free testing. I left her with the promise that we'd see each other soon and saved my tears for riding home.

After running tests, the Institute gave me several medications and antibiotics to fight the constant infections that still stopped my wounds from healing. Within three days, I was feeling better. And better still when I looked in the flat bowl of a Dutch toilet to see a 30-centimetre-long pale worm. I wondered how long that had been inside of me.

Michael wrote, telling me he was coming to Amsterdam, and Billie told me of a squat I could move into on the eastern side of the inner city, above a row of shops. Squatting was common in Amsterdam. People claimed the spaces left vacant by breaking in and setting up homes. I loved my new quarters of two rooms with a small kitchenette and a mattress on the floor. I didn't love the fleas that left me covered in bites after my first night. The woman above my floor loaned me her vacuum cleaner and I began a twice-daily routine of sucking them up.

Billie introduced me to the women's scene in Amsterdam, taking me to the women-only cafés and bookstores. The shelves were full of lesbian love stories, many in English. We went dancing at the gay clubs, which were open from 11 pm until early morning. We'd come back to my squat via a bakery on the corner, buying loaves still warm from the ovens. The mouth-watering smell of fresh bread walked us home. I marched in the gay pride parade through Amsterdam, one among thousands of dykes, gay men and allies.

Although we were having a good time, it dawned on me that Billie wasn't happy. She was torn between Rosa and me and told me she wanted a break from both of us. It woke my abandonment issues. I was struggling to find work, and with nothing to hang on to, I fell into the bottomless well that was always waiting for me.

When I stared into my eyes in the mirror, I saw an empty nothingness. I couldn't settle to meditate. My mind tormented and criticised me, worse than any external bully. In my isolation, I lost the hard-fought-for-good feelings that I'd briefly found.

I started drinking cheap red wine, buying a new bottle in the morning and downing it quickly. I hid in the next bottle and the next, swallowing it down in big gulps. I didn't care. I put on weight and stopped exercising. The only walking I did was to the bottle shop. Lost, and slowly drowning in wine, I drew a series of self-portraits on the walls of my room, mapping my descent into oblivion. Into this walked Michael, still wearing a lungi, with his bicycle and hammered dulcimer, to busk in Amsterdam. He strolled in, took one look, turned around and left.

It was appropriate. I wasn't fit for company, but I'd misread his face. It wasn't disgust but shock, because he came back with a load of healthy food and hassled me until I started eating. He pushed until he found a spark of life and then he fought with me some more until I reacted. He was determined to wake me up. He fed the spark, and over days of not leaving me alone, I began to fight for myself.

I stopped drinking and started moving. In the flat, I sobbed as Michael held me and let me talk. Outside, I sat and watched as he played the tin whistle and dulcimer on the streets of the city.

'You're a beautiful, strong woman, simply lacking direction, that's all,' Michael kept repeating. 'I know all the signs from my years of travelling. Why did you think I wanted to stop when we got to Bangkok? It wasn't because of you. I'd just had enough.'

He looked at me, his eyes soft. 'It's uprooting to leave your own culture, cut all the ties and spend this long on the road. You need to work out what you want.' We discussed it over cups of tea. I needed to let go of Billie. It wasn't working, this great love I thought I'd found.

Plus, I needed to get to an English-speaking country. With my stammer, it was difficult for me to learn foreign languages. I often avoided speaking. I told Billie I was leaving, going to England. She looked relieved.

I'd managed to find a job in a bicycle shop, building myself a new touring bike as payment. Billie and I rode south to Calais in France, where I planned to catch the ferry to England. It was a mellow, quiet togetherness, cycling side by side, holding hands. It felt healthy. The gentle pace settled the pain of our coming separation. I was going to be OK leaving her.

I hugged Billie one last time and left for the ferry to Dover. I looked back to give a final wave, and wondered if I'd ever see her again.

Chapter 17

Living, not dying

My first night in England was a drizzle-free one. This land was the home of my father. I refused to acknowledge my heritage through him but it did allow me special privileges, like claiming a British passport.

I made my way towards London and A Woman's Place, which was situated on Victoria Embankment. This was a women-only space I'd heard about from other lesbians. Once I arrived, they showed me the list of women willing to give lodgings to those needing a bed for the night. I found a room in Brixton and rode there, through the scarred streets and past the shop fronts showing the evidence of the recent riots between the local gangs and police.

The woman was welcoming, Jewish, highly intelligent and living alone. After checking I had a genuine need, she offered me her spare room for free, saying I could stay for the week, and gave me a key. I was surprised and touched by her generosity.

I'd left a message at the main post office for Michael; this was still my only way of communicating with him. When he visited me at the flat, Michael, who loved all things Jewish, especially the women, immediately connected with my host. She laughed and invited him to stay as well, enjoying his tales of living at the kibbutz. They were both big personalities. I didn't try to compete but took myself off, exploring the local neighbourhood.

I discovered a fair being held in the deserted Battersea Power Station. It had a multitude of stalls, one of which had a large banner saying, 'Greenham Common Women's Peace Camp'. Different kinds of women of all ages were grouped around: young punks with faces full of studs and safety pins; older women wearing long skirts, crystal necklaces and turquoise rings; and women my age, with short, cropped hair dyed the colours of the rainbow. It felt like a message for my heart – that maybe I could fit in too, and learn how to find the peace I was longing for.

The Greenham Common camp was a women-only space, fighting for freedom against the tyranny of men. Men who wanted to blow each other up. Men with guns, with their threats of violence. I was sick of violence. I wanted to find another way, another choice. I decided I was going to Greenham.

But first I listened to a talk from a practitioner of traditional Chinese acupuncture. She explained about meridians and this system's view of healing, building on what I knew from Shiatsu. The woman showed us how to feel our pulses. It was what the Tibetan medical practitioner in Nepal had used to diagnose me. This woman said westerners could train at a college in Royal Leamington Spa, England.

I sat against a wall of the vast hall and let it sink in, planting the ideas and imagining a future. I wanted both: to go to Greenham, live in a community of like-minded women and learn this Eastern system of medicine.

Graeme's death had derailed me but it also highlighted that there was more for me to sort out. I was caught in a cycle of despair, falling into a bottomless nothingness, then, exhausted, having to haul myself out, almost against my will, to start again. This grim emptiness was familiar. I'd been sitting in it since I was a little girl. There was one part of me who never left.

It hit me that in some perverse way, I was still waiting to die. I wasn't able to manage it directly. Graeme had asked me to live, but I didn't know how. I'd been caught in a passive version of that first year of grief. I'd somehow scrambled to always stay alive, yet not live, finding other people to get lost in. Other countries to try.

I'd never learned how to live for myself because I'd existed through Graeme. Any entitlement I had to life was borrowed from him and lost when I lost him. I knew at that moment that I was stuck in a prolonged grief made worse by my poor attachments to life.

I took a breath and saw the struggle spread out in front of me, like a map that I could finally read. My individual thoughts came together into a sense of knowing what I needed to do. An 'aha' moment.

On the map was the faint idea of a path – understanding my grief and my attachment issues – that pointed me towards what healing and living might be. But what did it mean? To live? Asking myself this question woke up the hole at the core of me. I felt its raw need. I looked into the deepest layers of myself for the first time. Instead of fear, I felt curious.

My curiosity was alive. Was it the secret? I was now eager and interested and wanting to know. I followed the thread of curiosity and it solidified into a solid knowing. Yes.

'Trust yourself,' it seemed to whisper. 'Listen deeply to who you are.'

It felt like a lump of stone that I could lean against – the beginning of my being – like a solid, safe cornerstone of presence inside. Now, I needed to learn how to navigate the rest of the map.

*

I said thank you to the woman in Brixton and told her I was riding to Newbury, the village near the peace camp. Cycling into the village, miles from the Royal Air Force (RAF) base, there was evidence of the villagers taking sides: pro-establishment locals banning Greenham women from their shops, and supporters with welcoming signs.

Greenham Common Women's Peace Camp began on 5 September 1981, two years before I arrived. The camp was set up against the fence of the base, RAF Greenham Common in Berkshire, after a Welsh group, Women for Life on Earth, arrived. They were protesting the British Government's decision to allow the USA to use the base to store, and potentially use, nuclear weapons during the Cold War with the Soviet Union.

The women stayed, setting up camps named after the colours of the rainbow at most of the base's gates. The first camp formed was called Yellow Gate, at the main entrance of the RAF base, where mostly young women congregated, many calling themselves anarchists or punks.

That first morning, when I rode towards the base, I found Blue Gate. It was a small, isolated camp just outside a gate on the far side of the base. It felt perfect for me, as it claimed a new age focus. The women were slightly older than me and wore sturdy boots, well-worn jeans and simple jackets. I immediately felt comfortable.

Each gate named its own identity and attracted women aligned with that theme. Green Gate, the only gate not accepting male visitors, exuded a decidedly witchy feel. The women there played with the idea of evil witches, and how women who dared lead independent lives had been targeted for centuries, such as during the witch hunts that occurred across Europe from the 16th century.

The women broke into the base for the first time on New Year's Eve, 1982. Forty-four women climbed on top of the newly built silos where cruise missiles were to be housed and danced for hours. All were arrested, with thirty-six imprisoned. Two hundred women later entered the base dressed as teddy bears, to highlight the need to protect the land for children. On 1 April 1983, 70,000 protesters formed a 14-mile human chain from Greenham to Aldermaston and the ordnance factory at Burghfield. This inspired the creation of other peace camps across Europe.

It was restful the morning I arrived, with several women sitting quietly around a fire. Blue Gate had a single large teepee where the women slept. I was welcomed and joined them at the fire as the women explained how the camp worked. It was leaderless, working on a cooperative system: all donations of food, clothing, supplies and money were shared. I locked my bike to the fence and settled into the teepee. It was October and the start of autumn. The forest around me was turning to brilliant yellows, reds and oranges. The air was crisp, with a hint of winter and the cold wet months coming. The dropped leaves crunched underfoot.

Eager to explore, I wandered along the fence line to the next gate, Green Gate, a large camp deep in the woods. It was the healing gate, where women went to rest and rejuvenate. Here, they held pagan ceremonies to mark the turning of the year. The witches at Green Gate went to local points of power to raise energy to attempt to heal the land and end the violence of the people. They invited me to their next gathering at the Neolithic henge monument in Avebury.

It was exciting to explore these new practices and connect with the land itself, to embrace the strong Wiccan ideal of 'no harm to others'. I had found a space where I could be myself and not pretend. I was warned about the locals and the vigilante groups of mostly men, who walked through the camps at night. They spat on the women and slashed the tents and benders (young saplings bent into a sleeping structure that could later be untied). They overturned water bottles, threw mud and maggots, and sometimes set fire to the sleeping structures.

One woman told me how she and two other women were sleeping at a new camp when several soldiers came out of the base and threatened to rape them. The soldiers urinated on their food and belongings and threw rocks into the tent. The women were often beaten up when they were caught after cutting the fence and entering the base, but the officers in charge refused to acknowledge the soldiers' abuse. I was warned to never walk around the base during the night, and never alone, as rape was a real possibility.

A local group of Quakers went out of their way to aid the women by inviting them for showers or time away from the conflict. They brought food or much-needed supplies.

When I first arrived, the fence was made of single mesh, with three strands of simple barbed wire strung along the top. It was easy to cut and enter the base. I went in at night with other women. We would stay hidden until we were near major structures, at which point we would call attention to ourselves, to confront the mostly male base and its secrets. The men sometimes were kind, but often not, holding us in separate unheated rooms for hours and eventually calling the local police whose job it was to collect us. The police were often angry at the added burden of dealing with the women protesters and manhandled us. They would leave us in cells for hours and refuse to release us together – more games of power.

I was doing what my grandfather had feared all those years before – protesting against the government. Surrounded by daring women and saying no to men's rules helped set me free inside myself. I became committed to peaceful action as I witnessed its power. It seemed to incense some of the military who openly taunted and pushed the women to react. But the women supported each other and held the line of nonviolence, refusing to fight back.

We watched as the Ministry of Defence (MoD) Police prepared for the arrival of cruise missiles. They replaced the single fence with three rows of fencing. Razor wire now circled the top of each fence in strong spirals, designed to spring back in the direction of where it was being cut. It gave an ominous warning: the base was no longer willing to tolerate the women protestors.

The US military forces arrived in long convoys of covered trucks, taking over from the British personnel. The RAF base was now deemed American soil with the uniformed men who patrolled the inside of the fences speaking with American accents, and Dobermans and German Shepherds on leads at their sides. They would stare at us through the fences like we were a foreign enemy that needed to be destroyed.

One night, after cutting through the fences, we were chased down by two of these dogs and men in a jeep. The soldiers enjoyed our terror, separating us into small sterile rooms. A military woman and man played good cop and bad cop; the woman was kind and sympathetic, and the man threatening and demanding. I stammered when questioned. They were quick to think I wasn't telling the truth. It took time for people to comprehend that I had a speech problem. After several hours, they gave up trying to get any words out of me and called the police to collect us.

My stammer was worse with stress, especially when I was questioned by the military or police. They made fun of me, their frustration and anger finding a target.

One clear, sunny day, a minibus full of Scottish women pulled into Blue Gate, driven by a woman called Ava. They claimed the gate as their new home. Blue Gate was growing, also preparing for the arrival of the missiles. Ava and I immediately connected. She was practical and down to earth, and I loved her quietly spoken Glaswegian accent. The Scottish contingent stayed for a week and then regularly visited over the following months.

Ava and I started a romantic relationship. It grew slowly, spaced out by her visits. In between, we communicated by letter. In big sprawly writing, she told me she loved me, and that she missed me more than she could say.

The first batch of sixteen cruise missiles arrived at Greenham RAF base on 14 November 1983. In the following months, a total of ninety-six arrived. They were carried in long-platformed, specially built trucks, amidst heightened police and military presence. Our gate was one of the entry and exit points, as the military held regular full-scale practice runs to secret sites deep in the English countryside, often at night. We held night vigils to monitor the gate, ready to block the trucks if they attempted to leave. In the early days, we heard stories of the extra-large trucks getting stuck, unable to manage the tight corners through the villages. Someone hadn't done their homework.

That first arrival though, we were prepared. We lay down on the road, hundreds of us, refusing to move, fight back or struggle. The police came in force, hauling us up and throwing us to the side, but we'd return, stopping the trucks from leaving.

A squad of mounted police were brought in. The horses forced their way through the women lying on the ground. It was terrifying to see their hooves descending. Women were hurt, with dozens of arrests made. The police cells in Newbury were packed full. Many women chose to go to prison rather than pay the fine. Ava spent time in HM Prison Holloway in London, and a group of us went to meet her on her release. She looked diminished when she walked out through the grey forbidding gates. I held her in my arms and didn't want to let her go.

A month after the arrival of the first cruise missiles, on 11 December 1983, the peace camp held a silent protest called *Reflect the Base*. I watched with wild joy as the camp filled with more than 50,000 women. Pride filled my chest, to be one among the amazing mix of women who came to form rings of femininity around the base.

The day started with women holding up mirrors to symbolically force the military to look at themselves and their actions. It ended with hundreds of arrests, as large sections of the fence were pulled down. I was one of those arrested.

*

Over the next few months, life at the camp became more and more difficult. It was mid-winter and continually raining. The police and government were increasing their efforts to disrupt the peace camp by sending in bailiffs first thing in the morning.

Anything we couldn't hold in our arms was thrown into the rubbish trucks that arrived with the bailiffs. We sat on the ground for the rest of the day, unprotected from the weather. We couldn't stay dry or warm, as they took any firewood and destroyed the fire pits. We weren't allowed to enter the local shops. Peace camp women were now banned from the town. Many women were struggling with their mental and physical health. A group of kind London women invited me to their homes to give me a much-needed break, but it wasn't enough.

Ava was worried about me as I was continually sick with colds and had an aching back from sleeping on the cold ground. 'Hey lass, yer exhausted. I hate seein' ye like this.'

'Yeah, I think my b-b-body has had e-enough. It's t-too hard ... I'm feeling worn out.'

'Come home wi me.'

'Do you mean it? I d-d-don't have any m-money for rent ...'

'That's no' necessary. Ye can stay rent-free.' She laughed and reached for me, pulling me into her arms. 'I love ye and a cannae stop thinkin' aboot ye.'

I'd been at the camp for five months and on the road for two years when, in 1984, I packed my few belongings on my bicycle and moved to Scotland. Another country, another beginning.

Chapter 18

Being a bonny lass

Ava's basement flat on Hill Street in Garnethill was in the centre of Glasgow. I entered by a door under the stairs of the steps leading up to the tenements above. It was dim inside, with two rooms and a bathroom. A cloth covering the front window filtered any light, providing privacy from the people walking past on the street above. Gaps in the walls and floor showed the damp earth underneath.

Glasgow itself had little colour; the shades of the winter clothes of its residents were muted. The sandstone buildings had darkened faces, looming above and around me. Over the next few years, the city sand-blasted these buildings back to their brilliant creams, soft pinks and pale golden yellows, lightening the city dramatically. But when I arrived, there seemed to be only variations of grey and black. Spring was struggling to arrive, the days short and sombre, coated by constant soft drizzle.

Hill Street overlooked the west of the city, with Charing Cross on one side and the motorway on the other. The sides of the hill dropped off steeply, often iced over in winter. Garnethill was a mix of cultures: local Scots who had lived on the hill for years and families from Northern Ireland who had escaped 'The Troubles' in Belfast. A large Muslim family ran the local shop and laundromat. Many serious-faced young men walked the streets; gossip claimed they belonged to local triad gangs. One was murdered a few months later.

Ava introduced me to her gay and lesbian friends and the vibrant community of Garnethill. Glasgow School of Art was situated on the next street. The school was famous for being designed by Charles Rennie Mackintosh. It was next to St Aloysius' College – Scotland's only Jesuit school. It had been built to transform the lives of Irish Catholics immigrating to Scotland to escape the effects of the potato famine.

We continued our anti-nuclear protest in Scotland by climbing the walls and getting inside the fence at Faslane Naval base in Argyll and Bute. Once inside, we danced and sang in a large circle. All of us were arrested. I should have been used to the process by now, but I stammered through the interrogation. It was easier to break in than talk.

Over the next few months, life with Ava settled down. We were now a couple. I helped her learn how to save and took her stray cats to the vet to be desexed. We spent more on cat food and litter than on human food.

Occasionally, the sun managed to break through the thick cloud cover. It shone like it knew its presence had to count. I watched for the patches of washed-out blue and yearned for a little heat – anything to break the constant, relentless grey. My state of mind reflected the weather. I wondered what I was doing in Glasgow. The days marched on as I stood still.

The parched land of northern Australia seemed so far away. I ached for the heat and the red dust of Broome, the miles of flat ground that stretched out, the huge blue sky and me a speck. I longed for the pounding surf and to hear the breakers thrown onto the sand. To see the spray cast high above the jutting rocks of the headland.

I wanted to be hit by the steamy heat of Darwin, to have a solid wave of instant sweat covering my limbs. To see the dying sun strike the pools of tropical rain that collected in the hollows of freshly laid bitumen and smell how the water blunted the acrid scent of new tar.

I wanted to hear the possums and how they used the branches of the mango trees to slip into the ceiling of our house – how the roof space became their playhouse through the long nights. Then, as dawn broke, the galahs swollen with grass seed would rise as flecks of grey among the fluttering pink. They'd turn, as if on a wheel, to swoop and settle among the eucalypts.

Smiling, I remembered how the possums had first go at the mangos still on the tree. I'd hear the startling clank of a half-eaten mango as it fell on the galvanised roof of the house. The sound gathered as it rolled, guided by the ripples of metal to thud on the ground. The possums competed with the screeching fruit bats and flying foxes. They often spat out the skins, leaving them lying on the grass. In the new morning soft light, I often trod on the slippery skins by accident, mashing the slimy flesh between my toes. These memories woke my longing to bite into a ripe mango and feel the juice running down my chin.

In the basement flat in Glasgow, as raindrops raced each other down my window, I played at being the land itself. How the redness was my friend, holding me close, and the breakers thrown onto the sand were my playmates. The spray, sharing my tears; the pounding, hiding my shame. The galahs screeched their joy at my escape as I flew with them.

The feeling of sitting, nestled, held up by wings was familiar. I'd done this before but I couldn't remember when. And what had I been escaping from?

*

'What's this?' I asked Ava.

'It's a wee present for ye.' She grinned. 'I found it in a second-hand shop in Aberdeen.'

'There's n-nothing "wee" about it. It's a b-beast.'

'Aye, lass, it will take up most of yer desk. But I know ye wasnae one to talk, so I thought ye could write … make a wee start, ye ken …' Ava looked at me, a question in her eyes. 'Do ye like it? Get all of them words oot of yer heid …'

'I love it, b-but you'll have to t-teach me. I've never used one b-b-before.'

'Nae bother. Let's get ye started.'

The green lettering of the computer screen added an alien feel, even as it lightened the room. I started writing, saving it all on floppy discs. It helped. I transformed my bleakness into words.

I found a job as an attendant at a local art gallery – the Third Eye Centre in Sauchiehall Street – before joining Ava at Greencity Wholefoods, a worker's cooperative in Dennistoun in the east of the city. I worked part-time in the oiling bay, bottling cold-pressed oils arriving from France in forty-four gallon drums. I learned to drive the forklift and fought an ongoing battle with the temperamental labelling machine.

Ava worked in the warehouse, stone-milling the organic grains into different flours, packing, and driving the trucks. She was one of several workers driving the three- and four-day loops to deliver the foods to the health-food shops, communes and isolated communities in the far north and south of Scotland. She invited me to join her and introduced me properly to her rugged home.

As we crisscrossed the country, the land itself spoke in hushed tones. It embraced me, a foreigner, and its ancient magic opened me to different rhythms than the ones I knew. I listened to the blunted bare mountains of the west coast and they won my heart. They too were worn down by endless years. The heathers hugging their craggy sides spoke to me of tenacity. The soft mauves were broken by spiny thistles thrusting up their spikes, ending in delicate purple flower heads. They whispered of endurance and determination.

Here the earth was moist, with endless swatches of freezing water and mysterious lochs, calling to the hidden depths within me. Iced-over puddles that I punched through with my heavy boots brought out a playful me. I danced, crunching their tops. This land delighted me. Red poppies waved as we drove past and the yellow fields of swaying rapeseed on the east coast brought the sunshine I longed for.

I sat, high up in the truck, navigating the winding roads through the glens and muddy tracks heading into more remote places. I watched Ava as she handled the Scania, her steady hands and compact body, and the way she used her slash of dyed ebony hair to hide behind. She'd rather drive than talk. She glanced at me, grinned, then called me 'her bonny lass'.

*

Remembering the second dream that I'd had the day of the fair at Battersea Power Station, I found a traditional acupuncturist, Vicki, and started treatment twice a week. My stammer was worse than ever – any remnants of smooth speech, long gone. I was feeling more at home in Scotland, but still believed there was something wrong with me.

After about six months of treatment, Vicki said I might be depressed. I'd never considered the diagnosis before, but in many ways, I pressed myself flat, like the cardboard cut-out I still imagined myself to be. Vicki suggested I see a therapist, and recommended Lara. I went for an initial appointment.

I was nervous when Lara greeted me. She said, 'I need to see your body structure and how you hold yourself. It's how I work out what we need to do, so can you please strip off to your underwear?'

I reluctantly undressed and stood in front of her. She walked around me, examining me closely. I felt like a specimen.

'You're a mess, do you know that?' I had no words, only the shame that now cloaked me. I wrapped it close. It was familiar.

'I see how your energy is blocked in your muscles. It's trauma that's got stuck. Can you feel it? By the way you stand? How your hips are turned up. You've no curve in your lower back. And your chest is collapsed in. I use Gestalt therapy techniques to increase your awareness of the present moment. And bioenergetics.'

'WW-What are they?' I thought I'd better say something.

'Bioenergetics was developed by an American, Alexander Lowen. It uses breathing, movement and touch to release physical tension and trauma. Gestalt was developed by Fritz Pearls in the 1940s and works by helping you become aware of your behaviour and patterns. I agree with Vicki's diagnosis, by the way. You look depressed.'

Oh thanks, I silently said to myself.

'Do you always stammer?' Lara asked.

I nodded.

'And the squint? Has it always been there?'

'Yes.'

'OK.' She smiled. 'Your depression has probably been held in your body for a long time. It's become your normal state. I imagine it started when you were a young child. Children do get depressed, you know. Adults dismiss it, but you have all the signs,' Lara said. 'I think you're one of those.'

I attended therapy with Lara once a week, working with a range of exercises to unblock my energy, often directly into muscles that she wanted to be released. I was stilted and timid, embarrassed by my body, hesitant to make a noise or speak through my stammer. Lara challenged me on these issues, alternating between pushing and cajoling.

It was like being put through a washing machine ringer. Everything I did was wrong. I wanted it to work so I kept going.

In early 1985, I enrolled at the College of Traditional Acupuncture in Leamington Spa, England. I was excited to begin learning. Once a month, I took the train south to Leamington Spa for a block of work, returning on the overnight train from Birmingham, with the carriages often full of drunken Scottish football fans.

The weeks in between were spent completing assignments and taking the hundreds of pulses required on as many different wrists as I could find, with my fingertips gaining the sensitivity needed to feel the subtle pulse qualities. It involved constant learning to memorise the acupuncture points and meridians and practise how to locate them on different bodies.

The five-element acupuncture system offered a framework for understanding how the world worked, based on Taoist philosophy – the unplanned yet natural rhythms called 'the way', or Tao. Action without intention, spontaneity with compassion and humility. I fell in love with it as it consolidated the idea of peaceful action and what I had already learned at Greenham. It explained that human life is part of the cycle of nature: the seasons, the daily rhythms, and living and dying. If we don't listen, we fall out of balance, becoming disturbed or ill in some way. It's all about finding harmony and gave me a softer idea of order – a contrast to the pushing egocentric energy I was experiencing with Lara.

One acupuncture point stood out, called Spirit Burial Ground – a magical point on the kidney meridian. It's capable of resurrecting the deadened spirit of a person. This point is used when a person has virtually given up, the spirit almost unreachable. Vicki needled this point on me repeatedly.

I settled into the Tao, allowing it to teach me. My curiosity was being met and I was being parented in the truest sense of the word. The Earth element mothered me, the Metal element, my father, was improving my worth. The Wood element allowed me to grow and use my energy. Water helped me flow. Fire, my heart, healed the still bleeding wounds and my Heart Protector was now able to protect my heart.

I felt my place as a human for the first time, standing on the earth, the heavens above, the sky my friend, the wind in my face. The sun, shining down, warming and awakening my heart. I thrived. I was finding my voice, able to speak back to Lara.

Then, in September 1985, I received a letter from Jannette's mother. She wrote saying Jannette had been killed. She had been hit by a car while riding her motorbike to work in Sydney.

My world crashed in again. Graeme, and now Jannette. It was too much. She was 24.

*

Jannette had been a solid presence in my life for seven years. We'd helped each other through nursing and countless experiences – travelling in Papua New Guinea and then across the world. We'd danced our frustration out over countless weekends, drank green ginger wine directly from the bottle while sitting in front of open fires. We'd camped in the bush, slept in caves and on numerous beaches, to wake as the sun rose. We'd spotted dolphins curving through the waves. Jannette spoke to me of sun and smiles and adventure.

We'd snoozed side by side on dozens of overnight buses, skied all day, got stuck in soft snow, and helped prise each other free. We'd attempted to cross-country ski through the Snowy Mountains. When we'd stopped to rest, we'd built massive snowmen instead, to mark our return journey. We'd ridden her horse, Sorrette, in turns. Jannette's voice was still loud in my head, shouting at me to keep my heels down, my knees clenched and my hands loose.

I loved her and now she was dead. It was crazy. How could she be gone from this world? I couldn't take it in. I couldn't get my head around the words from her mother, telling me *she had been accidentally killed*.

I remembered all our ups and downs, our learning together and apart. We'd stayed in touch when she returned to Australia, writing each other long, personal letters. We had been at peace with one another and able to compare our different loves.

Her death activated memories of Graeme's. Both were killed by other drivers, and neither were at fault. Thoughts of their deaths crashed and swirled around my brain. I couldn't separate the two. I was never going to see Jannette grow old. I was never going to see Graeme. I wouldn't see her mature into the woman she could be, I could never know Graeme as a man. I couldn't understand this crazy life. The sudden stop of death.

The intimacy we had shared, Graeme and now Jannette, was gone. Only I knew it. No one else would understand.

I was supposed to be learning how to live, but there was no room.

My heart was filled with the dead.

*

I needed gentleness and understanding as I grieved for Jannette. Instead, Lara pushed, to open me up further.

I looked into her eyes and believed her message of direct therapeutic action, coming again and again to her door. Lara wanted me to scream, to act out the rage. She gave me a tennis racquet to hit the bed one hundred times, to release the tension held between my shoulder blades and hips.

I was shouting and trying so hard to be the perfect client that I couldn't hear my muffled sobs. There wasn't any space for quiet.

After about a year of weekly therapy to unlock my body, I began to feel present in myself. Then, Lara's nail accidentally sliced the skin above my belly button. She was attempting to release some holding in my stomach muscles.

With that single line of pain, the brown paper-wrapped package was cut wide open. My memories flooded out, all the forgotten.

With great silent shudders, an onslaught of scenes crashed into my mind, one after the other, like a dam opening that nearly swept me away.

Lara wanted to work more deeply into the trauma. She pursued the clues, suggesting I start drawing and painting the images, keeping a journal, and recording the scenes as each was unlocked.

I remembered being a child lying on a table and a man with a knife. I remembered him using the knife to trace the contours of my body and him wanting to cut me. How he too had sliced above my belly button.

I remembered his face and his eyes staring into mine.

I remembered the bossman holding me too tightly on his lap and the men queued up, waiting, lounging against the walls.

I remembered my father turning his face to the door.

I remembered seeing my mother standing at the kitchen sink, and how she glared at me.

I did hundreds of drawings, of the men, the room, my mother, and my father in Currajong.

The more I did, the more I remembered.

Part III

Finding

Chapter 19

Remembering

I need to thank Joan for her punishment of me as a two-year-old because it prepared me for the men. It taught me to isolate my feelings, retreating instead into my thoughts. I learned how to be vigilant yet hidden, making the shadows my friends, withdrawing from stress and dissociating from terror.

I knew what hate was and how to somehow tolerate it. It was normal – a daily slide into careful stillness. It set the blueprint for my life – the hypervigilance and silence only a breath away.

A month or so before my third birthday, my father came into the kitchen of the house on View Street in Brisbane, holding a dress. I'd never seen a dress like this. It was frilly and pink. He put it on me, refusing to speak to my mother. I could see her behind him, watching us. He had bought me a dress and not her. I knew I would pay later.

He walked me to his car, explaining we were going somewhere important and I had to do exactly what he said. If I did, it would be OK. I trusted him – he was my daddy who rescued me from the kitchen.

He drove for a short time and then parked in front of a house. Daddy took me by the hand and led me through the gate to a door. He knocked and stood waiting, his hand clenching mine. A man opened the door, grinning.

He said, 'I didn't think you would come,' and stepped back, letting us in. My father pulled me after him, saying nothing, sweating, holding me too tightly.

'Is this her?' A different man, bigger than the first, older, looked me over. I tried to hide against my father, but Daddy pushed me forward. I stood awkwardly in a space on my own. A line of men were leaning against a wall.

I came to call the bigger man 'the bossman' because he was the boss of what went on in the room. He smiled and told my father, 'Undress her. I want to see her.'

Daddy pulled the frilly dress off, along with my pants, and left them lying on the floor.

The bossman then told my father, 'Put her on the table.' He wanted to see me better. He told another man to hold his knife against my skin.

This man was younger, blue-eyed with shoulder-length, dirty-blond hair. He stroked me with the point of the knife, playing with the pattern of my ribs, outlining the shape of my body. The point left stinging lines, but I didn't dare move. The knifeman was watching me closely, waiting for the bossman to direct events. I knew I shouldn't try to get away. I felt him tense, ready to grab me if I did.

The first night they talked – the bossman and my father. The bossman enjoyed my father's discomfort. The system was being explained because at one point my father complained, but the knife was pushed harder under my ribs, cutting my skin. I started crying. I remember being told to shut up. And my father was told to shut it too.

The fight seemed to leave him and he left me to the men. My father stood by the door as the bossman picked me up and carried me to an armchair. He sat me on his lap. He loosened his trousers. He smiled. 'It's time.'

One by one, the men came, jerking off, pushing their erect penises into my mouth. They ejaculated into my throat. The bossman, becoming aroused under me, smiled and clenched my nose shut with one hand, the other holding my chin. Some of the men helped hold me still.

I didn't want to swallow, but I couldn't breathe. I tried to hold on but the bossman squeezed my lips tight around the man's penis, forcing me to swallow and swallow, watching me closely, smiling, always smiling. Only then, when I thought I couldn't go on, he released my nose and mouth and let me gasp for breath.

Then it would start all over again.

The first night I was being taught the rules, just as my father was. I tried to look at him. To look into his eyes, to ask for help, but Daddy turned his face away from mine. I saw him do it. He wouldn't watch. He left me to the men.

I was alone in a room full of men, one of them my father.

*

Somehow, my father had decided I could save him from what he'd gotten into. My understanding is that the bossman extorted my father into bringing his daughter, with threats backed up by the knifeman, but I never found out the true story.

My memories of the first night are clear. My father was almost distraught holding my hand as we walked up to the front door of the house. Whether it was a concern for me or his skin, I will never know. He tried to prepare me, but I remember seeing the shock on his face when he first witnessed their actions and how he looked away.

It changed over time, but I cling to the knowledge that in the beginning he seemed to care. In the beginning, he loved me.

I desperately hold on to this, because I have few kind memories. The child in me wants to believe he hadn't chosen to take me, but it's not true. He was an adult man who made the conscious choice to take me, his nearly three-year-old girl, and give me to a gang of men to use.

There was a clock on a wall in the room. I could see it when I was lying flat on the table. It ticked away the seconds. I heard it in the silences and between the grunts and talk.

I hid my heart behind the clock face, where they wouldn't think to look. My beating heart thudded in time to the second hand. My heart was safe, away from my hurting chest. In the space where my heart should have been, I placed all my unspoken words. I tucked them under my ribs – words waiting to be heard, to be believed.

Waiting became the dress I slipped on each week, sometimes more often; it seemed only a single day had passed. Waiting was the dress that smelled – the stale sick sweet caught in the threads. It was rinsed out by my mother and hung up again and again, waiting for me to slip on, for my father to take me to the men.

My father was careful with me on the first night, but it was the beginning of his descent into whatever the place was he eventually went.

I stopped being his little girl and he stopped being my daddy.

The first night was an abbreviated version of what was to come. At the end of the line of men, when they were all done, my father was told to take me away but to come back. Too fearful to disagree, he dressed me, left and drove home.

He didn't speak when he took me into the house. My mother was standing at the kitchen sink, her hands in the suds of washing up. She turned and asked where we'd been. She was angry about our special time together. She couldn't see past her jealousy and believed the outing should have been hers. My father didn't answer.

Instead, he took me through to the bathroom, ran a bath and washed me. This first night he was gentle – almost an apology. He dressed me for bed and tucked me in. He kissed me on the forehead, but never again.

From then on, he became removed and short-tempered, and it became my fault.

If I wasn't his little girl, he wouldn't have to take me to the men.

My dress got washed and hung up, waiting for me to put on, again and again. I was caught without end, with no concept of knowing I needed an end. I was too young. The evenings themselves, when I was taken to the men, lasted longer than the days spent waiting, the seconds prolonged; those seconds stretched further than the hours in between.

How do I capture this feeling of waiting so you can understand? As an adult, you know waiting has an end. I can't show you waiting with no end. It was the waiting that marked the end for each time, until waiting, Daddy comes and finds me and takes me by the hand and drives me to the men, for it all to start again.

*

The pattern of the night changed after the first time. From the second night, the ritual with the bossman was always first, almost like he was establishing his domination. He was already sitting in the armchair when we arrived. He beckoned, not needing to speak. My father undressed me.

I made the short walk across the room alone; my father had already turned away. The bossman smiled and invited me, but he had to pull me onto his lap because I couldn't take the final step on my own.

Each man took his turn. The bossman watched me closely, intently, enjoying the power of holding me, taking me further and further into suffocation and drowning. He was aroused under me, and this time no cloth separated us as he prodded against me.

The nights continued, again and again.

I remember the men, their faces and bodies and fingers. I remember the bossman, his shadowy mass in the armchair, demanding through half-closed lashes, his nod forcing me to take the final step, and his cold smile as I climbed refusing and lost onto his thighs. Then, pinned and struggling, the men came, my folds and openings their playthings. Again and again.

*

During a therapy session with Lara, I remembered another scene.

My father was with three other men. This was different from most nights because he joined in. I remember pleading with him, please Daddy no more. My throat was painful and constricted. I tried to keep it shut but I couldn't. My mouth was forced open for them to use. It was wide open, but I remember the struggle of trying to breathe.

My father wanted to be one of them.

*

I have always thought that they were mostly policemen but I have no proof.

The men would swagger in, put any guns and belts to one side, and drop their trousers or shorts, their shirts now hanging free. Then they'd wait for the bossman to tell them to start.

This was happening in Brisbane during the 1960s, at the same time that corrupt police officers were involved with illegal gambling and prostitution, demanding a cut of the earnings. This was proven during the Fitzgerald Inquiry, held in the late 1980s. The inquiry investigated the corruption within the Queensland Police from the 1950s. The reporter, Phil Dickie of *The Courier Mail*, had written a series of articles about police corruption, with *Four Corners* following up with a television report.

My father had been a policeman in Townsville, and my family had moved to Brisbane in March 1962 – a time that was thick with corruption.

*

I remember the men, their faces now blurring, but their skin colour and the angle of their penises dangling between their legs are clear. I remember the way each would stiffen in turn to the call of the bossman and by their different butting rhythms against my face.

*

There was another man, a sort of fatherly type, with smiling eyes and a gentle mouth, who took my hand and showed me how to stroke his dick. He showed me how to hold on firmly and squeeze, room for both my hands on his growing length, the way he liked it.

'Faster now, do it quicker!' he said, and his hand covered mine, crushing my fingers, getting angry – he stopped smiling. Jerking hard, he pushed my face down and forced my mouth onto his dick, 'Bite me now.'

Sharp liquid squirted into my throat; I twisted away but he fixed my head. This was the cue the bossman was waiting for. It was his turn now. The bossman bent down where I could see his smile. Winking, he reached for my face.

He used one hand to squeeze my lips tight around this man's dick, his other hand pinching my nose shut. My mouth was full of liquid, I couldn't breathe. Squirming, the other men moved in, pinning my wrists and ankles, a solid wall of flesh holding me still. The bossman watched my face and my attempts to breathe. Swallowing and swallowing and swallowing and still no air. Only then would he grin and remove his hands. The men letting go, me gasping, coughing, almost vomiting, sucking in air.

Each time, learning my tricks, the bossman took me further and further and further until I was drowning.

After they were finished, one of the men took me across the room to the table, lying me down. The knifeman had been leaning against one wall the entire time, playing with his knife, watching, waiting to have me on his own. Now he did.

*

His eyes are still in front of mine; even now, I can picture him.

When I was attempting to understand it, in my late twenties, I wrote a letter to the knifeman. I had nowhere to send the letter – it was just for me, but I needed to write it to tell him that, in a crazy, messed-up way, he had helped save me from the men.

I was caught in a bondage-power system with the knifeman. It was different from what happened with the other men. It seemed similar to what hostages talk about with hostage-takers, whom they are dependent on.

> *Dear Knifeman,*
>
> *Do you remember when we first met, in the room with the blokes, my father, and your boss? His armchair? How the bossman told you to hold your knife against my chest. How my father complained and you cut me, making me cry.*
>
> *On the following nights, you leaned against the wall, watching me. You didn't move or speak or grin like the others did. I remember your narrow shape, wispy blond hair, bony cheeks and your eyes, pinpoints of light staring at me.*
>
> *I lost you as someone else forced my head back.*
>
> *Then, when I was lying on the table on my back, you looked at me for a long time. I knew I had to wait for you and look into your eyes because when I tried to look away or blink, you tensed.*
>
> *You nearly smiled, then blew gently on my skin, like a reward.*
>
> *From the corner of my eye, I saw you bring out the knife. You held it in front of my face and watched my eyes. I waited.*

You tensed when you brought the point down into the hollow of my neck. A drop of sweat ran down your face. You paused, then pressed the point harder, but I knew now to keep looking and you smiled.

Do you remember your first real smile? I made you happy and you flicked the knife onto my chest.

Gently, you marked red lines across my ribs, outlining each curve until you reached my nipples. You cut me to prove you would and then my belly. I knew what you alone needed, my eyes, but still, you cut me.

You worked your way down my body, the fight inside you growing as I glimpsed your other hand working between your legs. You stroked me with the metal, letting the edge leave cruel trails along my inside skin.

I knew to stay still, lost in the depths of your blue mesmerising eyes. Nothing else mattered. Until your spasm, until you shook and gasped, sweat now running freely down your face, dripping on my skin.

You never varied, it was always the same struggle and I grew to know each line you would leave, stinging and cutting my skin. Red trails I looked at and stroked on the days in between, imagining your blue eyes. The only eyes who wanted mine. The horrible cold, winking brown of the bossman didn't need me; he wanted to see me drown.

My father had turned his eyes away and couldn't bear to look at me. My mother only snorted in disgust, hating me for going out with my father. Do you see? It was only you who wanted me.

You couldn't kill me.

I know what you did to the others. I remember hearing the men cheer you on, telling you to just do it, but you couldn't, not to me.

I remember them saying, 'It makes a change to have a white cunt.'

How they would say, 'It's easier to kill black cunts.'

I know what you would have done if I'd stopped looking. You would have reversed the knife and slammed the handle down on my head, again and again, smashing my eyes. But you didn't, because you were mine, as long as I kept looking. And I did. You alone saved me, your eyes looking into mine.

My relationship with the knifeman has taken me time to work out. He was a dangerous man. He easily cut me. My feeling of being important was only mine. I know now that what he did was a form of torture. He was the bossman's right-hand man, doing his dirty work for him.

The knifeman loved cutting. He lived for cutting, but I needed my childlike trust in the power of our connection to stay hopeful in some tiny way, because I didn't have any adults who seemed to care.

My father had stopped meeting my eyes. Whether it was from shame or not wanting to see my sadness, I don't know, but he avoided me until he came to get me to take me to the men. My mother had never looked at me with kindness. She resented my special outings, still making me pay, but now her malice couldn't break through the confusion and loneliness while I was waiting to put on the dress.

Time stood still until the moment came to drive me to the men and then, like clockwork, time started again. The clock ticking on the wall. My heart was up there behind its face, safe from the knife and the men.

When the knifeman was doing his thing with the knife and my skin, it was my eyes that I believed he wanted and needed. The bossman didn't care about connection, only the line of near drowning, swallowing and needing air. The line he controlled, life or death, smiling over me.

Children need steady eye contact, with kindness, to develop a robust self. It's called mirroring and it's how a child learns where they begin and end. I didn't have good mirroring to begin with. I was desperate enough to imagine caring with the only eye contact I had.

Finding this knifeman-torturer, who I thought wanted to see me and not just my skin, allowed me to hang on to myself. Together we seemed to create and exist in a space and time separate from all the others, who were more obvious about abusing my body and openings.

I was an object to be used and discarded, by my father now, too. I was what kept him safe from the bossman and he resented me for his dependency and powerlessness. Now I had both parents blaming and hating me for their lives.

I was floundering and hung on to the routine that outlined my life – that at the end of all the men was the knifeman, a little private space of him and me. The others moved on to playing cards, drinking and swearing at the other end of the room, which was now filling up with smoke and noise.

The knifeman saw me. For every second I lay on the table and he was stroking and cutting my skin, I consciously chose to look and therefore not to die. This was me escaping from being a pawn – a tiny achievement in a night of terror.

I was also choosing to swallow down the fluids of the men. Drinking, rather than fighting, was another choice, a decision of a child. Plus the one I made to put my heart up there on the wall, hidden from the men behind the clock face.

Maybe I was making lots of little choices through the night, which helped me to survive. Looking back decades later, I see how these choices mounted up. They set the foundation for my character. Somehow, I knew that choices count, no matter how small.

The wisdom of the victim.

The knifeman and I were joined in an intimate ritual torture that I believe prevented him from acting out the violence that was always waiting to erupt. I could feel it in his skin, his barely held-in restraint, wanting to be unleashed. But he couldn't and wouldn't kill me. For that short time, I believe I stopped him from acting out his rage, thereby saving a piece of his soul and finding my own.

When the bossman invaded our bond, the knifeman's allegiance switched. I lost my power. He'd have no compunction in cutting me if the bossman desired.

After the knifeman was finished, nothing was said. He turned away and joined the others at the far end of the room. I'd be left naked, mucky, feeling sick, stomach bloated and hurting from swallowing the men's fluids, trying not to vomit, my mouth and throat, my skin and between my thighs hurting, seeping red lines stinging my skin.

When the table stopped making ridges in my back, keeping small and silent, like water trickling to the floor, the wooden boards my map, I snuck to my corner. Careful, in case their attention was caught.

I squeezed myself behind a chair, curling up, trying hard not to cry or pee. Sometimes I had to but I couldn't make a noise. I hid the sound in their laughter. Then I held myself silently still.

I regressed to the only time I'd felt safe, being wrapped around Graeme in the fluid confines of the womb. This, after all, had been only a few years earlier, when we'd been side by side, safe within sacs of warmth, oblivious to the outside world. I closed my eyes and pretended I had him again, like how it was before we were born. Before I lost Graeme to our mother.

Graeme became my left arm. I hugged him close, holding my arm, imagining feeling safe and warm, remembering a time when it was Graeme and me tight together. I had him now. No one could take him away from me.

I was no longer alone in a room full of men.

Chapter 20

A child murder

One night was different.

Something had happened and the bossman was angry, standing up and shouting as soon as we entered the room. The bossman told the knifeman to put me on the table and use his knife to press up under my ribs, into where my heart should be. The bossman threatened my father, reminding him how easy it would be to kill me – a single push would do it.

I focused on the clock, ticking in the silence between the words. The bossman was waiting for my father to explain. The clock held my heart safely out of reach. I was nothing, an empty shell. It wouldn't matter if the knifeman stuck his knife in me.

I noticed spaces, of the floorboards and the lines defining them. I escaped across them when the men were done. I found the spaces between the men and the empty spaces inside me, between my ribs. I retreated deep inside, leaving my heart up there on the wall where the men wouldn't think to look. I sat inside my chest.

I gave my body up to them, to do as they wished. They would anyway. It wasn't mine. It only hurt.

I lost my father but I found Graeme and I had the knifeman's eyes. It was enough.

*

One night is frozen within me.

There was a girl already in the room. She had fine curly hair and was about my size. I was entranced – a girl like me. I watched from across the room. I couldn't see who her father might be.

It was worse seeing her on his lap, the bossman's hands holding her tight, her nose clamped shut as he did to mine. She struggled for breath. She didn't understand. I wanted to shout to tell her she had to stop struggling. It went easier if you didn't struggle. He was worse if you fought him. He would punish her and take her further than he should, just to prove he could. And he did.

She fought him and fought him and tried to scream. He held her fiercely, holding her down. The other men joined in. And then she had to drink and drink and drink it all down, but he didn't take his hands away. He didn't stop.

I wanted to cry out to tell him to stop. It was too long. I knew it was too long. She stopped struggling. She stopped and went still. Limp.

Her life and beauty left her.

I was alone when for a moment there, I thought I had found a friend. The bossman was both disgusted and fully aroused. Jumping up, he flung her down and grabbed a towel to wipe himself. She'd peed on him.

He left her … a heap on the floorboards, discarded, her eyes open and staring. Fluids were dribbling from the corners of her mouth, making a mess on the floor.

I was empty, the men towering above and around me.

I never heard her name. I wish I had.

She had fought him and escaped him, but it cost her life.

I imagine her flying wild through the sky, singing out loud, singing her truth, her name, her song.

I see her as a beautiful grey and pink galah wheeling and gliding through the early morning light, screeching her escape.

He got me again and again. The consequences of our struggle for my breath have stayed with me. It has defined what I was but not who I am. I have escaped too, but at my own cost.

It has taken me my lifetime to be free. I fly with this other little girl and all the other children I know they used. I imagine us wheeling and crying out, a flock of pink and grey, in the freedom of dawn's soft hues. Dawn's swiftly changing colours reflected on our wings, the children used, children who I wish and hope fly free.

Tell-tale fingers, cerise and magenta, stroke the fading night's amethyst shell. Pools of crimson and coral flatter the oyster clouds as streaks of amber highlight tucks and crevices. Splashes of flamingo pink buttress the pastel curve of the rapidly lightening sky. A flush of ochre shimmering on the ocean suffuses upward through the lingering wisps of rose and orange. Champagne bathes the horizon, a silent fanfare as intense gold and white hot yellow together climb out of the sparkling sea.

*

My father ran soon after this. It became too dangerous even for him. He worried for his life, looking at me with a sharp bitterness in his eyes. Accusations were in his heavy-handedness, when he hauled the dress over my head at the end of the night, not even bothering to find my pants.

He blamed me for how I had destroyed his life, flinging 'cunt' and 'whore' at me whenever he could. I didn't know what the words meant. I looked at my father, but he was a stranger, even when I searched his face. A stranger who wouldn't meet my eyes except when he wanted to blame me, and then he looked like a monster. What did he do with his soul?

It was May 1965 when we escaped to Darwin on a jet plane. Our family had grown to six: I had a little sister – Sarah. John Denver's song 'Leaving on a Jet Plane', which Graeme used to sing along to and play on his guitar, makes me think of our flight to the far north. It was as far as my father could think to get away. He had a job with the Overseas Telecommunications Commission (OTC). A new start, he said. But the song is full of love and there was no love on this aeroplane ride.

Joan was busy with Sarah, leaving us three older kids free to escape to the streets. We formed the start of what became our little gang. My older brother Trevor had been having a rough time, too. He hadn't had the evening rides with Norm, but the parenting we were receiving was minimal and never kind. It was chaotic, full of Joan's screaming, then silences and slaps across the face.

In Brisbane, Norm had started grabbing us by the head or hair or throat, whatever was reachable, and bashing our heads against each other's. It left us dizzy and disorientated. Now, in Darwin, Graeme became Norm's regular target. My father lashed out at Graeme for the smallest thing.

Graeme was the sweetest of us. Trevor was tense and serious, lost in weighty thoughts with a frown between his brows, whereas Graeme was placid and dreamy. He was content to sit and pick his nose. He never thought to be on edge, so I took on the job of being his protector. When I heard Norm's tread, or his car entering the drive, I grabbed Graeme and we hid.

In Darwin, Norm continued morphing into the monster. Maybe before, in Brisbane, he'd been concerned about the bossman, who kept him in check. My father had never dared step out of line. It had kept him somehow powerless, like me, but now he was free. Something happened to his mind, especially when he looked at me.

If Graeme was his obvious target, I became the secret focus of his frustration. The wrongs in his life were because of me. Therefore, he needed to destroy me to release this frustration and wipe his mind clean. With this new ritual, it became a battle of survival between us.

Our house in Darwin looked on mournfully. It wanted to help me but ended up adding to my father's threat.

It was a typical Northern Territory fibro place, built high on stilts to catch the tropical breezes and cope with the monsoon rains. It was dingy inside. Massive mango trees brushed the sides and back of the house, blocking most of the light. The screen doors were often left half open, banging in the wind and frightening me.

Their squeaky hinges protested when I couldn't, as the house rose in an attempt to protect but only contained. The floorboards creaked underfoot in carefulness and shame. My silent screams were held captive in the spaces of their lines. The despairing rooms learned my father's patterns but couldn't stop him. The shadowy halls masked his intent. It didn't matter how careful I tried to be, he always found me. I hated myself for forgetting to watch or to listen. I hated that he found me.

But he did. Every few days, Norm grabbed me and took me to his room.

The bedclothes were strewn in his haste to start. I'd learned long ago to be frozen still, when, like clockwork, he began. First the taunting, it was all my fault, then the teasing of what was to come. And then the bottom drawer opened, his eyes never leaving mine. The white cloth object was removed and placed carefully on the dresser top. Unwrapped, he slid his thick, squat hand around the handle of the gun. Forcing the barrel into my mouth, it jarred my teeth and jammed up hard against my throat. The slow seep of gun oil mixed with my spit as I fought to not let the metal touch my tongue.

Then he ranted, blaming my cunt, as he promised to shoot dead my twin brother and fire the gun down my throat if I talked about the men. He pushed the fingers of his other hand into me, between my legs, his nails slicing the tender skin inside, as the gun was pushed further into my throat.

After he was finished, he washed his hands. He cleaned the gun, wrapped it in its cotton cover and replaced it in the drawer. He straightened the family photo sitting on the doily on top of the dresser and left me, lying there, alone.

I couldn't speak to adults; any words would stick in my throat. I only talked to Graeme and Trevor. We had a secret language that the grownups couldn't understand. Joan was frustrated with us but Graeme was still her favourite. She hated me and my influence on him, especially now she had Sarah. I was winning – I was with Graeme a lot of the time.

I couldn't get any whole words out. The gun worked. I knew my father would shoot Graeme first. Norm would destroy anything I loved to stop me from talking. It created a secret well of words inside of me. They sat, piled up, waiting for me to find a way to release them.

If I forgot and began to speak, my stammer gave me time to catch the word and change it to something more innocent. My father watched me. He listened in case I spoke. I felt the dangerous words coming that might make him shoot my brother and then come for me. I felt the sounds and caught them in the stammer. The word then got lost in the stuck syllables.

I hated how I looked, struggling to speak. The kids mocked me, mimicking my stammer, making it worse. It took me ages to work out how my stammer saved me.

*

Outside of the house, I roamed free. I lost myself in the vibrant colours and rain and giant cacti and wild stray cats whom I tried to befriend. Darwin was glorious with its squawking birds, wide skies and sunrises that changed the world into a better place. A place I could imagine I had escaped to – a place where I would never be caught, where I could keep Graeme safe. That is what I lived for.

*

After nearly a year in Darwin, my father flew us to Broome – a more remote town. Here, he seemed to relax. He stopped threatening me. I found my mother because she needed me and I turned into her helpful shadow. Broome became an island paradise in the sea of anguish. I almost had a rest from my parents.

A year later, we crossed the country to Townsville and stayed a few weeks with my grandparents in Rowland Street, before moving into the house in Palmerston Street, Currajong, at the beginning of 1968. After the strict routine of our grandparents' house, we were back to the chaos of our parents.

Joan and Norm battled continuously. Sarah demanded to be taken back to Rowland Street and Joan agreed to it most weeks. It left Trevor, Graeme and me alone again. Our gang survived by escaping next door to a neighbour's house, where a boy similar in age to Trevor lived. They became best friends. We would have moved in if we could, to escape the swearing and crying and hitting.

Dreamy Graeme irritated Norm, who tried to bash it out of him. I did my best to protect Graeme but I couldn't be with him all the time.

One day Norm looked at me. I froze. I knew that look. It was assessing and measuring. He realised I was big enough. I was six years old.

My father came into my room that evening, wearing his dressing gown with nothing underneath. He shut the bedroom door and walked towards me. He pulled my cotton pyjamas off me and looked at my naked hairless skin. Then he pushed me down and forced his penis inside of me.

I was breaking.

Something died. I never moved. I didn't speak. I had no voice.

It was the beginning of a new routine.

My father was now the monster. I couldn't separate the two – the monster who visited me in the night.

When these memories surfaced with Lara, I needed to write them in my child's voice, my child self who desperately needed to speak, to say what he'd done. My six-year-old self wrote the following words, after my adult named them:

The Penis Monster: *big ones, little ones, ones that bite you in the night, sneak up on you from behind, to go bang and it goes dark and hairy and sweaty and wet sticky stuff dripping down my back, it's not mine this stuff, but it's me now, it comes to me in the night, I never know when, sneaking up on me and bang there it goes again.*

BANG and BANG and BANG and BANG and BANG and I go dark.

Father Monster: *pushing so hard, I hurt, deep in my heart, sometimes I see its face and it reminds me of someone long ago, but now it's the monster with grimacing sharp eyes, I'm stuck to my bed, sheets wrapped between my thighs to try and stop the monster, but no, my bed is now the monster's place where can I go? it doesn't matter the monster will always know.*

Sarah and I shared a room, with twin beds against opposite walls. She spent a lot of time at Rowland Street but came home for days at a time. One day, the monster came into our room when Sarah and I were playing. I don't know why he came in the light. I glanced at the monster to work out what he wanted.

He looked at my little sister, who was three. I was nearly seven. I went cold. She was now the age and size I was when he had taken me to the men. He realised it too. I couldn't let him have my sister. She was a gleaming star in my murky world.

The Monster and My Sister: *I saw the monster look at her and I knew what monster thoughts appeared to it that day I knew the monster it's not that we were friends, but I knew the monster in a way I'd seen it change from silly child monster to big and heavy and pain monster she can't* *have the big monster, not the pain and horror, she's so tiny, she'll get squashed her noisy chatter will get squashed and leave her, dripping down the bed she's my precious sister her laughter keeps me laughing it's the sparkle I see in her eyes and the demand I hear in her crying, that lets me know I'm still alive*

I stood up and against my will, I walked forward and took his hand, pulling him to my side of the room and onto my bed. I let him do what he wanted. Sarah escaped. I started watching out for her, too. She started spending most of her time with our grandparents. I don't think she ever knew.

The Monster Visits: *I die a little more inside each time I wake to find my sheets wet and twisted around my legs, the monster visited I know, it leaves a slimy trail I find it when I wake, down my legs one time it went to sleep in my bed, I lay stiff and still, careful least I touch it, which is difficult when it's lying on top of me it was hot having the monster stay on me I didn't know what to do, it should leave I need a tiny patch of dry to breathe but it didn't leave, I was drowning in the sea, a huge weight too hot and sticky drying wet, I couldn't breathe but it had to leave I die each time it visits, how will I be when it stays, sleeping on top of me?*

*

These memories came back in great chunks, leaving me reeling. I didn't know which way was up. I struggled to understand the feelings and sights repeatedly playing in my head. I came up for air then plunged back in again, into the remembered scenes, allowing them to swamp me.

*

The monster again threatened me with the gun.

The secrets left a terrible taste in my mouth. Terror wrapped through their unsaid sounds and became my way of life, knotting my tongue still. The scenes I was forced to not name silenced me. The monster smiled at my silence, nodding in approval.

But I was forced to speak by unseeing teachers and the speech therapist. It ripped my voice apart, stammering in an almost continuing stuck sound, not a single word formed, stammering against the truth.

The monster visited me almost every night. And then, when Joan was in the last trimester of her pregnancy, she went to the hospital to rest for the last months before giving birth. Sarah was living at Rowland Street with our grandparents, as she was too young to be left without Joan. It was the boys and me again, left alone in the house with the monster to fend for ourselves.

Now the monster didn't need to pretend or be careful. He could come and go into my room as he pleased. I was exhausted and often fell asleep on my desk at school.

In the daylight, I dissociated from the night before, forgetting the monster as I walked across the road to school. It was a packed-away system of escape where I created a barely functioning daylight child to keep me safe from the horrors of the night. My night-time child I cut off, shutting her away from me and disowning her pain. I lived this way in thorough separation from myself.

I was sitting at my desk in class when I looked down at my hand. One of the monster's curly black hairs was glued to my skin. I froze and then silently screamed as my wall of careful separation crumpled apart. He couldn't invade my days. Not the monster. He couldn't come to school.

I was forced back into the night-time horror and felt the pain and pressure and sweat and gunk. It tipped me over the edge as my night-time child collided with my daylight one. It caused my put-together self to break apart.

That afternoon, I sat on the floor in the kitchen with the banana leaves watching, the knife in my hand. I attempted to end it. But I failed. I failed at everything.

Chapter 21

Bullies

In Glasgow, nearly twenty years later, in 1988, I mourned for my little girl self – my eight-year-old. I mourned for her and held her close.

*

Lara's system worked in many ways, loosening the trauma held in my body. My posture changed and I began to stand up straight, with my chest less caved in. My lazy eye also corrected itself. My eyes drifting out of alignment was always worse when I was tired, like my stammer, but now I seemed stronger.

Lara mentioned that abused children sometimes have strabismus because they need to turn their eyes away from what is happening – an unconscious defence mechanism. Or it may have been caused by my low birth weight, or the years of head bashing. Who knows.

I slept with a sharp knife I'd bought from a specialist knife shop at the Barrows in Glasgow. It looked like the one the knifeman used. I couldn't fall asleep unless I held it in my hand. It helped. I felt in control of the blade when I pressed its edge to my skin.

Sometimes I felt I was going mad, the memories crazy in my head, caught in the past yet having to live in the present. I didn't have any proof of what had happened, only my memories. The knife was a solid presence to confirm it had. It made it real.

Ava was freaked, finding the knife difficult to deal with. She moved in as my rescuer and mothered me. I leaned on her, needing her care. Our relationship worked when I was dependent.

One night I was angry with Lara, expecting to fight. Instead, she said, 'I'm here for you. It's OK. You're going to have erratic moods. It's all part of the therapy, of working it out. You have trust issues too, so of course you don't trust me.'

'But I wwant to. The ww-week ww-waiting to see you is too long. I think I'm l-losing it. I'm t-t-terrified of being psy-psy-psychotic. Like w-what happened in P-Puri. What if you p-push me over the edge?'

'You have more control than most people. I'm not worried about you. If I was, I'd take your knife away. But I don't believe you will hurt yourself or anyone else.'

'Are you sure? I don't tr-trust myself.'

'Look, I'm amazed you've made it this far. You're a beautiful person. Do you realise that?'

'I'm a mmess. I'm on the edge all the t-time, wwwaiting to break. It's all still l-locked inside me. I can't g-get away from it.'

'So, permit yourself to be as shitty as you want. Let it out.' She grinned at me. She liked me when I was heightened.

I performed Lara's exercises, shouting my 'No'. It was the first time I felt it in my eyes as well as my voice. I was joining up.

'I'm amazed you could even have relationships with men,' Lara says. I fight her when she wants to hold my head and release the tension in my jaw, telling me to scream. I can't let go, not fully. It's still a game. I'm still trying to please her.

*

In 1988, I decided to visit Australia for the first time since I left in 1982. I wanted to ask my mother about the sexual abuse. My family had moved to the western suburbs of Sydney. I refused to even think about visiting my father, who still lived in Queensland.

When I told Joan about what I remembered, she dismissed me. 'You're lying. You know, you always used to lie to me, ever since you were a little girl. I could always tell when you were lying. You stuttered.'

I stared at my mother, shocked into silence. How could she think my stammer was because I was lying? I tried again. 'I'm n-not lying. My f-father really did do those th-things to me.'

'I refuse to talk to you about it.' Then she leaned in close to me and almost spat the words, 'He was horrible to me, you know. You never want to ask about that, do you? It's always about you. But what about how he treated me? He was a horrible man. But you never cared about me and how bad it was. Graeme was the only one who did and he's dead.'

The next day, I tried again. 'Can you re-remember very much about living in Cur-Currajong?' I was standing with my mother in the garage, going through my tea chest of belongings. 'About how N-Norm came into my rrroom? And what he did …'

My mother turned and looked at me. She stood still for a moment, then said, 'Of course I knew. I was happy he did it to you. It left me alone!'

I knew her words were true. More tumbled out in her rush to say them. 'Don't you understand? He always wanted sex. He never stopped wanting it. It gave me a break. I was tired. Why shouldn't he do it to you, too?'

My mother was winning, back in her old battle with me. She continued, 'The Currajong School sent a lady to the house to ask if anything was wrong. They were concerned but I told her you were stuttering because you were stupid. I said there was nothing wrong and sent her away.' She smirked at me, waiting for my response, but I had nothing.

I needed a mother to protect me, a mother who never was.

I persisted in asking her questions. 'What a-about the g-gun? Do you re-remember that?'

'Do you know about the gun? I thought he always kept it safe from you kids. When did you see it?'

'He used it against me in Dar-Darwin. He shoved it in my m-mouth. Then he threatened me with it.' I waited for a 'sorry' from my mother, but none came.

'It was Norm's from when he was a police constable in Townsville.' I'd found a moment when Joan wanted to piece the story together. 'He took it to Brisbane with him. Do you remember the special outings you had with your father? When he left me behind?' I nodded. 'He used to take it with him then.'

'Will you hh-help me sssort out the t-timeline?' She nodded. It was the first time she wanted to help and talk about what she knew.

Norm grew up in Islington in London, joined the British Navy as a Morse code operator and was stationed in the Coral Sea, off Townsville, on a British aircraft carrier during and after World War II. He stayed on in Townsville after the war, meeting Joan at a dance. He went back to

England but returned to marry her in 1955 when she was twenty-four and he was twenty-nine.

Soon after they were married, Norm told her no wife of his was working and stopped her dressmaking apprenticeship. When she had friends to visit, he set an alarm clock on the kitchen table between them, set to go off in an hour, at which point it was time for her friends to go. Norm joined the Queensland Police as a constable, and was later promoted to second in charge of the Townsville branch of North Queensland Police Radio Intelligence, before transferring to Brisbane.

I learned pieces of information but, overall, I was speaking when my family didn't want to listen. My grandparents brushed it aside, unable to comprehend what I was saying. I didn't want to burden my siblings with my memories. I escaped on a 7000-kilometre round bus trip to explore the country.

On my return to Sydney, I telephoned Ava. She said, in her beautiful Scottish lilt, 'My dearest wee one, life's nae the same. I miss ye passionately. I'm terrified ye think there's nothin' fur ye here and ye dinnae want tae come back … please come home. I adore ye.'

*

Ava was too uncertain to meet me at Glasgow Central Station when I returned, as this had been our first big separation. She'd holed up in our flat, waiting.

When I walked in through the front door Ava was standing in the hall. After a long hug, she said, 'I wasnae sure what ye would say … how ye would feel aboot livin' with me. I couldnae face ye in public.'

'It's OK sweetheart. I love you.' I kissed her softly and said, 'I w-want to live here, in Scotland. I w-want to be here, with you.'

*

I continued weekly therapy with Lara, joining up the inside me to my surface self. Pieces of memory still returned at odd moments. Lara suggested I do the four-year Gestalt training course, to speed up my therapy. She was one of the trainers. The course involved intensive weekends of group work.

The trainers thought they knew what was best for me and were quick to tell me. They, like Lara, wanted to bring out my aggression. The problem was I rarely felt aggressive. It was the terror that I needed to resolve. They couldn't grasp this.

I'd been young when my trauma started. I hadn't had time to form a self and had fragmented instead, being unsafe from the beginning. Safety was the basic issue I struggled with: being held and protected, and learning how to trust. I'd survived my mother, the men and my father by being compliant. Aggression would have gotten me killed.

Group work and being in any sort of group touched my family-of-origin issues because the patterns of the past were re-enacted in the present. With the pushing from the trainers and members of the group following their lead, I was feeling isolated, abandoned and criticised. All the issues from my childhood were being resurrected and played out.

In the first few years with Lara, I thought I'd found the mother I longed for. I projected my need onto her, desperate for her soft, nourishing touch. At first, she met me, holding me as I cried, telling me I was dealing with it all wonderfully. She called me special. But over time, she became frustrated with my traumatised childhood place, demanding this part of me grow up.

Lara, a trainer as well as my therapist, became angry when I stammered. She was now behaving like my mother – another bully. I didn't feel safe enough to be real. Ganged up on and trapped again, I became two people, with one forever locked inside just as I had when I was seven years old. My young one was distraught but more real, with the outer me only a frame – a pretence of a person trying to gain Lara's approval.

I had one friend in the group, Judith. She noticed my unease and sat next to me, putting her arms around me. She was what I needed. The others thought she was sharp and prickly when she lashed out with her tongue, but inside, she was the most understanding person I'd ever met. She saw me.

*

One afternoon, in a group training session, I became heightened when one of the men acted out his rage against me. It felt like his words were swords, thrust into my side. It took me back to the room with the knifeman, and I disassociated, leaving my body. The trainers were unaware. I drove home without being present. I wasn't in the car. I couldn't find me.

During my private session with Lara the following week, I attempted to tell her. In my nervousness, my stammer was worse.

She stopped me. 'Speak fluently! What are you avoiding? It's time you stopped this stammering nonsense. You're choosing to stay a child. You want to stay a victim, don't you?'

I lost any words, just as I had with my mother. Lara thought I stammered when I wanted to hide something, just like Joan, but my stammer was worse with words that I wanted to say but was scared of saying out loud. Those words, those naming words, were the hardest words for me to say.

Lara continued, 'You don't want to get better. Come on, speak properly.' She pushed, believing she could force the words out of me. But the more she forced, the worse my speech became.

'I-I-I c-c-c … a-ca …'

The simple ways of healing – listening, sitting still and sharing – were all seen as inadequate.

*

I was in my final year of acupuncture training. The course helped ground me. It gave me purpose, but any fluency deserted me there too, especially when I had to speak to powerful men, such as Professor JR Worsley.

JR, as he was affectionately known, had formed the Acupuncture College after learning from the Chinese Masters of Acupuncture, who fled China and the communist regime under Mao Zedong. He was teaching about the fire element. It was a rare event to hear him speak and the room was packed with students.

I sat near the front and dared to ask him a question. 'H-How d-does the heart pro-protector recover from tr-trauma?' What he'd been explaining was what I struggled with most: how to protect my heart yet open myself enough to risk loving. Most of my issues were centred around the fire element.

Instead of answering, he asked me, 'Where are you from? You're not English, are you?'

'I-I'm from TT-Town …' I couldn't get the naming word out, Townsville. I was stuck. The professor didn't see my upset or understand my stammer.

'Where are you from? I can't hear you. Speak up.' He demanded, smiling, thinking it was a joke. The fire element, after all, was the element of fun. Of joy. But I was frozen. He missed this completely.

I fragmented, losing myself. In a room overflowing with students, I couldn't get the word out. I got up, left the class and got the first train home. I was too ashamed. I would never be an acupuncturist. It was stupid of me to even dream. I would never be able to talk with my patients. Just give up. I refused to go back to the college and wrote telling them I was leaving.

My sense of self disintegrated. An imploding. Whenever I thought I was doing well, something would happen to knock me down. I couldn't trust myself and I broke apart. Lara termed this a deconstruction and said it was necessary. She demanded I stop being scared and get angry instead – find my sadism. She told me I was hanging on to my stammer. And that it was all my fault.

I've since learned that there is no cure for stammering – it's a lifelong condition – which is why I couldn't fix myself. It's made worse by stress and can only be managed, but at this time I was still blaming myself and buying into Lara's judgement.

I was struggling on multiple fronts: failing in therapy, as well as the Gestalt and acupuncture training. My lesbian friends were also finding me difficult to be around. I couldn't explain myself to them. I went out to dinner with other couples and smiled. Several people suggested I needed to forget the abuse and pretend it didn't happen. But I couldn't find the off button to put it behind me, as they suggested.

I wanted to shout at them, 'Do you think I'd be like this if I'd found the button to switch me off?'

They used this button when they'd had enough – when they got tired or bored, or their attention got caught on something else. I couldn't do that. In my waking minutes and my dreams, the smells and tastes and pressure of the men were in me, pressing tight, filling all of me.

It was the wedge that separated me from my friends: an undercurrent of watchfulness, a wariness of shadows and rooms, feelings of shame, of waiting and knowing the world as a place of invasion and suffocation and being alone.

No amount of talking soothed me. I began to wish my father had killed me. I trained at the gym daily to exhaust myself. My friends didn't understand the consequences of the complex trauma my body had attempted to forget but now remembered. I needed to understand this mess to be free.

Ava was struggling. She wanted my father out of our bed as abusive memories often inundated me when we touched. Attempts at intimacy left me cut off from my feelings because I had to shut them down to be close. I was scared to be truthful yet frustrated I couldn't be real. I felt dirty – the men's forms and the knife constantly inside me, my mouth, my vagina. I couldn't escape the memories. It was an ongoing torment of never-ending invasion.

*

The Acupuncture College asked me to return. They said sorry. It had been a mistake to put me on the spot. I was a good student and it was OK if I stammered. We all have flaws. They quoted the idea of the wounded healer and said they believed in me. Their kind words helped and I returned to class. With their compassion and understanding, I completed the training. While I often stammered with my practice clients, I saw that my patients related to me. My vulnerability allowed them their own.

I was surprised to receive the College's special award on graduation: the Twigg Nixon Award Citation, 'For overcoming adversity and excelling in the training. And doing so with humility and dedication to the spirit of this system of medicine.'

It settled the raw place inside: the shattered part that believed my flawed self was too damaged to ever be any good.

*

By chance, I heard a talk on the radio. Joan Woodward was speaking about how she'd spent her life trying to be more than only a half, having lost her twin. She used the same words I used to describe myself. She had completed the first major study into twin bereavement and loss, presenting it to the International Congress of Twin Studies in Amsterdam in 1986, which published her work. She'd coined the term 'the lone twin' and wanted to set up a network for lone twins.

I went to one of the first meetings she organised in England. I held Graeme close, hugging my left arm. Eighty-six of us sat in circles in a room, all lone twins, all only halves. I felt Graeme's grin. Joan used John Bowlby's attachment theory to explain the trauma of losing a twin and wanted to publish a book of lone twins recounting their loss. I sent her my story and it was published in her book, *The Lone Twin*.

A reporter I knew also published my story in *The Herald*, a Scottish newspaper. I needed the publicity to set up a Scottish branch of the Lone Twin Network.

Joan's work validated my memories of communicating with Graeme in the womb because scans now showed twins interacting with each other before birth. She wrote about mothers who form a strong attachment with one twin and not the other, and how this leaves the other twin with the only choice of accessing the necessary attachment to the mother via the attached twin.

She said this is what occurs when the mother values a boy twin at the expense of the girl. The girl twin is only able to find herself via her brother – exactly my experience. Her words reached in to confirm a truth I'd always known.

*

In December 1988, Ava and I went with other women from the United Kingdom to Belfast to join a women's peace march through the streets of the city. It was another attempt by Northern Ireland women to stop the continuing violence between unionists or loyalists, who were mainly Protestant, and nationalists or republicans, who were mainly Catholic. The women were taking action and saying they'd had enough: enough of their sons dying and of plastic bullets destroying their families.

We stayed with a family in a Catholic area of the city. On the first night, I was walking on the Catholic side of one of the streets that marked the boundary line, with a woman from London. A white-skinned man on the Protestant side of the road ran across to stand squarely in front of us, pulling out a handgun and pointing it in my companion's face.

He said, 'I shoot black cunts like you.'

On hearing those words, a near-perfect copy of what the paedophiles had said, I reacted without thinking, stepping in front of the woman.

'Then you'll have to shoot me first,' I said to the man.

I stared him in the face, the gun now in front of my eyes, familiar, remembering my father's gun and how the barrel had tasted in my mouth. But here, at this moment, I could separate the two. This gun wasn't in my mouth. I could do this, protect this woman when I hadn't been able to protect the little girl.

I was silent and steady, still, waiting to see what he would do. Staring into his eyes. After another long moment of waiting, he laughed, turned and walked to his side of the street. As if he'd won. But he hadn't. I had. I'd chased down my past. Found my voice and my feet.

I'd stood up to a threatening man with a gun.

The woman was shaking. I took her hand, and we walked back to the house.

Chapter 22

Saying no

'I'd li-like to explore my gr-grief around Gr-Gr-Graeme. I still mmiss him,' I said to Lara when I arrived for my next therapy session.

'How long has it been now?' Lara asked me.

'NNine years …'

'Don't you think you should be over this by now? It's time you let him go. You're doing the same as you are with the abuse, and holding on to it. You're playing the victim.'

Lara didn't understand, but I couldn't tell her that.

'Stand up and say you're glad Graeme is dead.'

'What? No…'

'He is dead to allow you to live. There wasn't enough life energy for the two of you to survive. He had to die.' Lara stated it, believing her own words.

I stood in front of her, shaking my head. She'd crossed a line.

'You're wrong,' I told Lara. I was finally able to stand up to her. I could fight for Graeme when I couldn't protect myself.

But she was correct about me – I was playing the victim, but I was playing it with her. I allowed her to bully me. I'd wanted Lara to be the mother I'd always longed for, but ended up re-enacting the same submissive patterns of being with my mother with her. In that moment, I grew up and took responsibility for my actions. I saw how I gave my power away.

I'd needed to learn how to stand up for myself, to say enough. Enough of the abuse in what was supposed to be therapy. I told Lara she was abusive, but she refused to listen and became angry instead. I told her I'd had enough of her bullying behaviour, and left both her and the Gestalt training. I said no for the first time to the misuse of power. It was exhilarating.

When I said no, I built another cornerstone for the person I was becoming. Assertiveness joined curiosity as stones of my being. I felt open and aware, speaking calmly as I stammered. I needed to understand my trauma, not blame or stay in anger. Those were Lara's systems. I wanted to go to places Lara herself had not explored.

Lara should have applauded me. I was doing what therapy was meant to allow: personal empowerment. Instead, I was criticised by the Gestalt trainers and ostracised from the friendship groups I thought I'd found. They refused to deal with the issues I raised regarding the misuse of power within their organisation. But I didn't need their approval – I was finding my own.

In 1990, I enrolled in a writing course. I needed to write about my struggles – with Lara, my parents and the men, but my first words described the spaces.

> *Tightness at my temples, screws winding their way in, bulges at each end. But I'm oblong. No longer. I mimic the eternal egg timer. Who's*

going to turn me over? I've been walking on my head forever. The pounding, rhythmically pushing, winching me in.

The hooks press deep into my skull – fine twin pieces of straining metal. The only way to escape – go deeper, I find my spaces and tuck myself safely under the crevices. Let them have my flesh, my body of steel overhangs, protrusions of roundness and holes. It's yours. Turn me over when you're finished. I'll wait forever, the sands falling through, relentless. I can wait forever, waiting in the spaces.

I then wrote about my experience of therapy. My words came out as poems, short sharp lines naming various scenes. I attended a week-long intensive workshop with Liz Lochhead and Roger McGough at Moniack Mhor, Scotland's Creative Writing Centre. They encouraged my writing and Liz helped me edit and refine my book of poetry. I sent it to a publisher. He asked for the story in between the poems, but it was too early to find those words.

*

I'd heard about other clients of the Scottish Gestalt system who had been abused in therapy. The television station Channel Four made a documentary recounting the stories of several who were left damaged. One of the people speaking up was Kay, who'd followed a similar path to me, being a client and then doing the Gestalt training. Kay worked with the survivors of those abused in therapy and I started with her. She was gentle, encouraging and centred in her heart.

Kay and I unpacked the last half dozen years, undoing the damage done by Lara and the other trainers. We reframed it. My biggest breakthrough was learning about my victim place. I fell into the victim whenever the world became too much. Lara had tried to force it out of me, but the more she'd forced the more victimised I'd felt.

I often woke up after weeks of being blanked out and dissociated; this was still my main survival mechanism. In the early days, I was present about one week in four – the other three passing in a blur. But I now became more present, disassociating less and less until I could catch it happening. I learned how to ground myself and come back. I'd spent years blaming dissociation for the wrongs in my life, but now I could honour it. It had allowed me to escape when I couldn't leave the room. It had provided my only chance of getting out alive.

Kay sat with me, curious, waiting. It was always in my time. She listened to any words I might find. When none came, we sat together in silence. Her presence allowed me to trust my own. When I stammered, she named my stammer as my saviour. She suggested it grew from a disability to a protective mechanism – to keep me safe from naming what my father was doing. It allowed me time to catch any words that might be escaping – catch them in the stammering sounds before they were fully formed, and stop that dangerous one from spilling out. To stop my father from carrying out his real threat of killing me and my twin brother.

Kay suggested that I listen to my stammer when it happened. That I was stammering in reaction to some underlying trauma trigger, so I shouldn't force it but become inquisitive. It was the beginning of a friendlier relationship with my voice – one of interest amidst the panic and shame. My stammer was my ally, not the bane of my life. It was my early warning system of approaching danger.

We explored my scary places, my real victim, dropping into the horror and abandonment. We worked through the subtle layers, into the bottomless well of powerlessness … of being a little girl in a room full of men. I allowed my terror of the bossman to surface, to feel how he held my life or death in his hands. How he held my nose shut, how I couldn't breathe and had to drink in the fluids of the men.

I remembered the little girl being killed in front of me, lots of fine details, the scenes filling in: the men, my father, my mother. I felt my little girl in me and I grieved for her and the other children. I made friends with this place of utter powerlessness.

Centred in it was strength: a flexible strength like bamboo that didn't break. It leaned with the wind, allowing me to adapt and survive the men. I didn't have to defend against it or run from it. For most of my life, I'd been living above it in its casing of brittle strength, which often cracked, leaving me in pieces.

For the first time, I appreciated my helplessness as a strength. A pure, peaceful, settled, quiet, constant strength. All these words were like round, perfect stones deep within me, as I claimed this place and called it mine. The heavy comforting stones dropped into the lake of my being, to settle on the bottom. They formed a solid foundation between my first two cornerstones: curiosity and assertiveness.

I was learning to navigate the roadmap of my being. It was now my home. I found my belly. I found my heart. I found my way in and stopped running away because I now had an alternative to offer my victim place. The victim – the trauma place – and absolute quiet still presence. We became friends.

My task had been to understand my suffering. I had been submerged in it, overpowered by the suffering itself. Now, with these new thoughts, my suffering bore wings and I could bear it willingly, free of the despair. With this fundamental shift in my attitude, life was no longer about waiting for someone to save me, but what I could offer to life itself.

This sensitive monitoring of my power became my purpose. I'd found my meaning. I drew a line in the sand and stepped in front of it – to guard against the misuse of power in all its forms.

I now knew what my job was. If meaning needed to be found in life, then meaning needed to be found in the suffering of life itself. Purpose out of suffering, the gold, the alchemy of life.

My little girl inside was a victim. I didn't need to force her out, as Lara had suggested. If I did, I was repeating the pattern of force on myself – the one I had swallowed down when I swallowed the fluids of the men. Internalising their system of abuse made my mind my worst enemy and left me hating myself.

Instead, I reached out to my little girl place and held her safe in my arms in the present. The lack of mothering was a gaping hole where a mother should be. It needed to be met when I was a child and therefore went unfilled, but in the present, I was doing it differently. I embraced my wounded self, keeping her safe for the first time.

She now had me and was no longer alone. Together, we became a team. I mothered her in the way she longed for. I knew what she needed because she was me. I offered it to myself and stopped being dependent.

When I learned how to mother and love my most distressing of places, it set me free. I could catch the disconnect, the old pattern of thoughts rising, and replace them with this new pattern, of these allowing thoughts. I was aware of my underlying need and could tolerate the pain.

With Kay's gentleness and patience, I continued learning how to listen. And in my growing trust in myself, I began to spot a way through the pain itself. I found my healing.

I didn't need to throw my learning about the therapies away. I could say no to the abuse and keep the magic of different techniques. Chair work, for example – the technique Henry had originally done with me, planting the seed for further therapy. Henry had used it differently from Lara. The varying styles of therapy offer frameworks and methods to understand and work with trauma. It's our own bias or blind spots, our unresolved issues, that influence how we use the techniques and behave with other people.

Lara didn't trust me to find my way. She assumed she knew best and wouldn't let me influence her. She refused to reflect on her issues, even when I named them, blaming me instead. This is how she misused her power, by believing she was right and I was wrong. This was her defensive system to avoid dropping into her place of helplessness. She couldn't take me to places she hadn't gone.

At these moments she bullied me into submission until I said no and could hold my ground, but it destroyed our relationship. I couldn't trust her. She wasn't safe.

It's wonderful working it out. It taught me respect for my clients when I started working as an acupuncturist and massage therapist, and later as a counsellor. I'm continually aware of this: the dependency, and the difference between the person asking for help and the person helping.

It's a theme of my life and what I work with every day – this line of power. And holding the other person sacred – trusting them to find their knowing place with my support.

I'm still standing in front of the line I drew in the sand.

Chapter 23

Trusting my knowing place

In 1991, I returned for another visit to my family in Australia, this time empowered. I knew my mother was narcissistic, having worked this out with Kay. It helped explain how Joan could first deny knowing about an event and then later say she knew all along – because she picked what would hurt me the most.

I went on a road trip to western New South Wales to see a relative I'd known as a child. She stood in the harsh sun of the morning at her clothesline behind her home, pegging out her washing.

'C-C-Can we t-talk about Cur-Currajong? What do you rremember from that t-time?' I asked her.

'Can you shut up about that! Just shut up about your childhood. I'm fed up with you going on and on. Just put your head in the sand like everyone else. Forget about it, for fuck's sake. I don't want to know.'

I left and lost myself in the outback, the wide-open skies, the heat. I watched the cockatoos soar, a white wheeling mass of flapping wings with flashes of yellow. They screeched, reminding me, 'Remember, you have escaped.'

I filled myself up with the land, the rocks and the dirt, allowing it to settle within my bones. It dried out the damp, lush green of Scotland. I now had two lands to hold me. I claimed them both and returned to the faded colours of the Scots, the mist and the rain.

From Scotland, I sent Joan a series of letters asking her questions. She replied, 'I'm not happy, it's over twenty years ago. It upsets me terribly to remember these things. I'd rather forget.' Another time she wrote, 'I must put a stop to all this nonsense, it's all in the past. You were never neglected. It's a shame you had to wait until now to tell me.'

When I asked about the paedophile gang, she replied:

> *It's knocked me around terribly, the shock of your letter. You chose not to tell me all those years ago. I know you and I were having the same terrible life and he used me as often as he used you. I too was planning to end my life. I often took 2 or 3 boxes of Bex a day. I wanted to go to sleep. You and Trevor never treated me well, not like Graeme did. I always felt like I was a good mother but I must have let you down somewhere along the way.*

This was the only apology I got. I couldn't pierce her heart. I couldn't get in.

*

I didn't need Ava to save me anymore. I was growing and I wanted her to grow with me. Secure in my gay identity, I wanted to walk the streets of Glasgow out as a lesbian, but Ava wasn't comfortable and refused to take my hand in public.

We had been happy for many years. She'd provided stability, with space and time for learning new skills as I set myself up in private practice. She said she loved me, but repairs on her car or going to the gym always seemed to come first. She'd restored an MGB Roadster from scratch and it took all her earnings. I wanted her to travel with me, but money was always scarce.

I started pushing, demanding we go on holiday. Ava kept promising then putting me off. I was tired of waiting. I needed time with her where the sun shone and I could swim in the sea. Did she love me or need me to need her? I started confronting the rescuer system we were stuck in. The tension had to give. I didn't want to be a victim or dependent on her.

Ava withdrew but it fed my sense of isolation. She didn't get me. I started sleeping with other women to find what I needed. This high-risk behaviour woke me and I felt alive. It held a flavour of what I'd been seeking in Puri, but this time I understood it.

My sense of self hadn't developed normally and I didn't know how to bond healthily with others. Buried at the core of my self was this need for connection. It had to do with my twin but it was also a consequence of the sexual abuse itself. The times I'd connected were when I was under threat and in a hyper-aroused state. I was confusing this with feeling alive, as this was the only time when I could feel myself and the other.

I didn't live the motto: I think therefore I am. For me, it was: I feel therefore I am. But this could only be accessed when I was under threat or acting out in risky behaviour – then I could exist. When I did this, I found a sense of the other.

Ava found out about the other women. We managed to come back together and I shut myself down again, finding my self-controlled adult part. It was a relief, as the wild affairs scared me and left me feeling ungrounded. We moved to a small village north of Glasgow, making a new start, mixing with well-established couples and having a mortgage of our own. It was an external change that cemented over the cracks in our relationship.

I found hurt wildlife on the road as I commuted to and from Glasgow. In the back green we built a run for the hedgehogs, who hibernated there over the winter months. During the warmer weather, they joined our cats in front of the coal fire in the kitchen – a bundle of fur and spikes, their wounds healing. We released them back into the wild.

Ava came home one day with a chinchilla that was too old for breeding. We named her Ruby for her beautiful eyes. She was the softest thing I'd ever touched. She needed a metal pen as she chewed continuously, needing to wear down her growing teeth. When we released her for a run in the front room, we found splintered bits of skirting board.

Ruby loved perching on my shoulder and nibbling my ear, content to ride around as I walked between rooms. One day, she chewed through one of the electrical wires I'd tried to hide from her. Her fast-beating heart stopped. I breathed into her mouth, laid her on one hand and did heart compressions on her chest with two fingers. After long minutes, she twitched, lifted her head and started moving.

I gave silent thanks for my training as a nurse. Every life, even one as small as Ruby's, was worth fighting for.

*

A sign in a shop window advertised windsurfing lessons at Loch Lomond. I missed the sea desperately, and this seemed like the next best thing. I invested in a 5-mm-thick wetsuit and joined the beginners' class, watching in astonishment as the trainer, Ian, displayed his skill as a windsurfer. I wanted his ease on the freezing water and spent the weekends learning. I quickly became hooked by the speed of sailing close to the wind, finding the line where the board lifted and started planing over the water. The camaraderie with the guys reminded me of my brothers, of our little gang. I missed the easy friendship with males. It woke something in me.

I dreamed about having sex with a man and woke up horrified but curious. I explored it with Kay. For two years I'd been working with her to understand my relationship with Ava and knew I should leave, but I kept avoiding it.

My previous trauma was still taking me by surprise with sudden flashes of crystal-clear scenes. I remembered fine details that transported me to distant rooms – the men in front of me once more. Then my father's hands were on my shoulders forcing me down. I'd need to carefully separate the present from the past. Ground myself, feel the wind, my feet, breathe. Come back.

My senses betrayed me though. A smell or touch would set me off – its suddenness, overwhelming. It was different from memories. When I was caught unaware, I lost contact with the present. I wasn't seeing flashes of the room. Instead, I was in the room. The man was pinning me down. I never knew when it would happen.

Sometimes the two would set each other off – memories and being in the past. I couldn't sort them out or stop them from coming. I lived this hidden struggle while getting on with life. Some days, I used the excuse of swimming pool chlorine to explain my red-rimmed eyes to my clients.

I approached a group of lawyers who wanted to support adults going through the legal system who'd been abused as children. I asked if they'd work with me, a foreigner. They said yes, but nothing came of it.

I imagined how JT Edson would have written it. He'd have found justice, with an estimate of damage and a price put on my father's head, like old-fashioned bounty hunting. If the cops or sheriff didn't get him, someone else was sure to shoot him dead, dragging his body in to clutter up the floor and claim the bounty. Sweet revenge for my seven-year-old self, seeing him stiffen, blood money for a stranger, his death my prize.

I was dreaming of this outcome at thirty-one, longing for Dusty Fog to hear and come galloping, with Mark Counter and the Ysabel Kid close behind.

*

Ian told me about another windsurfing week he was planning to run on Tiree, in October 1993. I'd loved the first, a year before. Tiree was a windswept island four hours' ferry ride west of Oban, the most westerly island in the Inner Hebrides of Scotland. I invested in new second-hand sails, one of which was child-size. The year before my sail had caught too much wind coming in from the Atlantic and overpowered me. This time I was going prepared.

We packed our gear into a trailer and climbed into the minibus to drive to Oban. I'd seen a white Honda pull up with a stranger who joined us. He sat in the seat behind me and started chatting, introducing himself as Cameron. His brother, who sat beside him, I knew from the year before. Both gingers. Cameron had decided to come at the last minute, driving up from England where he lived and worked.

The ferry ride was stunning, the view of Tiree growing as we pulled into the main harbour of the low-lying island. It was ideal for windsurfing, as no matter which way the wind was blowing, we could still find a bay with an onshore wind so we wouldn't be blown out to sea. We settled into the Outdoor Adventure Lodge.

The wind came up, a force eight gale – perfect to try out my new baby sail. I rigged up and went out with Ian while most of the group stayed warm in the van. Thrashed by the wind, I spent most of the time trying to stop the sail from being ripped from my hands, finding the odd exhilarating run. Cameron told me later I had balls. Praise indeed from a man.

I ran a class on the pier before breakfast – a mix of Tai Chi and stretches, energy work. A bit weird, the guys said, but they felt the difference. I was aware of Cameron and looked for him at breakfast. I tried to chat with him after dinner, angling for a seat beside him, enjoying his voice and his calm ways, especially his hazel eyes. They were greener in the morning's sharp light, changing as the clouds swept in, with rings of brown through the green, then glints of gold as the late afternoon sun showed its face. He didn't draw attention to himself, but I noticed he was the person who jumped out of the van to open and close the gates, often taking care of the equipment and cleaning up.

On the last night, I went to the pub with the group. We played pool and joked until I nearly wet my pants, high on laughter and sparkling water. One of the men surfed the van home, balancing on the roof and then falling into the ditch when it stopped. He was unhurt.

Back at the lodge, Cameron walked away into the gloom and the wind to the end of the pier. I stood, watching him. I knew something important was happening. It tugged in my belly. I needed to listen. I could let it pass and regret it, or I could step up and grab it. I decided to grab it.

I approached Cameron as he came back. He was drunk but not too much, the cold sobering him slightly, enough that we could talk. We stood in the dark on the shore next to the pier and spoke for hours, my hands in his pockets to stay warm. Our first real conversation. Intimate. It confirmed the feeling I had. This man was important.

We shared a brief kiss on the stairs, a fleeting meeting of lips. I wanted more. The next morning we packed up and left the island. Cameron found me. Sitting close together in the minibus, we created a warm bubble of semi-privacy and talked the entire ride back, filling in the pieces of our lives. I told him I lived with a woman. He said he didn't know if he'd ever met a lesbian before. He had a girlfriend but wanted to break up with her.

We left each other at Milngavie. He drove away after giving me his number. I felt the emptiness where I already wanted him to be. I knew I had to be the one to pursue it. If I left it to him, nothing would happen.

When I went home, I told Ava I'd met someone – a man. I didn't know if anything would happen, but I wanted to explore it. I was sorry but our relationship had been over for some time. Whatever happened with Cameron, I knew I had to leave Ava. I'd been with her for ten years. She'd given me love when I had nowhere else to go. I'd grown up with her and found my love for Scotland. I wanted to stay friends and pleaded with her, but she couldn't. She hadn't seen it coming.

I shook my head, confused. How could she not? The signs of struggle had been there and I'd been asking her to work with me. Maybe if I'd said I'd fallen for another woman it might have been different, but to say it was a man was too much of a betrayal.

I said goodbye to the cats and Ruby and moved into a bedsit across the park from my work. In the meantime, I'd telephoned Cameron and arranged a visit. He'd split up with his girlfriend, too. I needed to see him and check he was real.

He was who I remembered and more.

It was strange to lie next to a man, to have him get up and leave me in his bed as he went to work, leaving me with instructions on how to make the Italian red sauce for dinner, making sure I didn't skimp on the olive oil.

I had the house to myself. It had a big, old-fashioned bathtub, standing alone in the bathroom, no shower. The spaces were single male with no frills but lots of plants and cookbooks leaning together in the kitchen. The semi-detached dwelling was roughly finished, the fraying carpet not meeting the edges of the room, and the long narrow yard was overgrown at the back.

It was another beginning. I trusted this knowing. Over the next six months, as we took turns driving the five-plus hours up or down the country, our relationship grew, becoming a solid presence I carried in my heart. The days in between I spent waiting to see him, to hold him, to touch his skin and look into his eyes. I wanted to be with this man, and desperately missed him when he had to leave. I found it difficult to separate when I had to drive back to Glasgow. I watched for his letters – long pages of loving words, sharing his life in between our meetings.

My lesbian friends disowned me. My identity from the moment I arrived in Scotland had been built on being a dyke. I'd been delighted to flaunt it – the marginalisation satisfying a need in me. I didn't want to belong to mainstream society, but now I was plunged back into heterosexual contact when I turned up with a man at my side. I wasn't heterosexual – I was still a dyke. A dyke who had fallen in love with a man.

I fell in love with a person, not a sex. I cried out my confusion with Bernard, the acupuncturist whose house I worked from. Not knowing where I belonged, Judith, my friend from Gestalt, told me to trust myself. With Kay, I once again started doing the painstaking work of dismantling and putting myself back together into this new shape – a shape I felt distant from. I wasn't what other people assumed. I wasn't straight.

Cameron accepted me and I could be myself. He joked as we walked the streets; it wasn't men he was nervous of, but women catching my eye. He read the poems I'd written. He cried, shocked, unable to comprehend the agony, happy to let me talk as he listened, holding me close. The words slowed. I'd talked my way into the present. To him. Words eased, stopping, leaving a comfortable loving silence.

I needed to do relationships differently – to be honest outside and in. We decided not to bottle anything. Cameron knew he avoided conflict but, with my ability to talk through most things, we made this openness part of our bond. It worked. Cameron didn't play the drama cycle. He didn't move in as my rescuer but let me be, trusting me to sort it out myself. I struggled with this as it was too abrupt a change, even as I recognised it was good for me. It forced me to grow up some more. I needed to take responsibility for my actions, to find my voice and ask for what I wanted.

When he first pushed inside of me, I went still. I couldn't feel him, his weight pressing on my hips, rocking to a rhythm I should know. I tried to match him but found instead I was watching us from across the room. When he slowed and slipped out to lie by my side, the child in me remembered and looked at him confused. I wasn't hurting.

I talked it through and let him close, trusting him to stop if I was scared. He respected my pace. I settled into knowing this man was for me. I wanted it all: marriage and commitment. I was thirty-two and didn't want to wait for Cameron to ask me to marry him. One night, when I was talking with him on the telephone, I said, 'Will you marry me?'

After a moment's pause, Cameron said, 'Yes!' He loved that I took the lead.

Cameron returned to Scotland after a decade of working in England. He found a job in Dundee, where we rented a flat and moved in together.

He introduced me to his parents, who I hoped would be the parents I longed for. I invested in trying to please them.

His mother was horrified we'd allowed six weeks to organise our wedding – a simple, straightforward affair. I opted for a soft, fawn wool dress that I already had, and tan boots. A fine piece of cream lace was draped around my head and shoulders. Cameron's mother helped me pin it into place the morning of the wedding. Cameron wore his kilt – the ancient Buchanan tartan – long, knitted wool socks, a sporran and a heather-green jacket. We celebrated with our wedding party, drinking champagne in the wind on St Andrews Beach.

Cameron and I had fun, honeymooning in Israel, driving through Germany, skiing in France with his mates, windsurfing and trying to surf on the small waves of the North Sea. Life was lightening, silliness stepping in, smiling. We bought our first home as a married couple – the ground floor of an old sandstone house across from Balgay Park in the middle of Dundee. I fell pregnant and arranged a water birth at Ninewells Hospital. I was thirty-five.

I screamed so loudly with the pain of labour that a midwife came in to tell me to quieten down. I was scaring the other women. I found out later the pain relief gas had run out and I was sucking air. The room was now a flood of water as I moved with the contractions, creating waves that splashed over the rim of the pool. Towards the end of the long labour, I was told to leave the pool. I lay on the bed, my body now heavy with gravity. The final pushing nearly defeated me, but in the end, we had a little boy.

Within two years, I had a little girl. Another water birth. Her birth was easier as my body was stretched. I warned the midwife the baby was coming but she didn't believe me, telling me it was too soon. I was able to stay in the pool. This time, I floated in the water until I felt my baby rush out of me. Standing up, I caught her slippery form and brought her to my chest, sliding back into the pool and holding her close.

Cameron and I were in and out of the hospital in four hours, home for lunch and to introduce our little girl to her brother. She gave him a brilliant train set. He was happy to have a sister who gave him such wonderful presents and played with nothing else for the next six weeks.

I was content. I had my family.

But I questioned myself in the anxious moments before sleep and when I woke in the night.

Could I be a good mother after experiencing the mothering I'd had?

Chapter 24

My words are round perfect stones

To imagine myself as a mother was terrifying. I bought numerous childrearing books and ploughed my way through them, visiting the girlfriends and wives of Cameron's workmates who were expecting or already had a little one. I invited myself into their lives, watching what they did. I could do nothing else but be a full-time mother because I didn't trust myself.

Cameron was steady and fell easily into being a dad. He loved his new role and was protective of me, but I needed more. I struggled with breastfeeding and suffered from post-natal depression. I was good at pretending and the visiting midwives didn't pick it up. What saved me was that Cameron worked close to home. I regularly phoned him, at least two or three times a week, telling him he had to come home now – I wasn't coping. It was too frightening, this new life.

I slowly settled and learned to walk away for a few minutes when it became too much – to put my son in his pram and go for long walks through the park. I worked at making friends with new mothers in the area, joining playgroups and continuing to watch what the women did, copying their actions. I noticed how relaxed they were, how unbothered. I attempted to be the same.

I could feel my mother in me – a false presence. I could feel her rise, especially if I was tired and alone in the house when I first had my son.

Those times were scary because that was when Joan had been her worst. I could feel her straining to get free in my hands, to act out as she had. It would be easy to let loose. I imagined my face getting angry, contorting into shapes I remembered on her, seeing her tongue clenched between her teeth in her rage.

I remembered being on the receiving end of her look, her hands hurting and pinching and holding me too tight. Throwing me through the air.

No. I refused. I wasn't her. I wasn't going to do what my mother did: blame my child. I fought with myself, hating myself. I hated that I wasn't like the other mothers, who were joyful, easy and relaxed. I struggled to find myself in the mass of her.

It gradually dawned on me that I didn't need to act out my frustration and tiredness. I could be exhausted and upset and stop before the line that Joan had crossed. I could do it differently. Be gentle. Soften my hands. I surprised myself.

I could feel angry and know it would pass. Frustration I could use up by doing exercise. I had choices I could make, different from those of my mother.

I wasn't my mother.

I fell in love with my son once I could trust myself.

*

This learning was strengthened after my daughter was born. I knew how to do it. I loved having a little girl and a chance to mother her differently. I promised her I was breaking this message passed through generations of women in my family. Girls were not going to be bad. I consciously worked at welcoming, loving and appreciating her.

I made it through those scary early years, reliving my trauma when my children hit the ages I had been. When I passed each of those dates I relaxed, my confidence growing. *I can do this.*

The worst was when my son hit eighteen – Graeme's age when he'd been killed. I was on edge the entire year, waiting for something bad to happen, but it too passed.

I was intense because, for me, mothering was serious work. I couldn't take my actions for granted. I learned about the British paediatrician and psychoanalyst DW Winnicott and read his famous book, *Home Is Where We Start From*. I hoped I was one of those good-enough mothers he wrote about.

Having children brought out the best and worst in me. I wasn't a bad person, though my behaviour wasn't good enough at times, but I learned to be gentle. It gave me hope.

In this small way I was changing my world – the waves of caring rippling out, like when a rock is thrown into a pond and the ripples find the surrounding shore. The water touches the grains of dirt and sand, washing them clean. My choices to do it differently, to be kind and take responsibility, were calming my fears and self-doubt. Another cornerstone to add to my foundation.

Cameron was the play master in our house. He knew how to laugh, the kids giggling in his arms. It warmed my heart to see them together but I felt separate, lacking, alone. I didn't know how to play or join in.

I suffered from severe premenstrual tension. I put a provisional driver's red P plate sign on the fridge each month, to help warn Cameron we were entering a difficult week. He needed to be careful and express his appreciation for all I tried to do. I needed his words, like the food I swallowed down, to fill the empty pit inside of me, to settle the constant questioning of whether I was good enough. With his love and reassurance, it too eased.

*

Events hadn't worked out so well with Cameron's mum and dad. The first occasion I met his parents was Hogmanay in 1993, when I watched his father flirt with women on the dancefloor as he downed straight whiskies.

Horrified, I turned to Cameron, who said, 'He's always like this.'

'Does anyone tr-try and ss-stop him?'

Cameron just shrugged, then said, 'Mum pretends it isn't happening.'

On family visits thereafter, the man often drank until he couldn't stand. The drunker he got, the more sexual and obnoxious he became, his wife mopping his chin and eventually putting him to bed.

They were doting grandparents though, so when I was pregnant with our daughter, I suggested I stay with them while Cameron went for a week skiing with his brother in France. He left and I settled into a week with his parents.

On the first night his mother was absent, working at an event at an old people's home, leaving her husband unsupervised. He'd taken the opportunity to escape to the local pub and indulge in an extended session of drinking. He arrived back at the house in the afternoon, stumbling and slurring his words. He attempted to sit on the sofa but fell off.

I'd never been alone with Cameron's father. We were in new territory – one he took advantage of. He struggled upright, then demanded, 'I'm gonnae bathe ma grandson.'

'No, it's al-already d-done.' I stood up, my son in my arms.

'Naw, am gonnae do it.' He reached for my son. I stepped back, retreating into the kitchen. He followed me.

'Yer aff yer heid! He's ma grandson! Give him here.'

'He's already b-bathed and re-ready for b-bed. Can't you see?' I appealed to reason.

Cameron's father stopped, wobbled a bit on his feet, and then peered at my son. His face changed when he looked back at me.

He leaned closer and said, 'Cameron's probably in bed with some French whore by now. Enjoyin' himself.' He leered at me, watching to see my reaction. He made a grab for me, rather than my son. I stepped around his hands and locked myself and my child in the sunroom.

He banged on the glass door, shouting and swearing. He was furious that I wouldn't let him in. It went on and on. I waited for hours, until it was quiet, before I crept out. He'd passed out on the sofa in the front room. I thought about what I was going to do.

The next morning, I went for a long walk through the village, making sure of my decision and trying to guess the consequences. I wasn't going to swallow my words and be silent. I refused to pretend and play happy families. Those days were gone. I returned to the house and asked to speak to both of Cameron's parents.

They stood in front of me, side by side, in the kitchen.

I told them what had happened the night before. What he had done. How he had acted and how scared I'd been. I said it simply, not blaming. Within moments of me finishing, Cameron's mother stepped in front of her husband, protecting him, as if I was going to physically attack.

She said, 'He's nice when he's sober, but he's even nicer when he's had a drink.' She then told me, 'You're making it up. He wouldn't behave like that.'

Cameron's father stepped up to her side, red-faced and angry. 'Yer heid's fu' o' mince! How dare yer make somethin' like that up! Accuse me of such things. Yer disgustin'!'

'I'm not ly-lying. It hh-happened just as I said. You were dr-drunk and sssexual. Why w-won't you be-believe me?' I appealed to Cameron's mother but she was having none of it.

They refused to listen, closing ranks instead. I stood silently in front of them, remembering my mother. Her doing exactly what Cameron's mother was doing when I'd first tried to tell her what my father had done. My mother later contradicted herself by saying she'd always known, but Cameron's mother didn't. My father never owned up to his abuse, and neither did Cameron's father.

The pattern repeats. Couples colluding. Refusing to see the damage they were doing. Refusing to see their actions. Blaming, always blaming. It's always my fault.

I packed my bags and went home to Dundee. I told Cameron what had happened when he called from France that night. At first, he was shocked but then said that whatever I needed, he was there for me. He was pleased it was out in the open. He and his brother had wanted to confront their father for years but somehow had never managed it. It took an outsider to do it. His brother's girlfriend backed me up, saying she'd experienced the same sexual harassment. She too was glad someone had spoken up and confronted his behaviour.

It took time for Cameron to realise his mother had her part to play. She aided her husband's chronic alcohol use. It was a family system built around denying his alcoholism. Cameron himself had learned to shrug it off, accepting it as normal. Years of playing on different pub floors as a child, as his mother joined his father in drinking, had paid off. The unit was trained to turn a blind eye and condone the father's behaviour. The alcohol acted as a depressant, reducing his anxiety, inhibition and feelings of guilt – hence the sexual acting-out.

When I found the courage to speak, I attempted to repair our relationship and rebuild trust, but they refused to discuss it and wouldn't speak to me unless I first admitted I'd made a mistake. They demanded an apology and kept telling me I was lying.

I refused to back down. I needed them to say sorry. Yes, he had a problem with alcohol, and yes, his behaviour changed when he was drunk. It needed to be out in the open. I didn't expect it to change.

Under my hurt, I was heartbroken that my second attempt at finding parents had been as dismal as my first. We sat in this stalemate for six months until my daughter was born; Cameron's parents wanted to see her and pretended things were fine. I let them visit and we sat in our lounge room with the great-grandmother and aunty, and ate the cake Cameron's mother had made.

Feeling trapped, I couldn't bear to see them or stand the lies. Cameron agreed with me and suggested we spend a year in Australia to see what it was like to live there.

We told his parents we were moving to Sydney. They were white-faced but said nothing. I was taking their grandchildren and son away. It was my fault; Cameron was free of any blame. The boy was good, the girl was bad – the old messages from my family, resurrected.

Their rage came to a head the week before we left. I'd made a special 'Leaving Dundee' book to help my three-year-old cope with the move. I wanted his grandparents and aunty to write a personal message in it, but they refused. I pushed them, demanding. Cameron's aunty broke first. She shouted at me. Cameron's parents joined in.

Their hatred spilled out into the open, all projected at me. Their pretend smiling faces cracked apart, showing the people behind the masks – real at last.

*

We flew to Australia in October 2000 and stayed with my mother for the first few weeks. I could tolerate short periods with her. She seemed to know that she needed to behave. She had bought her own home in western Sydney after my grandparents died and lived with her rescue collie Jessie, her goldfish, pot plants and roses. She'd joined a creative sewing group and seemed happy.

The month we spent with her was one of the few times she came through for me, providing me with a base from which Cameron and I could decide what to do. Cameron found a job and bought a second-hand car, and we moved to the southern end of the Central Coast. It had a sheltered bay with small waves, perfect for young children. We settled into a rented apartment across from the beach.

The summer was one of the hottest on record. Cameron left early in the morning for the long commute into central Sydney, taking the car. I was left with two young children, aged one and three. We'd sit for hours playing with toys in a shallow bath, trying to stay cool.

I found the local playgroups and started the slow journey of making friends, building links with other mothers, finding playmates for the kids and filling the hours. After six months, Cameron suggested we stay permanently. He was enjoying the beaches and outdoor life, but it was confronting for me. I was struggling, flooded by the images of my past. They pressed too close in the heat and the screeching of the galahs and cockatoos.

My father had died the year before. Trevor had stayed in contact with him and had let me know. I imagined myself standing in the room looking down on my father as he lay dying, his olive skin and black hair dulled by sickness, his eyes slightly glassy with pain, the heaviness dropping away from his bones as the cancer ate away at his flesh.

There were many things I'd wanted to ask him. Mostly why and how he could have allowed himself to be pulled into a child paedophile ring. Why did he give me to them? How could he even imagine I would be OK? I knew, though, that he would never have given an honest response.

He'd escaped into a make-believe world where he was a victim of circumstances, and blamed me for all of it. His last few aerograms from Australia years before, sent while I was travelling, had been full of vitriolic hate and accusations. His life would have been perfect if I hadn't been the child I was. It was always going to be my fault.

A relative had boarded with Norm for a time. She told me the story of one night with him. It occurred after I'd sent the photograph of me in my nurse's uniform, taken when I first arrived at Westmead.

Norm had come into her room, waking her up. He'd ranted at her, totally losing it, she said. Norm had taken the photo of me and waved it in her face, blaming me for all the wrongs of his life. He'd sworn, calling me a whore and a cunt, and ripped the photo up in front of her. She'd been terrified and had packed up and left the next day to find herself a cheap rental.

This woman's recounting of those exact words confirmed my memory of how Norm used to talk to me as a three- and four-year-old child. I could hear him shouting them in my face as he jammed the gun into my mouth.

I couldn't get my father out of my thoughts or contain the memories, and fell into an all-consuming depression. Those around me didn't understand, and I couldn't find the words to explain myself. My eyes turned inward to remembered scenes – nightmare rooms full of male forms that no one else could see.

The more I struggled to put a smile on my face, the wider the yawning split opened inside of me. I was tumbling round and round and didn't know how to stop myself or find any ground to stand on. There was no end. I missed Kay desperately.

It took several attempts to find a therapist who listened in a way I felt heard. Coming back to Australia had made me regress. I was three again – the age I was during the early sexual assaults. With this new therapist, I sorted through what was happening. She suggested I work with a dedicated counsellor from the sexual assault unit at Biala House in Gosford.

Biala House was the first professional service I'd used. I'd avoided the mainstream routes, maybe because the abuse occurred within the realm of professional men. It was a relief to have help without paying by the hour. The counsellor encouraged me to report the crimes to the New South Wales Police, to give police a chance to correct this injustice.

She introduced me to a detective from a special unit based at Tuggerah Police Station that dealt with sexual crimes. I spent a day with him and his team. I walked into the station hesitantly, unsure of what to expect, and left jubilant. He'd believed me. This detective sat with me for hours, piecing together the story, helping me find the words to write a report of the offences, even though my father was dead. I could still report Norm and the men.

I worked with their artist to make a Comfit (computer facial identification) picture of the knifeman. His face had been plastered inside my head for years, but now it was out there for others to see. I'd never been able to hold the bossman's face in my mind; he was too scary and has remained a terrifying, chilling presence within me.

The detective listened. He wanted me to succeed but he said he was sorry; he couldn't pursue the crime because it had happened in Queensland. He'd have to refer it to his colleagues in Brisbane.

I received a telephone call a few weeks later from a sergeant in Brisbane. He told me bluntly that the allegations I reported had happened too long ago. It was before computer records and not worth researching as I couldn't provide names. He laughed at me and said I was too young to remember what I was claiming. He sliced across me when I attempted to explain and stopped the conversation, refusing any chance of a further investigation.

That was it. End of attempt number one.

I put down the telephone and dropped into my familiar pit of nothingness. I'd been expectant and had dared to dream. Why did I always get my hopes up and expect that something would happen? I longed for that one person who could back up my story. To prove my words.

I gave up. It was exhausting – the rollercoaster of speaking through the stammer and hoping and waiting for someone else to step up and validate my memories, but I couldn't settle.

I heard about the Commission of Inquiry into Possible Illegal Activities and Associated Police Misconduct (Fitzgerald Inquiry), which had taken place between 1987 and 1989. The inquiry investigated corruption within the Queensland Police from the 1950s and '60s through to the 1980s. It came in response to a series of articles by reporter Phil Dickie in *The Courier Mail* about police corruption in the state. *Four Corners* followed up with a television report by Chris Masters, called 'The Moonlight State', which was shown in 1987.

Although the commission, *Four Corners* and the reporters dealt mainly with illegal prostitution and gambling aided by corrupt police, these events happened at the same time the paedophile ring was using me. If the corrupt police were controlling sex workers and gambling, they could also have been running paedophile groups.

I asked my brother Trevor about Norm's gun. I watched his face carefully. He was shocked when he remembered seeing the gun. He said it was wrapped in white cloth and kept in the bottom drawer, exactly how I remembered it. It was the proof I needed to try again.

I attempted to contact Phil Dickie to ask if he knew of any rumours of paedophile rings. I needed to find one person who had also been used – who was telling the same story as me. Phil Dickie didn't reply, for whatever reason; I couldn't get through. Attempt number two.

I became desperate. I contemplated contacting Amnesty International, daydreaming about their response – long-involved fantasies while I sat on the floor playing with my children.

Life settled. The pain receded. I forgot about the men, my father and my attempt to speak.

I put it away and started working with my mind, meditating and learning how to stay present. I found a place within a local Buddhist study group and started understanding the teachings in greater depth, delighting in listening to His Holiness the Dalai Lama when he visited Australia. His basic message of having a kind heart and a clear mind was balm soothing my wounds. It was another frame to understand my pain. He spoke a lot about suffering, the four Noble Truths and the path to Enlightenment.

Over the next twenty years, we settled into life in Australia. I embraced the teachings and the living action and behaviour of His Holiness, seeing in him the father I longed for. I made him mine. He was a distant figure but one I'd repeatedly bumped into. In Bodhgaya, he had arrived while I was there. I'd listened to him speak in a small audience of a hundred people at Kagyu Samye Ling in Scotland and attended a Yamantaka retreat with him in the Blue Mountains.

My daughter was five when she attended the weekly Christian religious education class offered by her school. The teacher asked the students who believed in God and my daughter was the only child not to put her hand up. The teacher gave all the children except her a lolly, leaving her out.

She came home in tears, not understanding why she couldn't have a lolly too. The next day I went to the school to speak up and the deputy head said if I could find a Buddhist teacher, she was willing to have one at her school. I couldn't find one so I became a Buddhist scripture teacher myself. I started teaching with only my son and daughter and a couple of their friends, but within a few months I had several classes with more than a hundred students at two different schools. I stammered in front of the children and they laughed at first but then it was fine. I'd found the courage to teach through my stammer. Other schools heard about my work and wanted me too, but two was enough.

The central teachings I shared with the children were the two precepts of having a kind heart and a calm mind – the two wings of the bird that allow us to fly. I used a singing bowl to stop the chatter and they learned to be still. I made it fun, teaching the children simple chants in Tibetan and mudras to use with their hands, to give thanks for our feast days celebrating the end of each term, with each child bringing a plate of food to share. I taught them juggling, investing in dozens of balls for the students to use. I brought in my juggling clubs and taught them how to pass to a partner.

I lived the words I taught, watching my mind and catching my thoughts, integrating the teachings into my being. It calmed me. As I distilled the essence of His Holiness's words, more waves rippled out, the children embracing the fun and happiness and chanting. I took some students to personally meet His Holiness on one of his visits – a blessing.

The ground of being, Prajnaparamita, the mother of the Buddhas, I took as my mother. This body of sutras and their commentaries are some of the oldest forms of Mahayana Buddhism – the female personification of wisdom. I'd found the parents I longed for and built my fourth cornerstone, completing my foundation – the stone of my being. I felt solid inside for the first time and could trust myself.

Yet, when I was in company, I felt like an outsider who always looked on. I watched closely, noticing tiny movements and unsaid words. I didn't know how to belong or play the game of chit-chat. Too many parts of me needed to stay hidden for me to be comfortable with other people.

I was making friends but I fell into the caretaker role, looking after their needs and leaving my own unsaid. There was so much of me I couldn't voice: the lesbian I'd been, the survivor of abuse and neglect. The stammer still kept me silent as others told their stories.

I didn't fit into the gay world yet I didn't identify as heterosexual. I threw myself into my work and volunteering with the school band, in the canteen and uniform shop, but only alone or with Cameron could I be myself.

Chapter 25

No longer hidden

I continued calling my mother by her name, Joan, as a grownup. It helped me distance myself from my childhood. By naming her Joan, I related to her as an adult rather than as a mother. It allowed me to see her with fresh eyes and stand firm before her. One adult with another.

It was a perfect system to disown the source of my pain: her mothering. A single-word way of confronting her to her face and not playing into her game of what a good mother she was. But I remember those silent years of struggle and the split inside, with the unending longing for her to be the mother I wanted, needed and craved with a quiet, empty desperation. I'd kept my need hidden to stop her from using it against me. On the surface, I'd toughed it out – the ugly child and the great disappointment in her life.

I refused to call her Mum. This was not for revenge but to protect myself. It's painful to name the role she should've filled. My little girl inside, who waits to be mothered, clings to me in terror when I imagine saying the word 'Mum'. The word dredges up hopelessness and reduces me to a shaking mess on the floor. I can't function. I'm a child again, abandoned and alone, dependent upon a mother who didn't care.

Joan did some things properly or I wouldn't be here, and I thank her for that. She and my father, Norm, were both invested in presenting the perfect postcard picture of a family to the outside world. They turned us out in neat, clean clothes, smiles stuck on our faces as we stared into the camera. But behind closed doors, I was the target of her unresolved rage.

When I use my therapist's eyes, I can see that Joan portrayed many signs of being a traumatised child. I see her unmet needs, a mirror of my own, and this is what kept me coming back to find a connection with her. But I couldn't find the bond of a loving mother and daughter. Our relationship only kind of worked if I did what she wanted. Even then, I never knew how to please her. I never could. She was a pit of need – one I couldn't fill from the outside. It was her job to meet it.

Joan saw me through the lens of her desires and unacknowledged trauma. I was a piece of her made real outside of herself – one she attempted to wipe out, as my presence unconsciously spoke to her pain and intense vulnerability. She needed to disown those fragile parts of herself as they were too overwhelming for her to tolerate. For her survival, she needed to destroy me.

Joan's child part, trapped inside her abusive acting-out adult, touched my heart. When Joan was in her sixties and seventies, she started reading the Mills & Boon romances – her first books. She became lost in the stories, later recounting them in detail to me. It pained me to see her delight and her little girl self, who was allowed to dream. She would read the stories softly aloud, stumbling over pronunciations, her index finger pointing to each word as she tracked the sentences, just like a child would do.

She couldn't see this split inside herself or take responsibility for her actions. It was always someone else's fault. She perfected the art of the victim, persecuting from the victim's position. Joan was a real victim, like me, but this adult victim behaviour was a defensive system, to avoid dropping into the pain and horror that allows us to start doing the healing work of integrating our personality. Without it, we remain flat, almost two-dimensional characters and unreachable. Our hearts are then barricaded to protect us from any more hurt.

This system, the drama cycle, thrives on drama. Joan needed a heightened emotional state to feel alive, and her life was lived this way. She was successful at finding people to look after her: social workers, doctors and the police came to her rescue. Joan wanted Norm to save her from being stuck at home with her parents, but then, years later, she needed her parents to save her from him.

This was part of Joan's demand of me. She loved Graeme in a possessive way, but my job was to look after her. I became her little helper because I was dependent and desperate to please. It came with some benefits as it allowed me to be intimately aware of my mother.

I became an instrument, sensitive and attuned to her needs, leaving my own abandoned and denied. By not making any demands on Joan, I lessened her need to destroy me. In this way, we reached a sort of truce during the year we lived in Broome, after those early years of full-blown hatred. My needs were met in a second-hand way by attending to her – the caretaker role. When I switched my allegiance to Grandma, it reactivated Joan's hatred and resurrected her wish to annihilate me.

In many ways, I was operating from what was called the fawn response but is now called the feign response – part of the fight or flight survival mechanism used when under threat. What was previously thought to be three responses – fight, flight or freeze – has now grown to include the fawn/feign and flop responses. The word 'fawn' was first used in terms of women's behaviour. It was seen as passive and people-pleasing, a way to placate any threat, but it came with a fear of expressing the self and difficulty fitting in.

When I use the word 'feign' instead of 'fawn', it implies a more assertive approach to my survival: pretending to fit in and doing what was expected to avoid retaliation. A choice. But, because of repeatedly doing it from a young age and over many years, this behaviour became my normal response to stress and threat, along with freeze and flop – hypervigilance and dissociation.

Although helpful at the time, it led to valuing my mother at the expense of myself and made it difficult for me to describe my feelings or speak. It exaggerated my sense of responsibility for others, including my mother, and left me out.

*

My mother was hospitalised in 2015 for a simple day procedure but this turned into months of care due to unforeseen complications. Her health deteriorated further. She was giving up. I spoke to the nursing team. They criticised me for suggesting my mother wanted to die and accused me of trying to get rid of her. They had swallowed my mother's stories about me being the bad daughter, even though I was doing most of the visiting, emotional comforting and washing her clothes.

Joan smiled into my face, sugary nice if she needed something, but behind my back, she destroyed my character. I left the ward silenced and isolated – another re-enactment of the pattern of our relationship. We were intimately bound in a terrible way.

On my next visit, I watched her refusing her meals, turning her head away when the plates were put in front of her. Choosing not to eat was the only control Joan had left. She was fading away in front of me.

*

I'd spent weeks visiting aged-care homes to find a suitable one. Joan arrived by ambulance to the temporary placement. She couldn't get out of bed, but as soon as she saw me, she raged from amidst the sheets.

She yelled, 'How dare you put me in a home, you bloody bitch! I knew you always wanted to get rid of me, you bloody hussy. Get me out of here. I want to go home!' She'd used some of Grandad's favourite swear words. It took me back in time.

When Joan had been lucid, she had agreed to the home, but she'd forgotten. The difficulties in her life were always going to be my fault.

I left.

Joan settled but I needed to find a permanent placement. I found one at Orana Aged Care Centre. I went for an interview with the head of nursing. She wanted to know about Joan and asked me pointed questions about my relationship with my mother. I gave evasive answers but she guessed it was a difficult one. She demanded the truth and I spent hours with her, almost recounting my life story. It was cathartic. The head of nursing finished the interview by saying, 'If your mother starts bullying you here, you are to leave and find a member of staff. They will deal with her. Do you understand?'

'Yes.' She'd bluntly named my mother's behaviour.

At the end of Joan's life, I was finding the recognition I longed for. Physically, my mother could no longer harm me, but emotionally, the wounding continued. This is what the head of nursing recognised. With her sanction, I stopped Joan's words from landing on me. When Joan spoke, it said more about her character than mine. I gave my mother's words back to her and felt free in the face of her bitterness. I offered her kindness even when it was not returned.

I'd brought my mother's favourite items, bedding and photographs, and arranged her room as if it were still her home. The warmth of the room helped me spend hours with her several times a week. When Joan knew it was me visiting, she grunted and turned her head to the window, ignoring me. I brought in the CDs she loved and played them while I worked through my feelings for this woman.

On one visit, I'd collected my nephew, Joan's grandson. I'd walked into the room first and Joan gave her usual dismissive growl. But then my nephew said 'Hi Grandma! It's me, I've come to see you.'

Joan turned her head and her face lit up with a huge smile. She reached for her grandson's hand. I sat in the corner, watching and listening to them talk over the top of one another.

It sparked memories of being put in the kitchen when I was two years old, my face pressed up tight to the slot under the door, listening to my brothers and mother playing next door. Nothing had changed. I was a fifty-five-year-old woman, still waiting for her mother to notice her.

This was my mother – the only mother I was ever going to have. And it was OK. I was OK. I'd survived her, grown and found my way. I let her be. It was peaceful.

When Joan died, I was released from the constant, overpowering presence of her. Relief was my predominant feeling. I took a full breath and expanded.

*

I needed to speak truthfully at Joan's cremation, so I wrote a measured account of the woman I knew her to be. I showed my eulogy to my brothers first and, with their reassurance, I spoke at Joan's service:

> *How to speak when I was never listened to? How to explain the bitterness of love never returned? How to say my truth when your truth squashed me? Joan, I realise this shame I feel is yours, not mine. It's your shame for not loving the child you brought into this world. You too, were wounded. And yes, you did your best, but it wasn't enough. You refused to take responsibility, you never grew up. You hid behind your charming childish ways and left everybody else to deal with your mess. I am speaking now to change the patterns of a lifetime. I am speaking now because I can. I am deeply hurt by your not loving me, for not seeing me for who I am. Yet, I am grateful for my painful heart. I am grateful for this chance to do it differently. I am grateful that now I speak. Please listen. Wherever you are, open your heart.*

Distant relatives and friends were shocked, some horrified, that I said such things. But I did. I spoke openly, in front of a large crowd with my stammer keeping me company.

My brother James said later, 'You were so brave to talk like that. I've never experienced such honesty before. Funerals are always so glowing, with only the positive stuff. When you started talking in a non-complimentary way, people were uncomfortable. Particularly those who never really saw those parts of Mum that you and I saw. I never felt the "love and compassion" that a child should expect from their mother. You spoke about her selfishness and the fact that she was a child who never really grew up. You were spot on. Thank you.'

Afterwards, in the RSL club, my cousins approached me. One asked, 'What was all that about?' So I gave more detail. It was liberating to have it out in the open, even as others tried to excuse or defend Joan's behaviour.

I've avoided the pain of never having a mother's presence by turning sideways and easing it through my attachment with my twin. Graeme's continual presence within me is like a soothing calmness – offering the warmth and love I long for. But I can now allow the grief of not having a loving mother's arms, of never being tucked up safe in bed or welcomed with a smile in the morning.

This is my original wound. The rest was piled on top. I've been so busy sorting through her hatred, the sexual abuse, my loss of Graeme and finding my identity and voice that only now can I face this pain – the absence of a mother's love. I'm down in the basement of my trauma.

At the bottom is this neglect and longing. It's come to the surface where I can face it. I have the strength to feel it, and in allowing the pain, I honour this wound.

*

I am sixty-two years old with peace in my days. The structures I've woven into my life hold me, the way the presence of my grandparents once did. I've integrated their love of routine, which saved my battered mind and body and made it mine.

I am the age my grandmother was when we arrived at her home. We've come full circle.

I wake early to the purring of my cats – my morning alarm. I feed them, make coffee and retreat to my workroom. My desk is ready, waiting for me to find the words to fill the pages with my story.

Then I do a workout and feel my body come alive, flowing even as I age. My body is mine now and no longer an object for anyone to use. I follow with a protein shake, shower and change, enjoying the warm water and being clean. I relax as I get ready for my clients, for the day, whatever it holds.

My mind is my friend. It no longer bullies me as I watch my thoughts. I am not defined by them as they come and go, constantly changing. Instead, I have a sense of infinite spacious awareness, of belonging and not the old stories of blaming and hate. Those stories have mostly stopped. If they return, I catch them and honour their roots, mourn for my little girl inside and keep her safe. She has me now. I know how to mother myself as I continue grieving for that space where a caring mother needed to be.

I am aware of the many pieces of me that were shattered but now work together as a team, compassionate and understanding, attuned at last, outside and in.

I've found my voice. Although a part of me wishes to be fluent, I've learned to live with my stammer. I know how to pick myself up and start again, until I find the words that speak directly from my heart.

Graeme is with me. I hold him close. The right side of me is protecting, facing out, as he continues to sit along my left side and faces in. The left of me will always be him. The two of us are fully one. I am fluid, non-binary, between and outside of the genders of male and female. Spaces and silence are now gentle places, calming the wounds that will always be there. I've given myself permission to be safe and recognise I am strong in a fragile, once-broken way.

Powerlessness is my friend, the ground to which I return, where my true power lies – a soft placid place. It holds me. This keeps my life simple and reminds me of how little control I have. Once cracked, despairing and lost, searching for the mothering I longed for and the mirroring I needed in another's eyes, I find my acceptance within this place.

I've always been here, but I never knew. I do now. I am mine. I feel my heart, quiet, open, beating. I've let myself in and found the path to myself. My endless paths out, searching, have led me in.

The path to my heart was always here but for so many years was not safe to find. The many pieces of my heart sat waiting, up there on the wall, safely ticking behind the clock face in the room and hidden from the men. But now it's safe to find and reclaim you, beating and cradled within my chest. I can say it simply, in one single line:

> *In longing to pierce my mother's heart, I was finding my own.*

*

In 2022, I heard about the Dig podcasts, *Sirens Are Coming* on the ABC app, with Matthew Condon reporting on corrupt Queensland Police. It was another journalist driving the story. He was finding women willing to speak up about how they were used and forced to give a cut of their earnings as sex workers to corrupt police from the 1960s through to the present. It seems there are remnants of corruption still going on in Queensland. Maybe I met one of them when the sergeant refused to follow up on my report, back in 2001. I'd recovered enough to try again.

I tracked down the producer of the Dig podcast, Clare, and told her a condensed version of being a child used by a paedophile ring, maybe run by corrupt police. She was happy I came forward and arranged for Matt to chat with me.

Matthew said he'd been searching for ten years to find a child used by the paedophile rings who was willing to speak. He'd heard rumours of the paedophile groups as he'd investigated police corruption but had never managed to find an adult who'd been a child victim. He said he was excited to find me.

My story fits with what he knew. The house where I'd lived in Brisbane was close to where he thought groups probably met, so my sense of the drive was consistent with Matt's information. He tracked down my father's police number and confirmed minute details. Another contact of his also mentioned the men playing cards and gambling after they finished using the children. How one of the main police officers fuelling the corruption was linked to childcare centres, with easy access to children. It was these little pieces of information that backed up my words.

But not enough. Not enough details. No names of the men. No actual addresses. The momentum faded. It was too costly to research further. Clare was sorry but my story alone was not enough without more evidence from other people. It was my third attempt to be heard.

With Clare's suggestion that I tell the story myself, this latest rejection was the catalyst to start writing. It poured out in a flood of pages. I have finally found the words between the poems that I started back in 1990.

Am I the only victim who wasn't killed by those men as a child or later through addiction or suicide? Am I the only one still alive who found the validation and safety to remember? Are any of the mourners of lost victims able to tell us who they were?

Where are those people who were on the edge of what was happening but who chose to turn away? Can any of these witnesses, who kept quiet out of fear or intimidation, speak up?

I can still see the row of adult male bodies lounging against the walls, waiting for the bossman to tell them they can start. Complicit, willing participants – a row of faceless men. Have any of these men reflected on how they behaved and owned up to their abuse? Is that possible for men like these?

As a society, we need to find the courage to speak, to break this silence.

I've never been able to find other children from this time. I hope to find one who survived, who says, 'Yes, they did that to me, too. I remember the knifeman, the bossman.'

Maybe the child made up different names for the men, and perhaps the child survived, grew up and learned how to live.

Where are the children, grown, adults, able to say what those men did, able to say, 'Yes, I too remember'?

Please come forward. My hope continues, with this book.

I am permitting myself to let free all my long-held words and sentences that were silenced, caught in the stammer.

I name my truth. My words find their special place on these pages, to be seen and read and heard. I am no longer hidden.

Epilogue

Gender as cure

My story has shaped my identity. Central to my identity is my gender. I cannot think of my gender separately from my story. In working this out, I changed my name from Wendy to Wen. Wendy was the doll my mother wanted and contained the child who was abused. I stammer on Wendy. Wen is cleaner, sharper and sets me free.

Currently, words like genderqueer, gender fluid and non-binary are commonplace. When I was working out my identity in the 1980s, gender and sexuality were seen in a binary system: male and female, heterosexual and homosexual. The in-betweens and outsides went unvoiced.

Being a girl with a boy twin fitted neatly into the binary notion. It was exaggerated by my mother's self-hatred projected onto me, her first girl child, with our twinship the ideal setup to make her female child bad and her male child good.

Dr Diane Ehrensaft coined the term 'gender creative' to describe those children who don't fit easily into the sex box assigned at birth. In her book *The Gender Creative Child*, she explains how biology, nurture and culture weave together to create a gender that can be fluid. Her writing has prompted me to find my true gender self. Reading her words and the stories of people identifying as non-binary, queer, fluid, enby or any other word they choose, has allowed me to work out my own.

When Graeme was killed, I spun out, as my identity was only possible through him. Since his death, I've reclaimed him and his maleness as my own, merging female and male, a spectrum, a moving fluid system. Some days I'm more on one end, on other days I'm neither. I'm outside, watching on. My web of nature, nurture and culture has crystallised into a realisation that I am one of the gender creative children Dr Ehrensaft writes eloquently about.

She explains gender can be a cure and a protection against trauma. The child chooses a unique gender web as a salve for injuries, such as sexual abuse, by rejecting the gender that causes the harm. In my case, it was both parents, both genders, who I was rejecting, plus rejecting my female form that attracted the abusive attention.

An 'aha' moment. I felt the correctness of her words within me. The gender I choose is my protection and healing from my trauma. It sets me free. My gender is not innate, not inborn and not forced on me. I create it and make it mine. My sense of myself refuses the extremes of male and female. I reject this mirroring in myself. Those systems were diseased in my family – abusive and punishing. I give them back to you, my parents – they are yours to own. They led to my anguish.

In rejecting this nurture aspect, I fly free of the binary and move in between.

I've crashed against the norms. Billie wrote in one of her letters, 'You are like the moon, outside, watching on, never wanting to be confined.' Wearing scrubs at my nurse's graduation, my silent rebellion for my grief not being seen. Graeme's death was the catalyst for my long search to find where I belong.

I found a voice for my internal struggle during the feminist wave of the 1980s, and safety living on the fringe in women-only spaces. It gave me the freedom to work out who I was. I firmed up my identity as a woman when this part of me was victimised. I found her first to later let her go – a step in my story.

Another step was fighting the patriarchy, being slapped with repeated charges of breach of the peace and thrown into police cells when it was peace I was fighting for. I will always be a Greenham woman, embracing anti-military campaigns, spirituality and feminism.

When I fell in love with a man, the ultimate crime back then if one identified as a lesbian, I was disowned and started again. I reinvented myself as a wife and mother – important steps when I didn't know the words I was struggling to find.

I wasn't bisexual or heterosexual and struggled with being a woman; those terms never fit. It took time to work out that my sexual orientation and gender identity are different. And it was gender, my innermost concept of myself, that I was struggling with. Then I heard a non-binary person speak and knew. *That's me. Those are my words.* This was another 'aha' moment.

Genderfluid is the word that sits gently with who I am. Genderqueer when I need to assert myself or hold my ground. I've found my place, my identity. In discovering the words, the trauma drops away. It's done. *I release you from my bones.*

I belong to myself. I've followed many paths over the world and those paths have led me in, to my heart. My mind is soothed. The many faces of my trauma – my mother, my father, the men, the bossman, the rapists – your faces blow yourselves out, the gale of your fury spent.

Your images are leaves settling in the soft breezes of my mind. I let you rest, face down in the dirt. The dirt that I thought I was, I now claim and honour, because this dirt becomes the ground on which I stand. And into this dirt, your images break down into clear thoughts.

Alchemy, the transmutation of matter into gold, transforms your faces, once telling me I don't matter into I do. I matter, and then into the gold of spirit, of finding an authentic self, a magical process of creation. Shaking my head free of you, I claim the sun and wind and rain, to break you down further, useful now, nourishing, fine lines of sense and understanding growing roots into the ground.

I once ran from your faces, lost and alone. Now, turning in, looking into your faces, I've found my own. My eyes are clear, settled and steady. And my face is the only face staring back into my own.

My Wish for You

May you connect with your heart,

and your heart be filled with kindness,

your hands gentle.

May you pause before you speak,

considering your words.

May your mind be calm, attentive,

allowing and accepting difference.

Listening, sensitive, present,

and above all, peaceful.

And for myself, my own two wings, compassion and open awareness,

free to fly,

and free to speak.

Acknowledgements

To my twin brother Graeme, my deepest thanks for our time together.

To Cameron, thank you for your forever love and constant encouragement. To Kyle and Anita, thanks for teaching me what love is and what it isn't. To Emily, for believing in me.

To Jo and Helen, thank you for your unwavering support, attention to detail and honesty.

Thanks, Trev, for being part of my first gang, and C, for teaching me about lifelong loyalty. Peter, your support allows me to pick myself up and keep going. And Kay, thank you for teaching me how to hold space for myself.

I am grateful to Julie, my first editor, for not giving up on me, and to Kev, Les and Ellen (Busybird Publishing), Maria, Cristin and Sarah (AudiobooksRadio) and their teams for saying yes to my words.

My sincere thanks to Assoc. Prof. Anthony Korner, Professor Warwick Middleton and Sharon Lawn for everything that you have done.

I am indebted to Liz Lochhead – Poet Laureate for Glasgow (2005–2011) and Makar, National Poet of Scotland (2011–2016) – for encouraging me when I first started writing. She believed in me before I could believe in myself. Liz, I am grateful for the time we spent going through my first poems at your dining-room table.

Thanks to my four-legged friends, Maxie, Charlie, Bonnie and Walter, for keeping me company during the early hours.

And most of all to you, the reader and listener, thank you for reading and hearing my words.

Learn more about Wen and
Stammering Against Truth by visiting:

wengibson.com

Further information for twins who have lost their twin can be found at:

lonetwinnetwork.org.uk

twinlesstwins.org

www.ingramcontent.com/pod-product-compliance
Lightning Source LLC
Chambersburg PA
CBHW030253100526
44590CB00012B/387